HENRY BRADSHAW SOCIETY

Founded in the Year of Our Lord 1890
for the editing of Rare Liturgical Texts

SUBSIDIA · I

PUBLISHED FOR THE SOCIETY

BY

THE BOYDELL PRESS

A HISTORY OF
EARLY ROMAN LITURGY

TO THE DEATH OF POPE GREGORY THE GREAT

G. G. Willis (†)

with a memoir of G. G. Willis
by Michael Moreton

LONDON
1994

First published for the Henry Bradshaw Society 1994
by The Boydell Press
an imprint of Boydell & Brewer Ltd
PO Box 9, Woodbridge, Suffolk IP12 3DF, UK
and of Boydell & Brewer Inc.
PO Box 41026, Rochester, NY 14604, USA

ISBN 1 870252 06 3

ISSN 1352-1047

British Library Cataloguing-in-Publication Data
Willis, G. G.
History of Early Roman Liturgy to the Death of Pope
Gregory the Great. – (Subsidia Series; Vol. 1)
I. Title II. Series
264
ISBN 1-870252-06-3

Library of Congress Cataloging-in-Publication Data
Willis, Geoffrey Grimshaw.
A history of early Roman liturgy to the death of Pope
Gregory the Great / G. G. Willis ; with a memoir of G. G.
Willis by Michael Moreton.
    p. cm. – (Subsidia, ISSN 1352-1047 ; 1)
Includes bibliographical references and index.
ISBN 1-870252-06-3 (alk. paper)
1. Catholic Church – Liturgy – History – Early church,
ca. 30-600. 2. Catholic Church – Italy – Rome – Liturgy.
3. Rome (Italy) – Church history – Early church, ca. 30-
600. 4. Italy – Church history – Early church, ca. 30-600.
I. Title. II. Series: Subsidia (Henry Bradshaw Society) ; 1.
BX1977.I8W55 1994
264'.02'009015–dc20   93-40141

This publication is printed on acid-free paper

Printed in Great Britain by
St Edmundsbury Press Ltd, Bury St Edmunds, Suffolk

TABLE OF CONTENTS

PUBLICATION SECRETARY'S PREFACE

The resurgence of the Henry Bradshaw Society in recent years has coincided with – and, in some sense, has perhaps helped to promote – a renewed interest in the medieval liturgy. This renewed interest is reflected both in the ever-increasing membership of the Society and in the amount of original research now being devoted to the medieval liturgy in universities and elsewhere. The Society's original series of publications was established in order to publish 'rare liturgical texts', that is to say, to publish scholarly editions of primary liturgical texts as they are preserved in medieval manuscripts. Monographs concerned with aspects of the liturgy evidently fall outside the scope of the original series so defined. Accordingly, the Council of the Henry Bradshaw Society, at its annual meeting in 1992, took the decision to establish a new series of occasional Subsidia, which could serve as the publishing outlet for book-length studies on all aspects of the medieval liturgy. The present volume is the first in this new series; it will, the Council hopes, serve to promote the publication of more such monographs in the future. (Scholars wishing to offer such monographs for publication in the HBS Subsidia are invited to contact the Publications Secretary in the first instance.)

When the Henry Bradshaw Society was founded in the late nineteenth century, some substantial part of its membership consisted of clerics in orders, from whom an understanding of the workings of the liturgy could be taken for granted. A century later, in the late twentieth century, such knowledge can no longer be assumed. Much of the present HBS membership is made up of students of the Middle Ages, many of them employed by universities, who realize that an understanding of the liturgy is essential to the proper understanding of that period, but who no longer bring to the subject the intimate knowledge of the liturgy which could be taken for granted a century ago. This is tantamount to saying that the aims of the Society must now be responsive to the interests of its twentieth-century membership; in other words, that its publications should attempt to clarify rather than obfuscate the complexities of the medieval liturgy.

As the Council was contemplating the establishment of a series of

vii

occasional Subsidia, it had (by happy chance) in its possession the typescript of a book on the early Roman liturgy by the late Geoffrey Grimshaw Willis, one of the most distinguished English students of the liturgy this century, and a former Vice-President of the Society. The Council was unanimously of the opinion that Willis's book would serve as an excellent harbinger of the new series, because, like all his liturgical publications – one thinks especially of *Essays in Early Roman Liturgy* (1964) and *Further Essays in Early Roman Liturgy* (1968) – it is written throughout in a clear, easily accessible style which masks the extraordinary range of learning, in Greek and Latin patristic and liturgical sources, which underlies it: it is a model, in other words, of what liturgical scholarship should be.

In preparing the volume for publication I have been aware that, during the nearly twenty years which have elapsed since the completion of the book, there have been important publications in the field of early Roman liturgy: the massive labours of Jean Deshusses on the Gregorian Sacramentary, or of Paul De Clerck on the *oratio fidelium*, for example, as well as many editions of relevant patristic texts in the series Corpus Christianorum. Yet on reflection I was not persuaded that such *aggiornamento* would necessarily import much improvement to the book as it stands. Here, as in all his liturgical publications, Willis's exposition is grounded solidly on primary sources, not on secondary scholarship (which by its nature is often transitory); and for much of his discussion it matters little whether (for example) Tertullian is quoted from the CSEL edition or from a more recent edition in the Corpus Christianorum. Willis's knowledge of the primary sources, particularly of Cyprian, Ambrose and Augustine, was truly comprehensive, and his exposition of the growth and development of the early Roman liturgy depends more on this knowledge than on up-to-date secondary scholarship. Accordingly, after some discussion with other members of the Council, I have decided to leave Willis's annotation more or less as he left it, in the hope that his voice will speak, clearly and unaided, to all students of the early liturgy, and will thereby serve as a helpful guide to one of the most difficult areas of liturgical scholarship.

M.L.
March 1993

GEOFFREY GRIMSHAW WILLIS
1914–1982

Geoffrey Willis was a north-country man. He was born in Manchester on 6 July 1914. He went to the University of Manchester, where he read Latin, graduating in 1935. Thus were laid the foundations for that command of ancient languages which, as Dom Botte once reminded us with some acerbity, are indispensable in the equipment of the liturgical scholar.

He was trained for holy orders at Lichfield Theological College, and was ordained to the diaconate in 1937, and to the priesthood in the following year. In those days 'research degrees' in Arts disciplines were not as readily funded as they came to be in the Robbins era, nor were benefices soon given to inexperienced priests as they are today. He served eight years in his first curacy, at Cotmanhay and Shipley in the Diocese of Derby, and two further short curacies-in-charge in New Mills, and St Edmund's Conventional District, Allenton, in the same diocese. It was not until he had been twelve years in holy orders that he was given his first benefice, when in 1949 Allenton was constituted as a new parish, and he was collated as its first incumbent. He was, however, collated soon after to the benefice of Fernilee, again in the Diocese of Derby – he married at this time Miss Stella Allen – where he stayed for nine years. He was a proctor for the clergy in the Convocation of Canterbury, and at the time of his election in 1945 he was the youngest proctor in the House and one of the only two who were unbeneficed. For a year, in 1946-7, he lectured in Divinity in Derby Training College.

During these years he was working steadily on St Augustine. He was awarded the degree of Master of Arts by the University of Manchester in 1939 for a thesis, not published, entitled *An Analysis, with Commentary, of St Augustine of Hippo's Treatises on Marriage*. There followed a further thesis, also not published, on *St Augustine's Text of the New Testament*, for which he was awarded the degree of Doctor of Philosophy by the University of Nottingham in 1951. His first published work was on *St Augustine and the Donatist Schism*,

ix

which appeared in 1950. Thus he established himself as an Augustinian scholar of the first rank.

His life soon began to develop into a period of what proved to be intense activity. In 1953 he was appointed Assistant Synodical Secretary in the Convocation of Canterbury, and editor of the Chronicle of the Convocation of Canterbury in 1957, both of which appointments he retained until 1969. From 1953 he was a member of the Joint Committee of the Convocation of Canterbury on the Lectionary, which eventually produced in 1961 a conservative revision of the 1922 office lectionary. The latter had reorganized the Anglican office lectionary on the basis of the ecclesiastical instead of the civil year. The most significant characteristic of the 1961 revision was perhaps the abandonment of the life-of-Jesus approach to the Gospels, represented by the conflation of the texts of the Synoptic Gospels, and the return to the reading of the Gospels separately in both gospel cycles of the year. In virtue of his familiarity with St Augustine's vast ouput, Geoffrey Willis himself carried out an examination of the lectionary traceable in St Augustine's sermons, the results of which were published in *St Augustine's Lectionary* in 1962. The information thus gleaned is considerably earlier in date than the evidence of the earliest known lectionaries.

His long absorption in the work of the greatest of the Western Fathers led to a thorough-going study of liturgy in the patristic and early medieval period. It was in recognition of his scholarship in this field that he was appointed to the newly-formed Liturgical Commission in 1955. He was its secretary for ten years. Concurrently he was appointed to the Standing Liturgical Commission of the Church in Wales as an assessor, a post which he held into the early 1970s.

The Church of England Liturgical Commission was, to begin with, answerable to the archbishops of Canterbury and York. Its first Report, on baptism and confirmation, was published in 1957. It had been preceded by a series of reports and debates in the Convocations on Christian initiation that started before the 1939-45 war. It was more the fruit of liturgical and theological scholarship, and less beholden to ecclesiastical politics, than any subsequent report, and was perhaps the best. It sought to treat Christian initiation as a three-fold sacrament – baptism, confirmation and the eucharist – and in this respect may be said to have anticipated the Roman *Ordo initiationis christianae adultorum* of 1972. Adult initiation in this threefold form was to be normative in principle, even though infant baptism without confirmation or the eucharist might remain more common in practice. But the Report met with much opposition, chiefly on the grounds, set out in Article XXV, that confirmation has not the like nature of a sacrament with baptism and the Lord's supper, having no visible sign or ceremony ordained of God. In consequence it was for some years put on one side. This outcome was ominous for the future course of liturgical revision in the Church of England. The *praejudicia*, inculcated in the minds of many if not most Anglicans by the liturgical schemes of the Reformers and the theological foundations on which they rested, would continue to resist and overwhelm the judgments of a disinterested and oecumenical scholarship.

From 1962 onwards the Liturgical Commission turned its attention to the revision of other Prayer Book services, including Morning and Evening Prayer, the Burial of the Dead, and the Order for Holy Communion. These services were published as *Alternative Services: Second Series* in 1965. Morning and Evening Prayer and the Burial of the Dead were conservative revisions, the Order for Holy Communion more radical. Geoffrey Willis continued to be Secretary of the Commission until March 1965. His resignation at that date was occasioned by more than one cause.

Like E. C. Ratcliff, who in the end preferred not to subscribe the 1965 Report, he was increasingly irritated and frustrated by the growing impact of ecclesiastical politics upon liturgical revision. The draft Order for Holy Communion was, in spite of its radical appearance, a compromise. Thus it included a thanksgiving section that owed its inspiration to Hippolytus, together with the Hippolytan oblation formula, after the narrative of the institution, at once the simplest statement of the meaning of the eucharist, and conceptually basic to all Catholic eucharistic prayers. On the other hand the Hippolytan epiclesis, which Geoffrey Willis like many others regarded as a fourth-century interpolation, was abandoned; and in its place were substituted the invocation formulae in the Prayer Book tradition, in which the change sought is not in the bread and cup, but in the hearts and minds of the people.

At this time the Joint Liturgical Group, quite unofficial in origin, was set up. Its influence was resented by Geoffrey Willis – 'What do they know' he once said 'that we do not ourselves already know?' – especially since it tended to give a lead to the Liturgical Commission in virtue of its supposed ecumenicity, as the question of the calendar and lectionary later showed. Moreover, the association of the Liturgical

Commission with the Joint Liturgical Group meant that schemes of revision tended to be slanted towards the churches in the Reformed tradition, and were less open to Catholic, and specifically Roman, tradition. Again, the proposal to appoint a full-time, salaried Secretary of the Liturgical Commission he regarded as an unnecessary extravagance, which at the same time seemed to promote liturgical revision as a fast-growing industry. In his growing disillusion with the way in which liturgical revision was developing, he was not alone. Both Ratcliff and A. H. Couratin subsequently resigned (or in the case of Ratcliff intended to resign, for his resignation may have been overtaken by his sudden death) when the Hippolytan oblation formula was rejected by the Convocations and the House of Laity in the Church Assembly in 1967.

It was in this period that he published two collections of essays, *Essays in Early Roman Liturgy* in 1964, and *Further Essays in Early Roman Liturgy* in 1968. Both series of essays are brilliant examples of liturgical scholarship. The subject is illustrated at every step by reference to evidence drawn from a wide range of primary sources, with extensive support from secondary authorities. It was in recognition of these works, together with the book on St Augustine's lectionary and other learned papers, that the University of Nottingham conferred upon him in 1969 a doctorate in Divinity. This gave him deep satisfaction at a time of great anguish.

In 1958 he had been instituted and inducted as the incumbent of the parish church of Wing in Buckinghamshire. It is, as is well known, one of the most important of surviving Anglo-Saxon monuments, for which he compiled a guide that is outstanding among parish church guides. This benefice made it easier for him to travel to London and back in connexion with his various commitments there. For some years too at this time he lectured in Liturgy at Cuddesdon Theological College, not far away.

But this decade and a half of intense activity was brought to an abrupt end in 1968 by the sudden deterioration of his eyesight caused by diabetes, and within a few months by blindness. He resigned his benefice and all his various appointments, and retired to Oxford.

From this devastating blow he soon began to recover. He continued to say mass, for he was able to recite the Prayer Book rite and the Latin canon of the Roman mass by heart. No stranger to his parish church, he also frequented the parish church of St Mary Magdalen in the centre of Oxford, which he could reach door to door by bus. (He once said,

'I have discovered what happiness is' – through the kindness of ordinary people in the streets.) His wife made it possible for him to continue to recite the daily office. On the academic side of things, he drew on the help of undergraduates and postgraduates who came to his house to read texts in Latin, Greek, Coptic, Syriac and Hebrew, as well as modern works in French and German. He learnt Braille with difficulty because of the insensitivity of his fingers, and relied heavily on his tape-recorder and typewriter.

A string of opuscula, some in the field of research, some by way of critical appraisal of revised liturgical services, began to appear. In regard to the latter, his standpoint was predictable, but his judgments were invariably founded upon great stores of knowledge. He had reason to criticize, for the developing process of revision steadily narrowed the ground in which liturgical scholarship could be in any degree influential, still less determinative. The Liturgical Commission prepared reports which were presented to the General Synod. *Ad hoc* revision committees would then be appointed to consider amendments, which might run into hundreds. Finally the revision committees' own reports would be returned to the General Synod, where again hundreds of amendments might be submitted. The results were what was to be expected from majorities in which comparatively few voters might be said to have a disciplined and sensitive knowledge of the history and theology of liturgy. Making up new liturgical forms to be authorized by popular vote is a way of proceeding that is distant indeed from the receiving of liturgical tradition from the remote past which has continuously for generations formed both belief and habits of prayer. Geoffrey Willis's reserves of patience and endurance in this situation were not unlimited.

Among his essays in liturgical scholarship from these years mention should be made in particular of two. There was first a critique of the corpus of eucharistic prayers in the Missale Romanum of 1970, which was printed in *The Heythrop Journal* in January 1971. Although he was critical of some modern critics of the *Canon Missae Romanus*, he regarded the pruning away of the accretions in the Canon, and indeed in the *Ordo Missae* as a whole, as 'pure gain'. But he was less than enthusiastic about the new eucharistic prayers, which he regarded as hybrid forms, especially III and IV conflated as these are from various sources. Secondly, he contributed an essay to the Festschrift in honour of Arthur Couratin in 1981 on the subject of the concept of the *sacrificium laudis* in the eucharist. It was marked by characteristic attention to the minutiae of texts, both scriptural and liturgical, a remarkable feat in view of his blindness.

One sustained work of scholarship, finally, was produced during these years – the work which now follows. It is fitting that this book should appear under the auspices of the Henry Bradshaw Society, a society which he served for many years as Vice-President.

He died, unexpectedly, on 8 May 1982. *Ipsi locum refrigerii lucis et pacis ut indulgeas deprecamur.*

Michael Moreton
The University of Exeter

ABBREVIATIONS

Andrieu	M. Andrieu, *Les Ordines Romani du haut moyen âge*, 5 vols. (Louvain, 1931–61)
CSEL	Corpus Scriptorum Ecclesiasticorum Latinorum (Vienna)
Gel.	*Sacramentarium Gelasianum*, ed. L. C. Mohlberg, *Liber Sacramentorum Romanae Aeclesiae Ordinis Anni Circuli* (Rome, 1960)
Hadr.	*Sacramentarium Hadrianum*, ed. H. Lietzmann, *Das Sacramentarium Hadrianum* (Münster, 1967)
HBS	Henry Bradshaw Society Publications
JEH	*Journal of Ecclesiastical History*
JTS	*Journal of Theological Studies*
Mansi	*Sacrorum Conciliorum Nova et Amplissima Collectio*, ed. J. D. Mansi, 31 vols. (Florence, 1759-98)
MGH	Monumenta Germaniae Historica
——AA	——Auctores Antiquissimi
——Ep.	——Epistolae (in quarto)
PG	Patrologia Graeca, ed. J. P. Migne, 162 vols. (Paris, 1857-66)
PL	Patrologia Latina, ed. J. P. Migne, 221 vols. (Paris, 1844-64)

I

The Pre-Nicene Eucharist

The earliest available text of the Roman *Canon Missae* dates back only to the end of the seventh century, where it is to be seen in the Bobbio Missal, the oldest surviving manuscript of the Roman rite of the Hiberno-Gallican family.[1] In the eighth century, texts of it are to be found in the other two members of this family, the Stowe Missal[2] and Missale Francorum,[3] and in the middle of this century the Old Gelasian Sacramentary (Vaticanus Reginensis 316) also contains a text of the Canon.[4] Knowledge of certain changes in the Roman Canon in the period between the death of St Gregory in 604 and the compilation of these sacramentaries enables us with some assurance to establish that the Canon of the Mass, as St Gregory left it, must have been very close to the text there preserved.[5] From the time of St Gregory until the revisions of 1969, which resulted from the *Consilium* set up by the Second Vatican Council, the Roman Canon underwent very little change. Other liturgical texts, however, changed and developed considerably. Information about Roman liturgy becomes more plentiful as the student advances through the centuries which followed St Gregory, but our task is to consider the development of liturgy at Rome in the period before St Gregory, and for this our knowledge is comparatively scanty. As we draw nearer to the time of St Gregory it becomes more plentiful, but at no point in this period is evidence as clear or as abundant as we should like it to be.

[1] *The Bobbio Missal: Facsimile*, HBS LIII (London, 1917); *The Bobbio Missal: Text*, ed. E. A. Lowe, HBS LVIII (London, 1920).
[2] *The Stowe Missal*, ed. G. F. Warner, 2 vols., HBS XXXI-XXXII (London, 1906-15).
[3] *Missale Francorum*, ed. L. C. Mohlberg, Rerum Ecclesiasticarum Documenta, Series maior, Fontes II (Rome, 1957).
[4] *Liber Sacramentorum Romanae Aeclesiae Ordinis Anni Circuli*, ed. L. C. Mohlberg, Rerum Ecclesiasticarum Documenta, Series maior, Fontes IV (Rome, 1960), nos. 1242-60.
[5] For critical editions of this text, see B. Botte, *Le Canon de la messe romaine* (Louvain, 1935); L. Eizenhöfer, *Canon Missae Romanae*, Collectanea Anselmiana, Series minor I (Rome, 1954); and E. Bishop, *Liturgica Historica* (Oxford, 1918), pp. 82-91.

Like all liturgy, Eastern and Western, Roman liturgy in the first six centuries is divided clearly into two periods by the Peace of the Church in the early fourth century, and by the subsequent development from an unofficial and semi-private to a tolerated and even state-sponsored cult. The second half of the fourth century saw everywhere in Christendom a formalization, enrichment and development of Christian worship. This was true of both East and West, and it is true of the Roman rite, though, as we shall see, the rite developed on different lines from those which it followed in the Eastern churches and in the non-Roman churches of the West. Unlike these churches, Rome had also a change of liturgical language, from Greek to Latin. This process was certainly complete by the time of Pope Damasus (366-84), though its precise dating is a matter for conjecture, as we shall see.

St Ambrose, in the catechetical lectures which he delivered at Milan about 390 and later published,[6] says that he desires to follow Rome in liturgical matters.[7] So it is possible to take his evidence as having some bearing on Roman liturgy, though he wrote at Milan. And indeed he quotes verbatim a eucharistic prayer which is closely related to the Roman Canon as we see it in the books of the seventh and eighth centuries which have been mentioned above, from the paragraph *Quam oblationem* to the paragraph *Supplices te rogamus*, that is, the core of the Canon. St Ambrose also gives us some information about other parts and ceremonies of the mass, and about baptism and confirmation. The only liturgical texts which proceed from Rome at a date earlier than St Ambrose are those contained in the *Apostolic Tradition* of St Hippolytus. He gives us, among other things, the text of an anaphora of the eucharist. The pieces of evidence are clearly a very scanty and meagre basis for writing a history of Roman liturgy in the first four centuries. Yet it is possible to supplement them with other information not comprising actual liturgical texts, and it is also possible to detect, and even to parallel from earlier centuries, a few features of the Roman rites of the mass, of baptism and of ordination which were in use at Rome in the sixth and seventh centuries. This may prove sufficient to give us some guidance about the early development of the liturgy of the Roman Church.

[6] *De sacramentis*, in CSEL LXXIII (Vienna, 1955), pp. 13-85.
[7] *Ibid*. III.i. 5-6 (*ed.cit.*, p. 40): '. . . ecclesia Romana . . . cuius typum in omnibus sequimur et formam . . . In omnibus cupio sequi ecclesiam Romanam . . .'

THE MASS

In obedience to Our Lord's command, 'Do this for my *anamnesis*',[8] the eucharist was from the earliest days of the Church the central act of Christian worship. But until the middle of the second century, when St Justin Martyr published his first *Apology* and his *Dialogue with Trypho*, practically no information of any kind has survived which throws light upon the rites and ceremonies which the Church used to celebrate the eucharist. And we have to wait until about A.D. 215 before we have, in the *Apostolic Tradition* of St Hippolytus, any text of a eucharistic prayer. It is, however, important to notice that the successors of the Apostles, the Apostolic Fathers, were teaching by the end of the first century, at a time before the later books of the New Testament were even written, and before any New Testament books were canonized, that the eucharist was an offering or sacrifice to God which Our Lord had enjoined upon the Church, and that in it was fulfilled the prophecy of Malachi, 'In every place incense shall be offered unto my name and a pure offering, for my name is great among the Gentiles, saith the Lord.'[9] In the spirit of this belief, St Clement of Rome, before the end of the first century, was describing the bishops as 'those who offer the gifts',[10] and calling Our Lord the 'High priest of our offerings'.[11] This title of Christ implies the existence of a heavenly altar[12] at which Christ the high priest makes his offering, and it suggests a connection between this heavenly offering and the earthly offering of the eucharist, which the bishops make at Christ's command. He is hinting at a doctrine which is explicit a century later in the words of St Irenaeus in southern Gaul,

> est ergo altare in caelo: illuc enim preces nostrae et oblationes nostrae diriguntur.[13]

It is precisely this doctrine which has for centuries been expressed by the Roman Canon, in *Supplices te rogamus*:

[8] I Cor. XI. 24, 26: τοῦτο ποιεῖτε εἰς τὴν ἐμὴν ἀνάμνησιν.
[9] Mal. I.11: καὶ ἐν παντὶ τόπῳ θυμίαμα προσάγεται τῷ ὀνόματί μου καὶ θυσία καθαρά, διότι μέγα τὸ ὄνομά μου ἐν τοῖς ἔθνεσιν, λέγει κύριος παντοκράτωρ.
[10] I Clement XLIV. 4.
[11] *Ibid.* XXXVI. 1.
[12] Apoc. VIII. 3.
[13] *Adv. Haer.* (ed. Harvey) II, 210; cf. IV. xviii. 6.

Supplices te rogamus, omnipotens deus, iube haec perferri per manus sancti angeli tui in sublime altare tuum in conspectu diuinae maiestatis tuae.

The holy angel here mentioned is none other than the Christ himself, the *angelus magni consilii* of Isaiah IX.6. who takes the offering which he made on the cross, and which he makes daily in the eucharist on earth, to God's heavenly altar, and there offers it to the Father.

The eucharist is essentially a thank-offering, a sacrifice expressive of thanksgiving for the mighty works of God which are enumerated in the eucharistic prayer. This is a primitive and universal feature of the mass. The eucharist is the Christian offering, and it replaces the offerings of the Levitical law. This is why St Irenaeus can say of Christ that he taught the new oblation of the new covenant: 'et novi testamenti novam docuit oblationem.'[14] So from the earliest times the sacrificial aspect of the Church's eucharistic offering is central; it is, in the words of St Irenaeus and others, the θυσία καθάρα foretold in Malachi which the Gentiles would offer all over the world, in contrast to the Levitical sacrifices which are offered only by the Jews and by them only in Jerusalem.

St Justin Martyr

St Justin Martyr, writing in the middle of the second century, about 155, gives no text of the eucharistic prayer, but he gives in his *First Apology* an outline of the structure of the eucharist, and that twice over. For he describes in chs. 65 and 66 the eucharist of Easter which was the first communion of the neophytes as well as the Church's regular offering, and in ch. 67 an account of the normal Sunday mass. These two descriptions, which have much in parallel, enable us to construct the following scheme of the eucharist, and some additional information may be derived from St Justin's *Dialogue with Trypho*, written about the same time as the *First Apology*.[15]

1 Lessons are read from the memoirs of the Apostles and from the Prophets.[16]

---

[14] *Ibid*. pp. 197-9.
[15] Ed. J. K. T. Otto, *Iustini Opera*, 2nd ed., 3 vols. (Jena, 1846-9).
[16] *Ibid*. ch. 67: καὶ τὰ ἀπομνημονεύματα τῶν ἀποστόλων ἢ τὰ συγγράμματα τῶν προφητῶν ἀναγινώσκεται μέχρις ἐγχωρεῖ.

2 The President delivers a homily based on the lessons read.[17]

3 Common prayers are said.[18]

4 The kiss of peace.[19]

5 Bread and a cup of wine and water are brought to the President.[20]

6 The eucharistic prayer. The President offers up praises and glory to God, through the Son and through the Holy Spirit, and gives thanks to him for these things.[21] The subject of this thanksgiving is the creation of the world and all that is in it, for man's sake, for the Incarnation, for the deliverance of man from sin, and for the overthrow of evil through Christ.[22] At the end of the eucharistic prayer the people respond *AMEN*.[23]

7 The Communion is ministered to those present by the deacons, and by them also carried to those not present.[24]

8 Contributions for the poor, etc., are given to the President.[25]

It will be seen at once that there is practically nothing here which is not to be found in the later Roman rite of the time of St Gregory onwards, though there have been many additions and some rearrangement.

1. Justin's description of the Easter mass shows that from the earliest times the service has begun with lessons from the scriptures. The

---

[17] *Ibid.*: Εἶτα παυσαμένου τοῦ ἀναγινώσκοντος ὁ προεστὼς διὰ λόγου τὴν νουθεσίαν καὶ πρόκλησιν τῆς τῶν καλῶν τούτων μιμήσεως ποιεῖται.

[18] *Ibid.* ch. 65: . . . κοινὰς εὐχὰς ποιησόμενοι . . .; cf. *ibid.* ch. 67. Ἔπειτα ἀνιστάμεθα κοινῇ πάντες καὶ εὐχὰς πέμπομεν.

[19] *Ibid.* ch. 65: Ἀλλήλους φιλήματι ἀσπαζόμεθα παυσάμενοι τῶν εὐχῶν.

[20] *Ibid.*: Ἔπειτα προσφέρεται τῷ προεστῶτι τῶν ἀδελφῶν ἄρτος καὶ ποτήριον ὕδατος καὶ κράματος; cf. *ibid.* ch. 67: . . . ἄρτος προσφέρεται καὶ οἶνος καὶ ὕδωρ.

[21] *Ibid.* ch. 65: καὶ οὗτος λαβὼν αἶνον καὶ δόξαν τῷ πατρὶ τῶν ὅλων διὰ τοῦ ὀνόματος τοῦ υἱοῦ καὶ τοῦ πνεύματος τοῦ ἁγίου ἀναπέμπει; cf. *ibid.* ch. 67: καὶ ὁ προεστὼς εὐχὰς ὁμοίως καὶ εὐχαριστίας ὅση δύναμις αὐτῷ ἀναπέμπει.

[22] *Dial. cum Tryphone*, ch. 41 (ed. Otto I, 134): Ἰησοῦς χριστὸς ὁ Κύριος ἡμῶν παρέδωκε ποιεῖν, ἵνα ἅμα τε εὐχαριστῶμεν τῷ φεῷ ὑπέρ τε τοῦ τὸν κόσμον ἐκτικέναι σὺν πᾶσι τοῖς ἐν αὐτῷ διὰ τὸν ἄνθρωπον, καὶ ὑπὲρ τοῦ ἀπὸ τῆς κακίας, ἐν ᾗ γεγόναμεν, ἠλευθερωκέναι ἡμᾶς, καὶ τὰς ἀρχὰς καὶ τὰς ἐξουσίας καταλελυκέναι τελείαν κατάλυσιν διὰ τοῦ παθητοῦ γενομένου κατὰ τὴν βουλὴν αὐτοῦ.

[23] *I Apol.* ch. 65: οὗ συντελέσαντος τὰς εὐχὰς καὶ εὐχαριστίαν πᾶς ὁ παρὼν λαὸς ἐπευφημεῖ λέγων Ἀμήν; cf. *ibid.* ch. 67: καὶ ὁ λαὸς ἐπευφημεῖ λέγων τὸ Ἀμήν.

[24] *Ibid.* ch. 65: οἱ καλούμενοι παρ᾽ ἡμῖν διάκονοι διδόασιν ἑκάστῳ τῶν παρόντων μεταλαβεῖν ἀπὸ τοῦ εὐχαριστηθέντος ἄρτου καὶ οἴνου καὶ ὕδατος καὶ τοῖς οὐ παροῦσιν ἀποφέρουσι; cf. *ibid.* ch. 67: καὶ ἡ διάδοσις καὶ ἡ μετάληψις ἀπὸ τῶν εὐχαριστηθέντων ἑκάστῳ γίνεται, καὶ τοῖς οὐ παροῦσι διὰ τῶν διακόνων πέμπεται.

[25] *Ibid.* ch. 67.

'memoirs of the Apostles' to which he refers might mean either their epistles or the gospels, and the mention of the prophets will proably indicate an Old Testament lesson. By the time of St Gregory, the prophetic lesson had disappeared from the Roman mass, which normally had only two lessons, preserving the Old Testament lesson as the first lesson in Lent, and retaining the epistle at other times of the year. But there were a few days, such as Wednesdays in the Ember Weeks, the Easter Vigil and that of Pentecost, which have preserved one or more lessons from the Old Testament down to the present, as well as an epistle and gospel in the normal way.

2. St Justin then tells us that the lessons were followed by a sermon from the President, that is, normally, the bishop, which was an exposition of the scriptural passages which had been read. There must have been many periods in the Middle Ages when the sermon had become obsolete, and its use seems to have depended upon the celebrant, so that some popes have left no sermons, and perhaps never preached any (for example, no sermon is mentioned in the description of the Roman papal mass of Easter Day which is contained in *Ordo Romanus Primus*), whereas others, such as St Leo and St Gregory the Great, have left large numbers of sermons, and in Africa St Augustine seems to have preached at every mass.

3. Common prayers are then said, the people standing. From their position it would appear that these are the *oratio fidelium*, as it was later termed. This name suggests that they belong to the *missa fidelium* and not to the *missa catechumenorum*, and that before they were said the catechumens were excluded, as they were in later times. In a way the prayer of the faithful, a general intercession for the Church and people, stands between the mass of the catechumens and the mass of the faithful.[26] The position of this general intercession was changed at the end of the fifth century, and in the time of St Gregory it disappeared altogether, but it has retained its primitive position in the Solemn Prayers on Good Friday only, and this position, though not the text of the *Orationes Sollemnes*, has been restored in the revision of 1969.

4. These prayers are followed by the Kiss of Peace. By the time of St Gregory this was in its present position at the Fraction, and a preliminary to the Communion, for which it seems most suitable. But the position before the Offertory mentioned by St Justin here is the

---

[26] See G. G. Willis, *Essays in Early Roman Liturgy*, Alcuin Club Collections XLVI (London, 1964), pp. 10-13.

primitive and original position, and the position in which practically every rite except the Roman still retained it in the sixth century.

5. Bread and a cup of water and wine are then brought to the President. This is the earliest mention of the Offertory, except what may be inferred from the description by St Clement of Rome of the bishops as those who offer the gifts. Justin does not state who brought the gifts to the bishop, though later practice may suggest that it was the function of the deacons, nor does he say who provided the gifts. In later times they were contributed by the people. The chalice is mixed, according to the immemorial tradition of the Church, doubtless derived from Jewish practice, which Our Lord would have followed at the Supper.

6. The eucharistic prayer follows. The President offers up praise and glory to the Father through the Son and the Holy Spirit. This prayer is described as praise and glory. It is primarily a thanksgiving, and its subjects are here defined as creation of the world and of man, the Incarnation of the Son and the deliverance of man from evil through Christ's Passion. At the end of the prayer the people say Amen.

7. The deacons deliver the communion to the people and carry it to those who are absent. The President, who has consecrated by pronouncing the eucharistic prayer over the gifts, appears to leave the administration of the sacrament to the deacons. It is also their responsibility to communicate at home those who are for any cause absent from the public eucharist.

8. The President receives gifts for the poor and other persons. It is not clear at which point in the rite these contributions are offered.

Various other considerations arise from Justin's account. In *Apology* ch. 63, he applies to Christ the title of angel of mighty counsel, μεγάλης βουλῆς ἄγγελος,[27] and this term becomes important in later Roman liturgy. St Hippolytus followed Justin in using it of Christ in the Eucharistic Prayer which he prescribes for use at the consecration of a bishop.[28] It appears again in the prayer *Supplices te rogamus* of the Roman Canon: 'iube haec perferri per manus sancti angeli tui in sublime altare tuum in conspectu diuinae maiestatis tuae . . .' It is probable that this phrase was in the Canon at Rome by the end of the fourth century, for St Ambrose in *De sacramentis* quotes a similar

---

[27] Isaiah IX.5 (LXX reading).
[28] *Ap. Trad.* IV.4; cf. B. Botte, *La tradition apostolique de saint Hippolyte*, Liturgiewissenschaftliche Quellen und Forschungen XXXIX (Münster in Westfalen, 1963), p. 12.

phrase: 'per manus sanctorum angelorum tuorum.' This form shows that St Ambrose misunderstood the Roman use, for it is most unlikely that in his day Rome was speaking of angels in the plural, but had before 700 recurred to the primitive form which perhaps it had in the second and third centuries. A far more likely explanation of this archaic phrase in the present Roman rite is that it was *per manus sancti angeli tui* in accordance with an Old Latin version of Isaiah IX.5, and that this was in the Roman rite from the time of St Justin onwards.

Another thoroughly primitive feature of the later Roman rite is the absence of an epiclesis. There is no sign of one in Justin, and the primitive form of epiclesis in the anaphora of Hippolytus is almost certainly a fourth-century addition to the original third-century text. (see below, pp. 13-14).

In ch. 66 of the *First Apology* St Justin quotes an account of the Institution of the Eucharist. It is difficult to say how far, if at all, it represents the liturgical text which was being used at the altar in Rome in the middle of the second century. The text of the account is as follows:

τὸν Ἰησοῦν λαβόντα ἄρτον εὐχαριστήσαντα εἰπεῖν · τοῦτο ποιεῖτε εἰς την ἀνάμνησίν μου, τοῦτό ἐστι τὸ σῶμά μου · καὶ τὸ ποτήριον ὁμοίως λαβόντα κὰι εὐχαριστήσαντα εἰπεῖν · τοῦτο ἐστι τὸ αἷμά μου.

Obviously this text is not close to any of the four New Testament accounts of the Institution, nor is it close to any known liturgical narrative. Professor Ratcliff has shown in an interesting study[29] that Justin's institution narrative is derived almost entirely from Matthew and Luke,[30] and that it was probably not compiled by him, but taken over from an existing catechetical tradition. It appears to be a generalised account designed for the eyes of the outside reader, although it is a little difficult to know what pagan readers would have made of it. It may be useful to compare some of its phrases with elements in the *Apostolic Tradition* of Hippolytus some sixty years later, and also with the earliest available form of the Roman Institution narrative.

[29] E. C. Ratcliff, 'The Eucharistic Institution Narrative of Justin Martyr's First Apology', *JEH* XXII (1971), 97-102.
[30] See Table *ibid.* p. 98.

Justin	*Hippolytus*	*Roman Canon, ed. Botte*
λαβόντα ἄρτον	accipiens panem	accepit panem
εὐχαριστήσαντα	gratias tibi agens	tibi gratias agens
τοῦτό ἐστι τὸ σῶμά μου	hoc est corpus meum quod pro vobis confringetur	hoc est enim corpus meum
καὶ τὸ ποτήριον ὁμοίως	similiter et calicem	simili modo . . . accipiens . . . calicem
τοῦτο ἐστι τὸ αἷμά μου	hic est sanguis meus	hic est enim calix sanguinis mei . . .

Hippolytus

The next Roman author after St Justin Martyr to give us any information about liturgy is St Hippolytus. The identity of this writer and the value of his polemical treatise Ἀποστολικὴ Παράδοσις for the reconstruction of Roman liturgy in the early third century, when the treatise was written, have been much disputed.[31]

Debate on these questions has continued for the whole of the twentieth century, but it is generally agreed among scholars that St Hippolytus was a priest at Rome who was the leader of a schism against Pope Callistus, but who is honoured as a martyr by the Roman Church because he died for the cause of Christianity in the penal mines of Sardinia; his body was brought back with that of Pontianus, the lawful bishop of Rome, and buried at Rome.[32]

It seems to be generally agreed that his treatise entitled the *Apostolic Tradition* was written as a polemical pamphlet against the pope, Zephyrinus, towards the end of the latter's pontificate, and about the year 215. The work is much more than a party pamphlet, though the

[31] In particular the student should consult R. H. Connolly, *The So-called Egyptian Church Order and Derived Documents*, Texts and Studies VIII.4 (Cambridge, 1916); *idem*, 'The Eucharistic Prayer of Hippolytus', *JTS* XXXIX (1938), 350-69; B. Botte, *La tradition apostolique de saint Hippolyte de Rome*, 2nd ed. (Münster, 1963), which has a critical edition of the Latin text and much information about the Oriental versions; Gregory Dix, *The Apostolic Tradition of St Hippolytus of Rome*, 2nd ed. rev. H. Chadwick (London, 1968); J. M. Hanssens, *La liturgie d'Hippolyte*, 2nd ed. (Rome, 1965), who argues for an Egyptian origin of the document. A good critical text of the Latin version will be found in Erik Tidner, *Didascaliae. Apostolorum Canonum Ecclesiasticorum Traditionis Apostolicae Versiones Latinae*, Texte und Untersuchungen LXXV (Berlin, 1963).
[32] Dix, *The Apostolic Tradition*, pp. xii-xxxv.

author avails himself of certain opportunities for launching attacks on his opponents. It is really the oldest extant example of a type of ecclesiastical literature which came to flourish in the East, though not in the West, during the fourth and fifth centuries. It might be fair to describe it as a handbook of Church practice, comprising canon law, regulations and discipline, together with regulations affecting divine worship and even prescribing texts for liturgical use. This last feature makes it of great interest to the historian of liturgy.

The *Apostolic Tradition* begins with some regulations for the ordination of bishops, priests and deacons, in the course of which it provides the text of an anaphora which the Sahidic version says elsewhere the newly consecrated bishop may offer if he is not of sufficient learning to compose his own text.[33] We are still in the primitive days in which there is no official prescribed text of the liturgy, but every celebrant has the right to say what he pleases at the altar, subject to the preservation of doctrinal orthodoxy, and probably also of one or two fixed parts, such as an institution narrative, in which he is expected to conform to agreed custom.[34] The book also sets forth an order of baptism, including what we call confirmation, and gives further information about the mass. If what is presented could be taken as the official text of the Roman rite in the early third century, it would be of surpassing importance as a witness of the liturgy at Rome in a period which otherwise is very dark. Yet how far is it safe to take it as such?

Fr Hanssens has argued at length that the Hippolytean liturgy derives from Alexandria and is not Roman in origin.[35] His arguments have failed to win general acceptance, although there is much to be learned incidentally from his book. Most scholars agree with Dix that the liturgy is Roman, and is the sort of thing which was being used at Rome in the writer's youth, say between 180 and 200. In other words, it was old fashioned at the time of the composition of the book, which must be somewhere around 215. This would fit the conservative tone of the treatise, which is a protest against innovation by a conservative who prefers the old ways. The theology and the main themes of the eucharistic prayer given by Hippolytus also fit very well with western eucharistic doctrine of the second century. It is in line with what we

[33] *Ap. Trad.*, ed. Botte, p. 29.
[34] See R. P. C. Hanson, 'The Liberty of the Bishop to Improvise Prayer in the Eucharist', *Vigiliae Christianae* XV (1961), 173-6.
[35] Hanssens, *La liturgie d'Hippolyte*.

have seen taught by St Clement of Rome, and the themes of the eucharistic prayer of Hippolytus are identical with those set forth by St Justin Martyr about 155, that is seventy years before the publication of the *Apostolic Tradition*, and are also in accord with the teaching of St Irenaeus, who stands midway between Justin and Hippolytus in time. Thus the prayer[36] is primarily a thanksgiving, in line with the type of thanksgiving for the mighty works of God used in the Jewish synagogue of the Dispersion. There are four main themes: 1. the Creation; 2. the Incarnation; 3. the Passion; and 4. the Lord's Supper. The fourth is out of its historical order so that it may stand in the eucharistic prayer immediately after the Passion, of which it is part, and may lead into the formula of oblation and the conclusion of the eucharistic thanksgiving. This pattern is clear in Justin[37] and in the prayer of the *Apostolic Tradition*, ch. 4. In the translation of the prayer which I give below,[38] the phrases italicized can be paralleled in the writings of St Irenaeus.[39]

It will be seen at once that this structure was drastically modified in the developed Roman rite after the end of the fourth century, by the truncation of the Christological thanksgivings. The scriptural narrative of the Institution of the sacrament has always held a prominent place in the Roman rite, and this makes its first appearance, so far as our documents go, in Africa in the writings of St Cyprian.[40]

Our main difficulty in assessing the value of the eucharistic prayer in the *Apostolic Tradition* is that we do not possess a text of what Hippolytus wrote in Greek in the third century. Fragments of the Greek may well be preserved in the eighth book of the *Apostolic Constitutions*, composed in Greek in West Syria round about 375, that is 160 years after the original work. These fragments are not certainly identifiable, and the *Apostolic Constitutions* as a whole express a liturgical tradition and an eucharistic doctrine very different from that of the work of Hippolytus. There have survived versions of parts of the work in Syriac, Ethiopic, Coptic, Arabic and Latin, none of which is less than about 150 years later than the original work. Of these the most complete is the Latin version found in a palimpsest at the Chapter Library in Verona.

---

[36] *Ap. Trad.*, ed. Botte, pp. 10-16.
[37] *Dial.*, ch. 41.
[38] See below, pp. 12-13.
[39] Quoted from E. C. Ratcliff, 'Christian Worship and Liturgy', in *The Study of Theology*, ed. K. E. Kirk (London, 1939), pp. 422-3.
[40] *Ep.* LXIII (PL IV, 392; CSEL III, 708).

The Latin appears to be a faithful version. The eucharistic prayer is set forth here in the Latin text and in Dix's translation as printed by Ratcliff.

(1)   Gratias tibi referimus d(eu)s, per dilectum puerum tuum Ie(su)m Chr(istu)m, quem in ultimis temporibus misisti nobis saluatorem et redemptorem et angelum uoluntatis tuae, qui est uerbum tuum inseparabile[m], per quem omnia fecisti et beneplacitum tibi fuit, misisti de caelo in matricem uirginis, quiq(ue) in utero habitus incarnatus est et filius tibi obtensus est, ex sp(irit)u s(an)c(t)o et uirgine natus. Qui uoluntatem tuam conplens et populum sanctum tibi adquirens extendit manus cum pateretur, ut a passione liberaret eos qui in te crediderunt. Qui, cumque traderetur uoluntariae passioni, ut mortem soluat et uincula diabuli dirumpat, et infernum calcet et iustos inluminet, et terminum figat et resurrectionem manifestet.

(2)   Accipiens panem gratias tibi agens dixit: Accipite, manducate, hoc est corpus meum quod pro uobis confringetur. Similiter et calicem dicens: Hic est sanguis meus qui pro uobis effunditur. Quando hoc facitis, meam commemorationem facitis.

(3)   Memores igitur mortis et resurrectionis eius, offerimus tibi panem et calicem, gratias tibi agentes quia nos dignos habuisti adstare coram te et tibi ministrare.

(4)   Et petimus ut mittas sp(iritu)m tuum s(an)c(tu)m in oblationem sanctae ecclesiae: in unum congregans des omnibus qui percipiunt sanctis in repletionem sp(iritu)s s(an)c(t)i ad confirmationem fidei in ueritate, ut te laudemus et glorificemus per puerum tuum Ie(su)m Chr(istu)m, per quem tibi gloria et honor patri et filio cum s(an)c(t)o sp(irit)u in sancta ecclesia tua et nunc et in saecula saeculorum. Amen.

[THANKSGIVING] We render thanks unto thee, O God, through thy Beloved *Child* Jesus Christ, whom *in the last times* thou didst send to us to be a *Saviour* and Redeemer and the *Messenger of thy counsel*; who is thy *Word* inseparable from thee, *through whom thou madest all things* and *in whom thou wast well-pleased*; whom thou didst send from heaven into the Virgin's womb, and who, conceived within her, was made flesh and demonstrated to be thy Son, *being born of Holy Spirit and a virgin*; who, fulfilling thy will and preparing for thee a *holy people, stretched forth his hands* for suffering, that he might release from sufferings *them who have believed in thee*; who, when he was betrayed to *voluntary* suffering *that he might abolish death* and *rend the*

12

bonds of the devil and tread down hell and *enlighten the righteous* and establish the ordinance and *demonstrate the resurrection*:

[INSTITUTION NARRATIVE] Taking bread and making eucharist [i.e. giving thanks] to thee, said: Take, eat: this is my Body which is broken for you [for the remission of sins]. Likewise also the cup, saying: This is my Blood which is shed for you. When ye do this, [ye] do my 'anamnesis.'

[ANAMNESIS] Doing therefore the 'anamnesis' of his death and resurrection, we offer to thee the bread and the cup, *making eucharist to thee*, because thou hast bidden us [*or* found us worthy] *to stand before thee* and *minister as priests to thee*.

[INVOCATION] And we pray thee that [thou wouldest send thy Holy Spirit upon the oblation of thy holy church] thou wouldest grant to all thy saints who partake to be united [to thee] that they may be fulfilled with the Holy Spirit *for the confirmation of* their *faith in truth*, that we may praise and glorify thee through thy [Beloved] Child Jesus Christ, through whom glory and honour be unto thee with the Holy Spirit in thy holy church now and for ever and world without end. Amen.

How much of this is from the pen of St Hippolytus in the early third century?[41] The language of the Christological thanksgivings in paragraphs 1 and 2 may well be original. It is not by any means certain that the Institution narrative paragraph is from the hand of Hippolytus, and it is very unlikely indeed that the epiclesis of the Holy Spirit in paragraph 4 is original. As Dix pointed out, the working theology of Hippolytus is patently binitarian[42] though he does mention the Holy Spirit in doxologies. Invocation of the Holy Spirit in the eucharist upon either the elements or the worshippers is a fourth-century development, and begins at Jerusalem in the middle of the century in the *Catechetical Lectures* of St Cyril of Jerusalem.[43]

Under the influence of the pneumatological controversies of the fourth and fifth centuries it spread widely in the East, and in most Eastern liturgies an epiclesis or prayer to the Father to send down the Holy Spirit was added at the end of the existing eucharistic prayer. It usually asked for either the immission of the Spirit on the bread and

---

[41] See E. C. Ratcliff, 'The Sanctus and the Pattern of the Early Anaphora', *JEH* I (1950), 29-36 and 125-34.

[42] Dix, *The Apostolic Tradition*, p. xxi.

[43] Ed. F. L. Cross, *St Cyril of Jerusalem's Lectures on The Christian Sacraments*, pp. 32 (Greek) and 74 (Eng.).

wine to consecrate them, and make them the Body and Blood of Christ, or else upon the worshippers to make them worthy partakers of the Body and Blood of Christ, or else it embraced both these themes. Clearly the epiclesis petition in *Apostolic Tradition* is more primitive than this. It asks for neither of these things, but that the Spirit may be sent upon the Bread and Cup in order that the communicants may be united.

All the same, it can hardly be attributed to the early third century. Professor Ratcliff, in the article cited, has argued very convincingly that the prayer as it stands cannot be the original work of Hippolytus. Paragraphs 3 and 4 are later. The lower script of the Verona palimpsest can be dated about 420, so the Greek from which it was translated may well be about 380. It is very difficult to imagine who would have wanted a Latin version of such a book at that period. The West had no interest in this type of 'Church Orders', which were very popular, on the other hand, in the East. And liturgical texts were not copied for historical or archaeological reasons, as Dr Cross showed,[44] but because someone wanted to use them for liturgical purposes. This means that they were adapted to the theological notions and liturgical habits of those who had them written. We are thus faced with the question, who on earth about 400 or a little later can have wanted a Latin text of such a book of two hundred years old? Some eastern churches had a text because they wanted to use it at the altar, and in Abyssinia a eucharist substantially identical with that of *Apostolic Tradition* is still in use.[45]

But it is hard to imagine who required one in Latin in the early fifth century. The liturgy of *Apostolic Tradition* has very few contacts with later liturgy in Rome itself.[46] Africa was using a Latin liturgy, but there is no sign whatever that it had anything in common with *Apostolic Tradition*, and the descriptions of the eucharist by St Augustine, with whom the Latin Verona version of *Apostolic Tradition* is contemporary, show no relation to it at all, and presuppose a much more developed rite. St Ambrose at Milan expounds in *De sacramentis*, near the end of the fourth century, a very different and more developed rite. Who then can have wanted a rite so primitive in its general outlines, and so Jewish in tone? Professor Burkitt seems to have been the first to suggest that it was some conservative Arian in north Italy, and he points

---

[44] F. L. Cross, 'Early Western Liturgical Manuscripts', *JTS* n.s. XVI (1965), 61-70.
[45] Dix, *The Apostolic Tradition of Hippolytus*, pp. xlix-li.
[46] See below, p. 16 and Table I.

out that Auxentius, a predecessor of St Ambrose in the see of Milan, and some other Milanese prelates, were eastern and Arians. Professor Chadwick and others have thought this suggestion worth considering, but in fact Burkitt produced no definite evidence in support of it, and against it it may be urged that there is nothing particularly Arian about the Christological thanksgivings, in the eucharistic prayer; indeed they are very orthodox. And also if this prayer were in use in Milan in its Arian days, before Ambrose's accession in 374, we may well wonder why anybody should have thought it worth while to publish a Latin translation of the Greek some forty or fifty years later, when as we know from *De sacramentis*, St Ambrose's catechetical lectures delivered about 390, an early form of the Roman rite, very different in pattern, was in use in Milan. The purpose which the translator of the rite of *Apostolic Tradition* into Latin had in view is one of the greatest unsolved mysteries of this puzzling document.

The *Apostolic Tradition* appears to have a single Eucharistic Prayer, like other early liturgies. It begins with the traditional versicles and responses:

V. Dominus uobiscum.   R. Et cum spiritu tuo.
V. Sursum corda.   R. Habemus ad Dominum.
V. Gratias agamus Domino.   R. Dignum et iustum est.

To the last of these three versicles the words *Deo nostro* were later added, but otherwise the section is identical in Hippolytus and the later Roman rite. The prayer then continues with the Christological thanksgivings for creation and redemption. These did not survive into the Roman rite after St Gregory, but were much curtailed, and in later times were represented only by the comparatively brief terms of the preface. In the fifth and sixth centuries the prefaces were much more ample than they have usually been since that date, and in the Leonine Sacramentary, compiled in the middle of the sixth century, probably during the pontificate of Vigilius (537-55), almost every mass has its own preface. But the elaborate thanksgivings represented in the *Apostolic Tradition* atrophied as time went on. Hippolytus's phrase applied to Christ, *angelum uoluntatis tuae*, is the exact Latin translation of the Septuagint of Isaiah IX.5, and it survived into the classical Roman rite of St Gregory's time, where in *Supplices te rogamus* the Father is asked to order the gifts to be carried by his holy angel (*per manum sancti angeli tui*) to his altar on high. This angel, in view of the history of the phrase, must be the Son himself.

15

The institution narrative of Hippolytus has not many close similarities with that of the final Roman rite, but a few parallels for comparison have been set out in Table I (below, p. 149). Hippolytus cites the words of administration. They are 'The Bread of Heaven in Christ Jesus' for the Bread and 'In God the Father Almighty, And in the Lord Jesus Christ; And in (the) Holy Spirit (and) in the Holy Church' for the Cup.[47] These forms were not used in the Roman rite later on. Nor was the custom preserved which Hippolytus attests of the communicant responding AMEN when he is communicated.

St Cyprian

After the *Apostolic Tradition* of St Hippolytus, which is to be dated about 215, there is a very long interval of over 170 years before the next substantial piece of evidence about the order of mass at Rome is provided by St Ambrose in his catechetical lectures, published under the title of *De sacramentis* about 390 (see below, pp. 23-32).

A generation, however, after St Hippolytus wrote the *Apostolic Tradition*, valuable information is provided by St Cyprian. This does not of course derive from Rome, but it is none the less significant for the history of Roman liturgy, since from the second century till the seventh, when African Christianity itself was swept away by the Arab invasions, there was a close relationship between African Christianity and Roman and such relations were significant in the sphere of liturgy. And when we examine the eucharistic teaching of St Cyprian we shall notice that it displays characteristic features which ally it to Roman more closely than to any other liturgy.

The classic source of St Cyprian's eucharistic teaching is his letter to Caecilius, *Ep*. LXIII.[48] The letter was written to controvert certain people who had an eccentric manner of celebrating the eucharist. They were very likely aquarians, who filled the chalice with water and used no wine, for Cyprian says that the sacrament is invalid if there is no wine in the chalice.[49]

---

[47] Ed. Botte, pp. 56-8 (§ xxi (L)). For the bread S(AE) has the words, 'This is the heavenly bread the body of Jesus Christ'; for the cup, 'This is the blood of our Lord Jesus Christ.'

[48] PL IV, 383-401; CSEL III, 701-17.

[49] PL IV, 392; CSEL III, 708: 'Unde apparet sanguinem Christi non offerri, si desit vinum calici, nec sacrificium Dominicum legitima sanctificatione celebrari, nisi oblatio et sacrificium nostrum responderit passioni.'

He insists that water and wine shall be mingled in the chalice, in conformity with what the Lord did at the Last Supper when he instituted the eucharist.[50] The celebrant's actions in the eucharist must in every respect conform with those of Christ – the mass must be a careful *imitatio cenae*. For Cyprian the Supper interprets the Passion, since Christ offered himself to the Father in sacramental form *sub die passionis*.[51] Through the church Christ continually offers this same sacrifice.[52] The Supper, the Passion and the Mass are therefore three parts of a single action by which Christ offers himself to the Father. To such an action a scriptural narrative of the Institution is indispensable.[53] St Cyprian then quotes *verbatim* the Institution narrative relating to the Cup only from Matthew XXVI.27-8 in the following form:

> calicem etenim sub die passionis accipiens benedixit et dedit discipulis suis dicens: bibite ex hoc omnes. hic est enim sanguis testamenti qui pro multis effundetur in remissionem peccatorum.[54]

The Matthaean narrative concerning the Bread is not cited in any of St Cyprian's extant works. But the earliest Institution narrative to be composed, that of St Paul in the first Epistle to the Corinthians (I Cor. XI.23-6), influences and supplements for St Cyprian the Matthaean narrative, which he regards as basic, and there is in his narrative none of the pious embroidery which is so prominent a feature of Eastern narratives of the Institution. St Cyprian's account of the Institution is even more scriptural than the Roman narrative as we find it in the Irish tradition at the end of the seventh century, though as we shall soon see, this tradition is closely related to the tradition of St Cyprian. Here is St Cyprian's text of the narrative from I Corinthians:

> Dominus Iesus in qua nocte tradebatur accepit panem et gratias egit et fregit et dixit: hoc est corpus meum quod pro uobis est. hoc facite in meam commemorationem. simili modo et calicem postquam cenatum est accepit dicens: hic calix nouum

---

[50] PL IV, 385; CSEL III, 702: 'Admonitos autem nos scias ut in calice offerendo Dominica traditio servetur, neque aliud fiat a nobis quam quod pro nobis Dominus prior fecit, ut calix qui in commemoratione eius offertur mistus vino offeratur.' Cf. also PL IV, 399; CSEL III, 714: '. . . nihil aliud quam quod ille fecit facere debemus.'
[51] PL IV, 392; CSEL III, 708.
[52] PL IV, 398-9; CSEL III, 714: 'Passio est enim Domini sacrificium quod offerimus.'
[53] See E. C. Ratcliff, 'The Institution Narrative of the Roman *Canon Missae*: its Beginnings and Early Background', *Studia Patristica* II (1957), 64-82.
[54] PL IV, 392; CSEL III, 708.

testamentum est in meo sanguine. hoc facite quotienscumque biberitis in meam commemorationem. . . . quotienscumque enim ederitis panem istum et calicem biberitis mortem domini adnuntiatis quoadusque ueniat.[55]

The nature of St Cyprian's text of the Institution narrative will be seen from comparisons set out in Table I (below, p. 149), drawn from Botte's text of the *Apostolic Tradition*, Hartel's text of St Cyprian's *Ep.* LXIII, and Botte's text of the early form of the Roman canon.[56]

A passage from St Cyprian's treatise on the Lord's Prayer which deals with the spirit of liturgical prayer is also of some significance in relation to the eucharistic canon. He says that restraint and discipline should be observed in offering such prayer, not with a windy and noisy style.[57]

> et quando in unum cum fratribus conuenimus, et sacrificia diuina cum dei sacerdote celebramus uerecundiae et disciplinae memores esse debemus, non passim uentilare preces nostras inconditis uocibus nec petitionem commendandam modeste deo tumultuosa loquacitate iactare quia deus non uocis sed cordis auditor est, nec admonendus est clamoribus qui cogitationes uidet, probante Domino et dicente: quid cogitatis nequam in cordibus uestris? et alio loco: et scient omnes ecclesiae quia ego sum scrutator renis et cordis.

It appears that St Cyprian here has in mind the excesses of extempore improvisations by exuberant celebrants. *Tumultuosa loquacitas* is a danger inseparable from improvisation. Extempore preachers and intercessors who make up the *orationes fidelium* as they go along are a menace to the modern church, and noisy and verbose improvisors of the eucharistic prayer must have been an even worse menace in the ancient Church. The turgid and repetitive Eastern eucharistic prayers which have survived from the fourth and fifth centuries show what had to be feared from such celebrants, and St Cyprian's plea for restraint bore fruit in Roman and no doubt in African liturgical composition of the succeeding centuries. Thus we see in the Roman Canon as it stood in the time of Pope Innocent I (402-17) and St Gregory (590-604) that the exuberant thanksgivings for the works of God have been reduced to very modest proportions.

---

[55] PL IV, 392-3; CSEL III, 708.
[56] Botte, *Le Canon de la messe romaine*, pp. 38 and 40.
[57] Cypr., *De orat. dom.*, ch. 4 (PL IV, 538-9; CSEL III, 269).

II

The Development of the Roman Mass between the Peace of the Church and the Death of Pope Gregory the Great

By about the year 700 the Roman eucharistic prayer had reached the form which has survived with no fundamental change down to the present day, and which continues in *Prex Eucharistica Prima* authorized in 1970 in the revised Missal which was produced as the result of the decisions of the Second Vatican Council.[1]

This *Canon Missae* is first seen in the Bobbio Missal[2] which is to be dated shortly before 700, and in the other members of the Hiberno-Gallican family, the Stowe Missal[3] and *Missale Francorum*[4] of the early eighth century. There is little difference of any moment between the text of the Canon in these books, and in the Gregorian books, which are more purely Roman, of the end of the eighth century and the beginning of the ninth. Since there was no important change during the seventh century, it is fair to claim that in the text resulting from collation of these two families in their earliest form, a text printed by Dom Bernard Botte,[5] we have something very close to the Canon as it stood at the death of Pope Gregory in 604.

The three hundred years between the Peace of the Church and the death of St Gregory were a period of liturgical development and settlement in all parts of Christendom, and not least at Rome. During

---

[1] *Missale Romanum ex decreto sacrosancti oecumenici concilii Vaticani II instauratum auctoritate Pauli PP.VI promulgatum* (Vatican City, 1970).
[2] *The Bobbio Missal: Facsimile*, HBS LIII (London, 1917); *The Bobbio Missal: Text*, ed. E. A. Lowe, HBS LVIII (London, 1919), pp. 10-13.
[3] *The Stowe Missal (MS Royal Irish Academy D. II.3)*, ed. G. F. Warner, 2 vols, HBS XXI-XXXII (London, 1906-15), II, 10-16.
[4] *Missale Francorum (MS Vat. Reg. lat. 257)*, ed. L. C. Mohlberg, Rerum Ecclesiasticarum Documenta Series Maior, Fontes II (Rome, 1957), pp. 31-3.
[5] *Le canon de la messe romaine* (Louvain, 1935).

this period the Roman rite was undergoing development and formalization which eventually brought it to something like its present state. The period of three hundred years begins with a state of affairs in which the eucharistic prayer is still at the discretion of the celebrant, and in which there is no fixed and authoritative form, and ends with fixed rites written in books. Unfortunately there is a considerable dearth of evidence about this important formative period in Roman liturgy, and a complete account of the development is not likely to be possible unless further evidence comes to light. Two questions in particular remain unanswered:

1. At what time did Latin replace Greek as the liturgical language at Rome?
2. When did the Canon begin to be said silently?

It will be convenient to defer discussion of the latter question, and to deal with it in connection with the two paragraphs of the Canon which begin with the word *Memento*.[6]

The change from Greek to Latin

As to the former question, a definitive answer is precluded by the paucity of the evidence. Preaching at Milan about 390, St Ambrose cites a Latin eucharistic prayer, which he says is Roman, and which is an earlier form of the traditional Roman *Canon Missae*.[7] But in the days of St Hippolytus, 170 years earlier, Rome, for which he was writing, evidently prayed in Greek. At the end of the first century St Clement of Rome is writing in Greek and quoting the Bible in Greek. St Justin Martyr is doing the same in the middle of the second century, but by the end of the second century there is at Rome, as in Africa, a Latin version of the Bible, and from that time onwards Latin versions diverge in two families, the African and the European, the latter developing mainly in Italy. As far as the Bible is concerned, the process seems to have been complete at Rome by the middle of the third century. By this time, too, the correspondence of the popes, which in earlier days had been exclusively in Greek, began to be conducted in Latin, at any rate for

---

[6] See below, pp. 39-40.
[7] Ambrose, *De sacramentis*, ed. O. Faller, CSEL LXXIII (Vienna, 1955), pp. 55 and 57.

correspondence in the West, including Africa, though Greek was still used in official correspondence with the East. About 250, for instance, the Roman clergy was writing to St Cyprian, the bishop of Carthage, in Latin, and at the same time Novatian, a Roman priest, wrote his *De trinitate* and other works in Latin, quoting an existing Latin version of the Bible.[8]

The change from Greek to Latin for liturgical purposes was evidently completed before 390, the approximate date of St Ambrose's *De sacramentis*, indeed by 382, the date of the treatise by Isaac the Jew, *Quaestiones Veteris et Noui Testamenti*, written at Rome. This treatise states that Melchisedech is referred to in the liturgy as *summus sacerdos*.[9] *Summus sacerdos* is the mistranslation of the Greek of Hebrews VII.1, ἱερεὺς ὑψίστου, priest of the Most High (*scil.* God) which appears in the section *Supra quae* in the Roman Canon, so its quotation by Isaac and by Ambrose a few years later shows that it was in the Canon, and that the Canon was in Latin, by 382. Some twenty years earlier the Eucharistic Prayer at Rome is cited in Greek by an African writer, Marius Victorinus, writing in Latin at Rome.[10] The passages of Marius Victorinus were written between 350 and 375.[11] These passages are *Aduersus Arium* II.30: 'sic rursus et Paulus in Epistula ad Titum' (II.14): populum περιούσιον circa substantiam hoc est circa uitam consistentem populum, sicut et in oblatione dicitur: Munda tibi populum circumuitalem, aemulatorem bonorum operum';[12] and *Aduersus Arium*. II.8: 'appellamur λαὸς περιούσιος. hinc sanctus Apostolus ad Titum: epistula sic dicit graece: . . . καὶ καθαρίσῃ ἑαυτῷ λαὸν περιούσιον ζηλωτὴν καλῶν ἔργων. latinus cum non intelligeret . . . posuit 'populum abundantem. hinc oratio oblationis intellectu eodem precatur eum' σῶσον περιούσιον λαὸν ζηλωτὴν καλῶν ἔργων.'[13]

[8] See G. Bardy, *La question des langues dans l'ancienne église*, (Paris 1918), p. 81; Christine Mohrmann, 'Les origines de la latinité chrétienne à Rome', *Vigiliae Christianae* III (1949), 67-106; T. Klauser, 'Der Übergang der römischen Kirche von der griechischen zur lateinischen Liturgiesprache', *Miscellanea Giovanni Mercati I, Studi e Testi* CXXI (Vatican City, 1946), pp. 467-82.

[9] PL XXXV, 2329: 'Similiter et spiritus sanctus quasi antistes sacerdos appellatus est excelsi Dei, non summus, sicut nostri in oblatione praesumunt.'

[10] See G. Bardy, 'Formules liturgiques grecques à Rome au quatrième siècle', *Recherches de science religieuse* XXX (1940), 109-112.

[11] See G. Morin, 'Formules liturgiques orientales en Occident aux quatrième et cinquième siècles', *Revue Bénédictine* XL (1928), 134-7.

[12] PL VIII, 1063B.

[13] PL VIII, 1094D.

Marius Victorinus was writing at Rome for Romans, and they evidently understood both languages, and performed the mass in Greek. In the light of these quotations from Marius Victorinus and the *Quaestiones Veteris et Noui Testamenti*, therefore, it is possible to fix the final change from Greek to Latin as the liturgical language at Rome during the pontificate of Damasus, 366-84, and it is a pity that St Jerome, who was closely associated with Damasus in the later years of his pontificate, tells us nothing about this fundamental change of liturgical language. What happened in the pontificate of Damasus was not necessarily, or even probably, a definitive change of language on a particular day. It is clear from St Augustine that in his time (bishop of Hippo, 395-430) there was still fluidity in the eucharistic prayer in Africa. The council of Carthage in 397 stipulated that the prayer should be addressed always to the Father,[14] which suggests that in the early years of St Augustine's episcopate other practices were known in Africa. These may have included the custom of addressing the eucharistic prayer to the Son, which was the case with the original form of the Anaphora of Addai and Mari in Eastern Syria at an earlier date.[15]

The quotation of the central part of the Roman Prayer by St Ambrose shows that at Rome about 390, or in the decade before, fixity was being approached, but what happened in respect of liturgical language under Damasus was the completion of a process which may have been going on for many years. Professor Mohrmann suggests that the baptismal liturgy may have become Latin before the Mass,[16] and Canon Couratin that Latin may well have been first employed at Rome by an African congregation as early as the third century,[17] but neither suggestion is supported by its author with definite evidence, so that the hypotheses, though quite reasonable and likely, are not proven. What is certain is that the use of Greek at Rome did not survive later than the pontificate of Damasus.

---

[14] Council of Hippo (397), Canon XXIII: 'cum altari assistitur, semper ad Patrem oratio dirigatur' (Mansi III, col. 884).
[15] See E. C. Ratcliff, 'The Original Form of the Anaphora of Addai and Mari', *JTS* XXX (1929), 23-32.
[16] C. Mohrmann, 'Les origines de la latinité chrétienne à Rome', p. 70.
[17] A H. Couratin, *The Pelican Guide to Modern Theology* II (Harmondsworth, 1969), p. 192.

The Canon cited by St Ambrose

It is therefore generally agreed that the latinization of the Roman rite was completed under the pontificate of Damasus (366-84), and the first substantial citation of any part of the Roman Canon in Latin makes its appearance very soon afterwards in the catechetical lectures of St Ambrose entitled *De sacramentis*, the attribution of which to St Ambrose is now universally agreed. Comparison of these six lectures with the similar work of the same author, entitled *De mysteriis*, shows that *De mysteriis* has been extensively revised and edited by the author, with a view to publication, as have certain of his other works, like the *Explanationes in psalmos*, which were originally delivered as sermons and which underwent literary revision before publication. This did not happen to *De sacramentis*, which reads like the *verbatim* report of a stenographer, such as we have in the *Gesta cum Emerito* of St Augustine, and in the case of many of that preacher's sermons. It is generally thought that the six catechetical lectures, entitled *De sacramentis*, which appear to have been delivered to the neophytes at Milan on the six weekdays of an Easter Week, are to be dated about the year 390, that is, three years after St Ambrose baptized St Augustine on Easter Even, 387.

In the course of these lectures St Ambrose states emphatically that he desires in all things to follow the use of the Church of Rome, and in speaking of the baptismal ceremonies he devoted special attention to the main point in which he diverges from Roman usage, namely in washing the feet of the candidates.[18]

So in treating of the Canon of the Mass it seems reasonable to take St Ambrose as a witness of Roman usage, especially in view of the fact that the central portion of the Canon, which he quotes verbatim in *De sacramentis* IV.21-9, has a fairly close relationship to the form which that Canon had assumed by the year 700, when we next see it quoted *in extenso* in the Bobbio Missal and in other, slightly later, members of the Hiberno-Gallican family. The three hundred years formed a period during which constant change was being carried out in the Canon, so that the differences between St Ambrose's Canon and the finally settled Canon are less remarkable than their similarities.

---

[18] Ambrose, *De sacramentis* III.5, ed. Faller, p. 40: 'Ecclesia Romana . . . cuius typum in omnibus sequimur et formam . . . In omnibus cupio sequi ecclesiam Romanam.'

It should also be borne in mind that it is quite likely that there were small local differences between Rome and Milan in relation to the Mass, just as there are known to have been in respect of baptism.[19] St Ambrose does not cite the whole Canon, but only the central part, parallel to the sections of the Roman Canon which begin with the words *Quam oblationem, Qui pridie, Unde et memores, Supra quae,* and *Supplices te rogamus.* Before citing these sections, St Ambrose refers vaguely without quoting any text, to two parts of the Mass which precede the sections which he quotes verbatim. His words are: 'Laus Deo, defertur oratio, petitur pro populo, pro regibus, pro ceteris'.[20] The praise will be the Preface, telling forth the mighty works of God in creation and redemption, with which the eucharistic prayer of the *Apostolic Tradition* begins, like every known eucharistic prayer. Until the time of St Gregory this Preface, as it was called in Roman liturgy, was much more extended than it has been ever since. But for long it continued to be at the discretion of the celebrant, and it is very doubtful whether by the time of St Ambrose it had been fixed. Almost every mass in the Verona or Leonine Sacramentary, compiled probably under Vigilius in the middle of the sixth century, has its own Preface. What happened is that the celebrant composed his Preface, which was often topical, and commented, like some modern sermons, on contemporary events, and then filed it in the *scrinium,* and from such collections of *libelli,* as they were called, the Verona Sacramentary was compiled. An indication that in the time of St Ambrose the celebrant still retained his discretion in this matter is the distinction which St Ambrose makes between the eucharistic prayer in general, which the celebrant devises, and the *uerba Christi,* which he uses in consecrating the sacrament.[21]

The section of the Canon quoted by Ambrose is doubtless the fixed part, containing the scriptural narrative of the Institution, while the variable part, still at the discretion of the celebrant, includes the Preface.

It is more difficult to be certain what it is to which St Ambrose refers in the words *oratio petitur pro populo, pro regibus, pro ceteris.* The verb *petitur,* 'is requested', would not naturally apply to the form of the later Roman Canon, 'Memento famulorum famularumque tuarum . . .'

---

[19] See below, pp. 118 and 134-6.

[20] Ambrose, *De sacramentis* IV.4, ed. Faller, p. 52.

[21] *Ibid.*: 'Ubi venitur. ut conficiatur venerabile sacramentum, iam non suis sermonibus utitur sacerdos, sed utitur sermonibus Christi. Ergo sermo Christi hoc conficit sacramentum.'

as part of the sacerdotal prayer of the celebrant, which makes prayer rather than seeks it. The verb *petitur* would more naturally suggest the deacon reading the diptychs, or lists of living and departed, for whom the people is told to pray. The forms *Memento* and *Memento etiam* of the final Roman Canon no doubt developed from this type of diaconal prayer, and St Augustine gives a hint that this form of intercession was known in Africa when he says, 'communis oratio voce diaconi indicitur'.[22] Alternatively, it might refer to a form of prayer which has survived, though on Good Friday only, in the Roman rite, in what are called *orationes sollemnes*.[23]

In the original form of these intercessions the biddings were proclaimed by the deacon, and they can be traced back to the fourth century, or perhaps to the third. The collects are said by the priest, and they can hardly be earlier than the accession of Xystus in 432, probably not earlier than that of Leo the Great in 440. These criteria as to date are based upon considerations of style, rhythm and content.[24] Of course in the time of St Ambrose, and indeed down to Gelasius (492-6), the *orationes sollemnes* were used daily and were not confined to Good Friday.

The fixed part of the Canon cited by St Ambrose may now be set out in the text of Faller,[25] side by side with the early Gregorian and Gelasian recension of the Roman Canon as established by Dom Bernard Botte.[26]

Ambrose	*Roman Mass*
Fac nobis hanc oblationem scriptam, rationabilem, acceptabilem, quod est figura corporis et sanguinis domini nostri Iesu Christi. Qui pridie quam pateretur, in sanctis manibus suis accepit panem, respexit ad caelum, ad te, sancte pater	Quam oblationem tu deus in omnibus quaesumus benedictam adscriptam ratam rationabilem acceptabilemque facere digneris ut nobis corpus et sanguis fiat dilectissimi filii tui domini dei nostri iesu christi. Qui pridie quam pateretur accepit panem in sanctas ac uenerabiles manus suas eleuatis oculis in caelum ad te deum

---

[22] Augustine, *Ep*. LV (PL XXXIII, 221; CSEL XXXIV, 209).
[23] See G. G. Willis, 'The Solemn Prayers of Good Friday', in *Essays in Early Roman Liturgy* (London, 1964), pp. 1-48.
[24] Willis, *ibid*., pp. 45-7; *idem*, 'The Variable Prayers of the Roman Mass', in *Further Essays in Early Roman Liturgy* (London, 1968), pp. 114-15.
[25] Ambrose, *De sacramentis*, ed. Faller, pp. 55-7.
[26] *Le Canon de la Messe romaine*, pp. 36-42.

omnipotens aeterne deus,
gratias agens benedixit,
fregit, fractumque apostolis
et discipulis suis tradidit
dicens: Accipite et edite
ex hoc omnes; hoc est enim
corpus meum, quod pro multis
confringetur. Similiter
etiam calicem, postquam
cenatum est, pridie quam
pateretur, accepit, respexit
ad caelum, ad te, sancte
pater omnipotens aeterne
deus, gratias agens bene-
dixit, apostolis et
discipulis suis tradidit
dicens: accipite et
bibite ex hoc omnes. hic
est enim sanguis meus.
quotienscumque hoc fecer-
itis, totiens commemorationem
mei facietis, donec iterum
adveniam. Ergo memores
gloriosissimae eius passionis
et ab inferis resurrectionis
et in caelum ascensionis
offerimus tibi hanc inmaculatam hostiam, rationabilem
hostiam, incruentam hostiam,
hunc panem sanctum et calicem
vitae aeternae. Et petimus et
precamur, uti hanc oblationem
suscipias in sublime altare
tuum per manus angelorum
tuorum, sicut suscipere dignatus
es munera pueri tui iusti Abel
et sacrificium patriarchae
nostri Abrahae et quod tibi
obtulit summus sacerdos
Melchisedech.

patrem suum omnipotentem tibi gratias
agens benedixit fregit dedit discipulis
suis dicens accipite et manducate ex
hoc omnes. hoc est enim corpus meum.
Simili modo posteaquam caenatum est
accipiens et hunc praeclarum calicem
in sanctas ac uenerabiles manus suas
item tibi gratias agens benedixit dedit
discipulis suis dicens accipite et
bibite ex eo omnes. hic est enim
calix sanguinis mei noui et aeterni
testamenti mysterium fidei qui pro uobis
et pro multis effundetur in remissionem
peccatorum. Haec quotiescumque feceritis
in mei memoriam facietis.
Unde et memores sumus domine nos tui
serui sed et plebs tua sancta christi
filii tui domini dei nostri tam beatae
passionis necnon et ab inferis resurrectionis sed et in caelos gloriosae
ascensionis offerimus praeclarae
maiestati tuae de tuis donis ac datis
hostiam puram hostiam sanctam hostiam
immaculatam panem sanctum uitae aeterna
et calicem salutis perpetuae.
Supra quae propitio ac sereno uultu
respicere digneris et accepta habere
sicuti accepta habere dignatus es munera
pueri tui iusti Abel et sacrificium
patriarchae nostri abrahae et quod tibi
obtulit summus sacerdos tuus Melchisedech
sanctum sacrificium immaculatam hostiam.
Supplices te rogamus omnipotens deus iube
haec perferri per manus angeli tui in
sublime altare tuum in conspectu diuinae
maiestatis tuae ut quotquot ex hac altaris
participatione sacrosanctum filii tui
corpus et sanguinem sumpserimus omni
benedictione caelesti et gratia
repleamur per christum dominum nostrum.

St Ambrose's citation begins absolutely: *Fac nobis hanc oblationem scriptam*, unlike the Roman form *Quam oblationem tu deus in omnibus quaesumus benedictam adscriptam ratam rationabilem acceptabilem-que facere digneris.* The relative in the latter form connects the section with the prayer which has preceded *Quam oblationem* since the sixth century and probably since the fifth, *Hanc igitur oblationem.*

Ambrose's form is not connected with anything which precedes it: indeed possibly nothing does precede it at his time except the Preface, and perhaps also some intercession, of which the precise form may not have been fixed. However, quite apart from the possibility that in the time of St Ambrose nothing did in fact precede *Fac nobis hanc oblationem scriptam*, there was a tendency in the development and formalization of the Roman Canon to introduce relative clauses to connect one sentence with another, instead of the simpler and less stylish parataxis of the early form. Another example of this may be noted further on, where *Supra quae* is substituted for *et petimus et precamur ut hanc oblationem suscipas*, which Ambrose has.

Tu Deus and *in omnibus*, which the Roman Canon adds, are embellishments on stylistic grounds, to make the form more rotund and graceful. The same may be said of the expansion to five of the original three epithets which govern the substantive *oblationem*. Ambrose puts *scriptam, rationabilem, acceptabilem*: the Roman Canon *benedictam, adscriptam, ratam, rationabilem, acceptabilemque*. *Ratam*, approved, is an adjective with a juridical sound, deriving from Roman pagan euchological forms rather than from Christian or biblical sources. This also applies to *puram*, which governs *hostiam* in *Unde et memores*. The phrase *quod est figura corporis et sanguinis Domini nostri Iesu Christi* has an Oriental rather than a Roman ring: it should be compared with προθέντες τὰ ἀντίτυπα τοῦ ἁγίου σώματος καὶ αἵματος τοῦ χριστοῦ in the Liturgy of St Basil.[27] In the Roman rite it was transformed into an explicit petition for the consecration of the gifts: *ut nobis corpus et sanguis fiat dilectissimi filii tui domini dei nostri Iesu Christi*.

Professor Christine Mohrmann is right in saying that the Gelasian Canon, that is to say, the Canon found in the Old Gelasian Sacramentary, Vaticanus Reginensis 316, is, as had already been argued by Mgr Callewaert, a stylistic modification of the forms found in the *De sacramentis* of St Ambrose.[28] Its most striking characteristic, she says, is the accumulation of synonyms, and a tendency to amplify, and to make the language more solemn. Paratactic constructions are replaced by either a relative clause, e.g., *Fac nobis hanc oblationem* by

[27] F. E. Brightman, *Liturgies Eastern and Western* (Oxford, 1896), p. 329, lines 23-5.
[28] C. Mohrmann, 'Quelques observations sur l'évolution stylistique du canon romain', *Vigiliae Christianae* IV (1950), 1-19; C. Callewaert, 'Histoire primitive du canon romain', *Sacris Erudiri* II (1949), 95-110.

Quam oblationem, etc.; *Et petimus et precamur ut hanc oblationem suscipias* by *Supra quae propitio ac sereno uultu respicere digneris*, both of them cited above; or else by an ablative absolute, as when *respexit in caelum* is replaced by *eleuatis oculis in caelum*, also cited above. Another tendency is the accumulation of synonyms. This is a feature strongly characteristic of Roman euchology, which has already made its appearance in the Canon as cited by St Ambrose, and becomes much more common in the developed Canon. From the former may be cited *scriptam, rationabilem, acceptabilem*; *fregit fractumque apostolis et discipulis suis tradidit*; *et petimus et precamur*. In the developed Canon may be cited (in *Te igitur*): *supplices rogamus et petimus*; *haec dona haec munera, haec sancta sacrificia inlibata*; *quam pacificare custodire et regere digneris*. In the Institution narrative we have *in sanctas ac uenerabiles manus suas*. In *Unde et memores* there is *de tuis donis ac datis*; *hostiam puram hostiam sanctam hostiam immaculatam*; in *Supra quae*: *propitio ac sereno uultu*. There are some tricks of style derived from Roman juridical language, e.g., *nec non et, sed et*, and *dignare* from curial style, often found in papal correspondence. This juridical pleonasm is not peculiarly Christian; it occurs in Latin pagan prayers.[29] This similarity with Latin pagan prayers is a matter of style only: it does not extend to vocabulary. The vocabulary of the Canon is fundamentally Christian, indeed biblical, as we shall see when we come to consider the sources of particular phrases and thoughts in the Canon.

In *De sacramentis* the opening of the Institution narrative is the characteristically Roman phrase *qui pridie quam pateretur*, 'who on the day before he suffered', which connects the eucharist with the Passion in general and not with the betrayal in particular. In this it contrasts with the Eastern rites, which all introduce the Institution by the Pauline phrase 'who in the same night in which he was betrayed'. Ambrose has *in sanctis manibus suis accepit panem*. The phrase about the Lord's hands is a liturgical embellishment of the gospel narrative, and is much more modest than the form it assumes in most Eastern liturgies. By the time of the developed Roman Canon it has been slightly amplified and has become *in sanctas ac uenerabiles manus suas*.

The phrase *respexit ad caelum* is an example of the addition of notions and phrases from scriptural sources other than the accounts of the eucharistic Institution: this one is derived from the narratives of the Feeding of the Multitude. Note that while Ambrose has the simple

---

[29] See Morhmann, *ibid.*, pp. 12-14, where she cites examples of this tendency.

paratactic verb *respexit ad caelum*, the Roman Canon has an ablative absolute, *eleuatis oculis in caelum*, which is purely a stylistic modification. In both the Ambrosian and the Roman Canons the same phrase is repeated in the narrative respecting the Cup: one of several examples of the desire to make the two parts of the liturgical narrative parallel to one another. The word *fractumque* is an addition to the gospel narrative peculiar to Ambrose, and not shared by any form of the Roman Canon. The phrase *tibi gratias agens* is an addition of the Roman narrative, not present in Ambrose, but due to parallelism. The Roman Canon reads *dedit discipulis suis*, but Ambrose has *apostolis et discipulis suis*, an expansion probably derived from Eastern sources, where it is common. Ambrose reads *edite* and the Roman narrative *manducate*. Similarly, the phrase *quod pro multis confringetur* is not in any form of the Roman Canon, but occurs in Hippolytus in the form *quod pro vobis confringetur*.

In the narrative respecting the Cup, Ambrose inserts, in parallelism, the words *pridie quam pateretur*, which the Roman sources do not. The phrase *apostolis et discipulis suis tradidit dicens* is repeated in the narrative concerning the Cup by Ambrose. The simple form of Ambrose, *hic est enim sanguis meus*, is expanded in the Roman rite to *hic est enim calix sanguinis mei noui et aeterni testamenti mysterium fidei, qui pro uobis et pro multis effundetur in remissionem peccatorum*. *Noui et aeterni testamenti* is an expansion partly scriptural, partly stylistic. The phrase *quod pro uobis effundetur in remissionem peccatorum* is scriptural (Matthew XXVI.28), and *mysterium fidei* is a scriptural addition (I Tim. III.9) from a portion of scripture not related to the eucharist, an addition evidently Gallican which looks rather late, though it was certainly in the text by 700. However, some of this may perhaps have been in the Canon at Milan in Ambrose's day, for after the words *hic est enim sanguis meus* Ambrose breaks off in his address to make some comments of his own, and when he returns, in ch. 26, to citation of the narrative, he goes on at *quotienscumque hoc feceritis, totiens commemorationem mei facietis donec iterum adueniam*. It is therefore possible that he has in fact omitted some words from the narrative in use at his time. Note should be taken of a significant difference between the Ambrosian and Roman forms of the final phrase just quoted. It is, of course, derived from St Paul's account (I Cor. XI.25-6), but in the Roman form it has been adjusted, by the change of *hoc* to *haec*, to include the eating of the Bread as well as the drinking of the Cup.

In the Anamnesis, the adjective *gloriosae* has appeared before *Ascensionis* in the Roman form, and *beatae* has replaced *gloriosissimae* as the epithet of *passionis*. A more elaborate modification is the amplification of the subject of the sentence, from *nos* understood to *nos serui tui sed et plebs tua sancta*, in the Roman form. The object of the sentence, too, has been modified in the later form. Ambrose has *hanc immaculatam hostiam, rationabilem hostiam, incruentam hostiam, hunc panem sanctum et calicem vitae aeternae*, which in the Roman Canon becomes *hostiam puram, hostiam sanctam, hostiam immaculatam, panem sanctum uitae aeternae et calicem salutis perpetuae*. Both these should be compared with the earliest known form of this prayer, seen in the *Apostolic Tradition* of St Hippolytus, *panem et calicem*. Notice another expansion after Ambrose, by which the indirect object of this verb *offerimus* is expanded from *tibi* to *praeclarae maiestati tuae*.

The rest of the citation by Ambrose, which is parallel to the sections of the Roman Canon which begin *Supra quae* and *Supplices te rogamus*, expresses two thoughts which are extremely primitive, and goes back at least to the second century, namely the mention of the pre-Mosaic sacrifices of Abel, Abraham and Melchisedech, and the petition that God's holy angel, who is the Christ, may be commanded to bear the Church's oblations to the heavenly altar.[30]

During the second century, at a time when the Church was asserting against its Jewish opponents, with whom was great strife, that the Levitical sacrifices of the Old Law had ceased to be acceptable to God, it would have been unseemly to cite those sacrifices as the antitype of the true offering of Christ or the true sacrifice offered by the Church, which the ancient Fathers regarded as the pure offering foretold by the prophet Malachi, which the Gentiles would offer in every place (Mal. I.11). From very early times, therefore, Christians used the sacrifices of Abel, Abraham and Melchisedech as types of the eucharistic offering. They were pre-Mosaic, and they fitted very well with the concepts of Christian sacrifice, for Abel offered lambs, the first-fruit of his flocks, and these were acceptable to God, as the offering of Cain was not; and Christians offer him who is the Lamb of God. Abraham offered his only son, as Christians offer the only begotten Son of God;

---

[30] See G. G. Willis, 'God's Altar on High', *Downside Review* XC (1972), 245-50; H. W. Codrington, 'The Heavenly Altar and the Epiclesis in Egypt', *JTS* XXXIX (1938), 142-50.

Melchisedech offered bread and wine, which are the eucharistic elements offered and prescribed by Christ. The other primitive notion enshrined in this section is the concept of the heavenly altar. The notion that there is a true altar in heaven, derived from Apocalypse VIII.3, the counterpart of the earthly altar at which the eucharist is offered, is of great antiquity. It is mentioned by St Irenaeus towards the end of the second century,[31] and indeed is implied by the language of I Clement XXXV.12 and XXXVI.1 at the end of the first.

It is therefore a very primitive notion, and one which, for all that we know, may have been Roman in origin, for Clement and Justin both wrote at Rome. Curiously enough, the form cited by Ambrose is not so primitive as that seen in the Roman Canon, for he reads *per manus angelorum tuorum*, but the primitive concept is of the angel in the singular, a term which in the first and second centuries, at any rate, could be applied to the Christ himself, and is derived from the *angelus magni consilii* of Isaiah IX.5 in the Septuagint and in the Old Latin. Ambrose's slip, in putting angels in the plural, is doubtless derived, not from Rome, but from some Eastern liturgy.[32]

Supra quae is a relative clause replacing the original simple phrase of the Canon quoted by Ambrose: *et petimus et precamur uti hanc oblationem suscipias*. In the quotation by Ambrose the two sections of the later Canon are conflated, and the petition for acceptance at the heavenly altar precedes the mention of the pre-Mosaic sacrifices. The Ambrosian form carries the suggestion that the offerings of Abel, Abraham and Melchisedech were accepted by God at the heavenly altar, like the sacrifice of Christ. This suggestion is not conveyed by the final form of the Roman Canon, which prays in *Supra quae* that God may accept the gifts, and in *Supplices* that they may be carried by the Holy Angel to the altar on high in the sight of his divine Majesty. At the end of the section *Supra quae* in the Roman Canon occur the words *sanctum sacrificium, immaculatam hostiam*, which are in apposition to the phrase *quod tibi obtulit summus sacerdos tuus Melchisedech*. The *Liber pontificalis* attributes this addition to St Leo the Great.[33]

---

[31] Irenaeus, *Adv. Haer.* IV.19 (ed. Harvey, II, p. 210).

[32] For example the Liturgy of St Mark, in Brightman, *Liturgies Eastern and Western* I, p. 129, lines 21-3; or the Liturgy of the Coptic Jacobites, *ibid.*, p. 171.

[33] *Liber Pontificalis*, ed. L. Duchesne, 2 vols. (Paris, 1886-92), I, 239: 'Hic (Leo) constituit ut intra actionem sacrificii diceretur sanctum sacrificium et reliqua'.

J. B. Thibaut asserted that the Institution narrative of *De sacramentis* was related to the narrative in the Liturgy of St James.[34] Comparison of the two in fact suggests that the differences are greater than the similarities, and that the similarities often prove to be such as would be shared by texts of the narrative other than those of St Ambrose and St James. To begin with, Ambrose has the note of time in the classical Roman form, which does not occur in any Eastern rite: *qui pridie quam pateretur*, and not *qui in qua nocte tradebatur*, which is universal in Eastern rites. His parallelisms between the narratives of the Bread and the Cup are not the same as those in St James, nor are his expansions and embellishments from non-scriptural sources. Ambrose's Institution narrative is by no means identical with that of the final Roman Canon, but it is much closer to it than it is to the narrative in the Liturgy of St James.

A striking difference between the portion of the eucharistic prayer cited by St Ambrose and the Roman Canon as found about 700 may be seen by comparing the rhythm or *cursus* of the two texts.[35] *Cursus* prevails in Roman liturgical composition from the time of Pope Siricius (384-99) until about 650, that is to say, half a century after St Gregory the Great. By the end of this period the Roman Canon had virtually reached its final form, but it only shows twenty-two rhythmical *clausulae* in its whole length from *Te igitur* to the *Amen* which concludes it. This is a much lower average than is found in the prayers of the three great Roman sacramentaries, the Leonine, Gelasian and Gregorian, most of the contents of which were composed within the period mentioned. The central part of the Canon, parallel with the part cited by Ambrose, has but seven of the twenty-two endings, and only one of these occurs in the citation of St Ambrose, namely *in caelum ascensionis* in *Unde et memores*. One or two rhythmic *clausulae* occur in the biddings of the *orationes sollemnes* which, by contrast with the collects of that form of intercession, are not on the whole rhythmic. This is what might be expected in a form of prayer which was composed in the last half, or even the last quarter, of the fourth century.

---

[34] J. B. Thibaut, *La Liturgie romaine* (Paris, 1924), p. 110.
[35] See Willis, '*Cursus* in the Roman Canon', in *Essays*, pp. 111-17.

Rhythm in the Roman Canon

The stylistic revision of the Canon between the time of St Ambrose and the final form, roughly between 400 and 700, has already been mentioned, and illustrated by comparison between Ambrose and the Gregorian Canon. Here it may be illustrated by reference to the *cursus*. It has just been noted that even in its final and developed form the Canon is not rich in rhythmic endings, producing only twenty-two examples, none of which occur in *Qui pridie*. Comparison with Ambrose establishes that the developed form of *Qui pridie* is later than Ambrose, but it can hardly be much later, since it has acquired no rhythmic *clausulae* whatever. The parts of the Canon which are known to be the latest turn out to be those richest in such endings. For example, the clause *diesque nostros*, which is known to have been added to *Hanc igitur* by St Gregory,[36] contains no fewer than three *clausulae* in the space of eighteen words. The rhythmic endings in the Canon, as printed in Botte's text, are as follows:

Te igitur	
rogamus et petimus	*tardus*
regere digneris	*trispondaicus*
orbe terrarum	*planus*
Memento, domine	
nota deuotio	*tardus*
Communicantes	
sanctorum tuorum	*planus*
precibusque concedas	*planus*
muniamur auxilio	*tardus*
Hanc igitur oblationem	
familiae tuae	*planus*
placatus accipias	*planus*
pace disponas	*planus*
damnatione nos eripi	*tardus*
grege numerari	*trispondaicus*
Quam oblationem	
deus in omnibus	*tardus*
facere digneris	*trispondaicus*
Qui pridie	
None	
Unde et memores	

36 *Liber Pontificalis*, ed. Duchesne, I, 312.

33

plebs tua sancta	*planus*
gloriosae ascensionis	*uelox*
salutis perpetuae	*tardus*
Supra quae	
respicere digneris	*trispondaicus*
Supplices te rogamus	
gratia repleamur	*uelox*
Memento etiam, domine	
indulgeas deprecamur	*uelox*
Nobis quoque peccatoribus	
donare digneris	*planus*
largitor admitte	*planus*

The Sanctus

It is not possible to say precisely when the *Sanctus* was introduced into the Roman Liturgy.[37] The earliest mention of the angelic song of the Thrice Holy in a liturgical context appears to be in the Epistle of St Clement I of Rome to the Corinthians,[38] but it cannot be definitely established from his words that the *Sanctus* was used in the liturgy, and the quotation by Clement may be a biblical citation.

In the early third century there occurs in Tertullian another inconclusive reference to the angelic song. A few years later, in the *Apostolic Tradition* (ch. 4) of St Hippolytus, there is no *Sanctus* at the beginning, or in any other part of the eucharistic prayer. The *Sanctus* was therefore no part of the prayer of *Apostolic Tradition* either in the first recension or in the developed recension from which the Latin version in the Verona palimpsest was translated about the year 400. Neither St Ambrose nor St Augustine ever mentions it as a liturgical feature, so that it is reasonable to conclude that it was unknown as a part of the eucharistic prayer at Milan and in Africa at the end of the fourth century. Two fragments of a Preface and the beginning of a eucharistic prayer composed by a Western Arian in the region of Milan were printed by Cardinal Mai in 1827, and the fragments which survive go far enough into the prayer to show that the rite had a Preface which led into the Canon without any *Sanctus* or any mention of the angelic song.[39] Exact dating of these fragments is impossible, but they are

---

[37] See Gregory Dix, *The Shape of the Liturgy*, 2nd ed. (Westminster, 1945), pp. 537-42.
[38] Ed. J. B. Lightfoot, *The Apostolic Fathers* II (London, 1890), p. 105.
[39] The text of the fragments is quoted by Dix, *The Shape of the Liturgy*, p. 540.

likely to be between 380 and 450. There is no mention of the *Sanctus* in the letter of Innocent to Decentius, bishop of Gubbio, in 416, though the pope there speaks of precisely the part of the Canon where the *Sanctus* was later to occur. It is unlikely, therefore, that the *Sanctus* had appeared in Milan, Africa or Rome before the middle of the fifth century. It was in the Gallican Liturgy by 529, when the third canon of the Council of Vaison in southern Gaul ordered that *Sanctus* should be said in all masses, weekdays, Lenten masses and masses for the dead included in the same order as was then used at public masses. The *Liber pontificalis* provides evidence that the *Sanctus* was known at Rome about 530. It attributes its introduction to Xystus I, who was pope from *c*. 117 to *c*. 127,[40] but as is well known, *Liber pontificalis* does not furnish trustworthy evidence of anything which happened before its original compilation. The attribution of this item of the mass to Xystus I, however, is of course evidence that the *Sanctus* was known at Rome in 530, and probably that it was by then a feature of some years' standing. Perhaps then it will be safe to assert that *Sanctus* was in the rite at Rome soon after 450. It is in the Old Gelasian (Vaticanus Reginensis 316), which, though of the mid-eighth century, contains much that was in use before St Gregory the Great, about 560. It is not possible to say whether the *Sanctus* was present in all masses, as in Gaul before the Council of Vaison, or was restricted to public masses or to Sunday masses. At Rome it was in use at all masses by 700, the date of the Bobbio Missal. Dom Gregory Dix is probably correct in believing that the *Sanctus* was in the Alexandrian rite in 230, at which time Origen refers to it, that it had spread to Jerusalem, where it is mentioned in the fifth Mystagogical Catechesis of St Cyril,[41] a little before 350, and that it replaced the Thanksgiving Series which originally began the anaphora in the East. This happened in Syria in the fourth century, and was imitated in Rome in the fifth. A significant connection between Syria and Rome is established by the fact, which Dix points out, that the Egyptian and all Eastern forms, except the Syrian, read, 'Holy, holy, holy Lord of Hosts', but the Syrian has 'Lord God of Hosts', and this is followed by Rome, which in all sources reads *Dominus Deus Sabaoth*.[42]

---

[40] *Liber Pontificalis*, ed. Duchesne, I, 128.

[41] Cyril, *Mys. Cat.* V.6 (ed. F. L. Cross (London, 1966), pp. 32 [Greek] and 73-4 [English]).

[42] In a famous article published in 1950 ('The Sanctus and the Pattern of the Early Anaphora', *JEH* I (1950), 29-36 and 125-34), Professor Ratcliff suggested that at

Silence

An important problem, which affects the interpretation of the Canon and the history of its development, and is particularly relevant to the Preface *Te igitur, Hanc igitur* and the two *Commemorationes pro uiuis et defunctis*, is the question when the Canon began to be said silently by the celebrant. The change from audibility to silence took place in different regions at different times, and conclusive evidence establishing the date when this change took place at Rome is wanting. From the ninth century onwards the Canon begins at the words *Te igitur*, before which there is often a title, *CANON MISSAE*, or *CANON ACTIONIS*.[43] By this time there is a clear distinction between the Preface, sung aloud, and concluded by the *Sanctus*, which the *schola* sings, and the Canon, which the celebrant says silently. In the time of St Ambrose and St Augustine it is clear that the Canon was said aloud in Milan and in Africa, and probably in Rome as well. At Rome in the time of Innocent I, as we see from his letter to Decentius, the Canon is said aloud. In Rome in about 750, the date of *Ordo Romanus* I, the Canon is said silently.[44] There is a difficulty about accepting the date 750 as the *terminus ante quem* for silent recitation of the Canon, in view of the fact that *Ordo* III, which is to be dated twenty or thirty years after this, *c*. 780,[45] envisages concelebration by priests with the pope's deputy in the absence of the pope, and concelebration can only be practised when the rite is said aloud. Indeed this *ordo* prescribes that the concelebrant assistants are to say the Canon in a lower voice than the principal celebrant.[46] Evidently silent recitation was not completely established at Rome in the eighth century, though it probably was by the ninth, and it may, of course, have been practised, at least on some occasions, before 750. It may be significant that curtains began to be put up at Rome towards the end of the seventh century, which may be connected with secrecy. If so the Canon was said aloud in Gregory's time.[47]

Rome, as perhaps at Alexandria, the *Sanctus* came at the end of the Anaphora, and not at the beginning, but there is absolutely no trace of it in this position in the Latin or in any other version of the *Apostolic Tradition*.

[43] See below, pp. 40-4, and Willis, *Essays*, pp. 121-2.

[44] *Ordo* I.88: 'surgit pontifex solus et intrat in canonem'.

[45] Andrieu II, p. 127.

[46] *Ordo* III.1 (Andrieu II, p. 131): 'Et simul cum illo canonem dicunt . . . ut vox pontificis valentius audiatur.'

[47] See P. Batiffol, *Leçons sur la messe* (Paris, 1927), p. 209.

There is an important Novel of the Emperor Justinian, dated 565, prohibiting the silent recital of the prayers of baptism and of the Mass.[48] This Novel has an official Greek and Latin text, and was intended to apply in both parts of the Empire. No man legislates against imaginary abuses which have not yet arisen, so it may be concluded that Justinian knew of the existence of the practice of silence, of which he disapproved and which he wished to restrain. Of course this need mean no more than that silence was then known in the East, and one would guess that, in common with other innovations, it originated in Jerusalem or Syria and spread to the eastern Mediterranean and finally to the West. It seems unlikely that it had reached the West by 565, in view of the fact that the old stratum of the Gelasian Sacramentary (Vaticanus Reginensis 316), which is to be dated just about this time, seems clearly to imply the audible recitation of the prayer. Here at the mass of the scrutinies of the third Sunday in Lent[49] *Memento Domine* is read aloud by the celebrant, who stops at the appropriate place while the names of the sponsors are read by someone else, and again at the appropriate place in *Hanc igitur*, while the names of the candidates are read by another person, perhaps the deacon. In the time of Innocent I the names of the offerers were heard by all at *Hanc igitur*, which is said aloud. Canon Couratin suggests that the Leonine text of the mass of the consecration of virgins[50] implies that *Hanc igitur oblationem* is being said silently while the deacon or somebody is reading *Memento Domine* aloud, with the names of the candidates. The words are: 'hanc etiam oblationem, domine, tibi uirginum sacratarum, quarum ante sanctum altarem tuum oblata nomina recitantur, quaesumus, placatus accipias'.

---

[48] Iustinian, *Novellae* VI.138 (ed. Schoell and Kroll, p. 699): 'praeterea iubemus omnes et episcopos et presbyteros non tacite, sed ea voce quae a fideli populo exaudiatur sacram oblationem precesque in sancto baptismate adhibitas faciant, ut inde quoque audientium animi ad maiorem contritionem et de domino deo praedictionem excitentur. Ita enim sanctus quoque Apostolus docet, cum dicat in priori epistola ad corinthios: Namque si benedixeris spiritu, quomodo is qui priuati locum obtinet post tuam gratiarum actionem amen deo dicet? quoniam quid dicas nescit? Nam tu quidem bene gratias agis, sed alter non aedificatur. Et rursus in epistola ad romanos ita dicit: corde enim creditur ad iustitiam, ore autem confessio fit ad salutem. Propterea igitur quae in sacra oblatione fiunt preces ceterasque clara uoce per sanctissimos et episcopos et presbyteros offerri par est Domino nostro Iesu Christo, deo nostro cum patre et spiritu sancto, sciantque sanctissimi sacerdotes, si quid horum neglexerint, et terribili iudicio magni dei et salvatoris nostri Iesu Christi se rationem reddituros, et ne nos quidem. haec cum comperiamus quiete passuros aut impunita relicturos esse.'
[49] *Sacramentarium Veronense*, ed. L. C. Mohlberg, Rerum Ecclesiasticarum Documenta, Series Maior, Fontes IV (Rome, 1960), XXVI.195 and 197.
[50] *Ibid.* 283.

But Canon Couratin's interpretation depends upon taking *recitantur* as a continuous present, 'are being recited', and it might equally well be taken as a simple present, 'are recited', in which case it could mean that the names were recited at the altar, at *Memento* or at *Hanc igitur*, by the deacon while the celebrant paused, as he evidently did in the case from *Gelasianum* just cited. The word *recitantur* could thus mean 'are customarily recited'. If this is accepted, then the evidence is that in the middle of the sixth century the Canon was still said aloud at Rome. It is therefore reasonably safe to assume that at Rome the Canon went silent between 560 and 800, probably in most cases between 560 and 750, and it is possible, but not certain, that the process was the work of St Gregory the Great, who certainly added the words *diesque nostros* etc. to the Canon, and transformed the *Hanc igitur* from a commemoration of particular offerers or objects of intercession to a general prayer on almost all occasions except baptisms.[51]

The Canon

Commemoratio pro uiuis et pro defunctis

St Ambrose's citation of the central portion of the Canon makes it certain that this part, represented in the present Canon by the sections beginning *Quam oblationem*, *Qui pridie*, *Unde et memores*, *Supra quae* and the first part of *Supplices te rogamus*, forms the oldest core of the Canon. It is almost certain that the sections *Te igitur communicantes*, *Hanc igitur* and *Nobis quoque peccatoribus* had been added by the time of St Gregory the Great. The latest sections to be added were the final phrase of *Supplices te rogamus* ('ut quotquot ex hac altaris participatione sacrosanctum Filii tui corpus et sanguinem sumpserimus omni benedictione caelesti et gratia repleamur'), and the two prayers which begin *Memento*. The former was added probably in the sixth century, when prayers for the fruits of communion were becoming popular, to a prayer which was one of the earliest in the Canon and represents a notion which was current in the second century.

---

[51] On the question of silent recitation, see E. C. Ratcliff and A. H. Couratin, 'The Roman *Canon Missae*: its Beginnings and Early Background', *JEH* XX (1969), 211-24, and Edmund Bishop, 'Silent Recitals in the Mass of the Faithful', in R. H. Connolly, *The Liturgical Homilies of Narsai*, Texts and Studies VIII (Cambridge 1909), pp. 121-6.

It is not possible to say with certainty when the two *Memento* paragraphs entered the Canon, but it is quite clear that they are additions, because they spoil the flow of the Canon, and if they are omitted the prayer runs much more intelligibly and smoothly, as will be seen when we discuss the sections of the Canon which precede and follow them in their present position. On the other hand, the language of the two *Memento* prayers is not of a late date: on the contrary it has signs of antiquity, specially the prayer for the departed. These two prayers did not enter the Canon at the same time. *Memento, Domine* was certainly there in the sixth century, before St Gregory, and no text of the complete Roman Canon is without it. Forms of the Canon which go back to a date earlier than the ninth century, for example, that of the Bobbio Missal, or the Old Gelasian Canon, do not contain the commemoration of the dead. This may be because they are intended for Sunday, and the section was used in requiem masses, and in weekday masses for a long time before it was used at every mass, including Sundays.[52]

Though the two Commemorations found their way into the Canon as fixed prayers recited by the celebrant at very different times, it seems fairly certain that they originated together outside the Canon. The fact that they both begin with the word *Memento* is highly significant, when we recall the frequent μνήσθητι as the opening word of intercessory paragraphs in the Greek liturgies.[53] They were inserted into different places of the Anaphora in different regions or different liturgical families, but they started as diaconal and not priestly prayers. The deacon kept the diptychs, or wax folding tablets, on which could be written on any day the names of those for whom the deacon would ask the prayers of the faithful during mass. Before the next mass the names could be obliterated by warming and smoothing the wax, and new names could be written. Thus the lists were kept up to date. The names of the living were inscribed on one side, and of the departed on the other. They were read out by the deacon in Rome as in Africa.[54] When the deacon's functions atrophied, the priest took on the *Memento* paragraphs and inserted them into the Canon, and in the Roman rite this

---

[52] Bishop, *Liturgica Historica*, pp. 109-15, and M. Andrieu, 'L'insertion du *Memento* des Morts dans le canon de la messe', *Revue des sciences religieuses* I (1921), 151-4.

[53] See, e.g., Brightman, *Liturgies Eastern and Western* I, pp. 55-6.

[54] Augustine, *Ep.* LV.xix.34 (PL XXXIII, 221; CSEL XXXIV, 209): 'oratio uoce diaconi indicitur'.

happened at different times with the two Commemorations. The Commemoration of the Living was inserted in the first part, where it ruined the connection, till then intimate, between the word *Communicantes* and its grammatical antecedent *papa nostro*, so that it should stand in the section concerned with offering: the Commemoration of the Living was concerned with the offerers and those on whose behalf they offered. The Commemoration of the Dead was inserted immediately before the concluding paragraph, *Nobis quoque peccatoribus*, because in that paragraph the offerers ask that they may be admitted, like the departed, into the fellowship of the saints in heaven. Since the dead no longer make the eucharistic offering, they are not fittingly associated with the *Memento* of the living, who are intimately concerned with offering.

In the Commemoration of the Living the phrase *pro quibus tibi offerimus* appears to be an addition by Alcuin in the ninth century.[55] *Signum fidei* in the *Memento* of the dead is an old phrase meaning 'baptism'. The phrase *dormiunt in somno pacis* also has an archaic ring, as does *locum refrigerii, lucis et pacis*.[56]

Te igitur and *Communicantes*

Having excluded as the latest additions to the Canon the two *Memento* paragraphs and the concluding phrase of *Supplices te rogamus*, the conclusion *per Christum dominum nostrum* at the end of four prayers, and one or two phrases which are known to have been added later, we shall find ourselves left with the prayer as it may well have been at the time of St Gregory or perhaps a little before his accession. It is a prayer with a clear theme and a logical sequence. It may be helpful to set out here the resultant prayer as we envisage it to have been towards the end of the sixth century:

Te igitur, clementissime Pater, per Iesum Christum filium tuum dominum nostrum supplices rogamus et petimus uti accepta habeas et benedicas haec dona, haec munera, haec sancta sacrificia inlibata, in primis quae tibi offerimus pro ecclesia tua sancta catholica, quam pacificare, custodire, adunare et regere digneris toto orbe terrarum, una cum famulo tuo papa nostro. illo. communicantes et diem sacratissimum celebrantes, sed et

---

[55] See Botte, *Le canon*, apparatus *ad lin.* 30.
[56] See Botte, *ibid.*, p. 68; C. Mohrmann, 'Locus refrigerii', in B. Botte and C. Mohrmann, *L'ordinaire de la messe* (Paris and Louvain, 1953), pp. 123-32.

memoriam uenerantes beati . . . et omnium sanctorum tuorum,
quorum meritis precibusque concedas ut in omnibus protectionis
tuae muniamur auxilio. Hanc igitur oblationem seruitutis nostrae
sed et cunctae familiae tuae quaesumus, domine, ut placatus
accipias, diesque nostros in tua pace disponas atque ab aeterna
damnatione nos eripi et in electorum tuorum iubeas grege
numerari. Quam oblationem tu, Deus, in omnibus, quaesumus,
benedictam, adscriptam, ratam, rationabilem, acceptabilemque
facere digneris, ut nobis corpus et sanguis fiat dilectissimi filii tui
domini dei nostri Iesu Christi. Qui pridie quam pateretur accepit
panem in sanctas ac uenerabiles manus suas, eleuatis oculis in
caelum ad te deum patrem suum omnipotentem, tibi gratias agens
benedixit, fregit, dedit discipulis suis dicens: Accipite et
manducate ex hoc omnes: hoc est enim corpus meum. Simili
modo, posteaquam caenatum est, accipiens et hunc praeclarum
calicem in sanctas ac uenerabiles manus suas item tibi gratias
agens benedixit dedit discipulis suis, dicens: Accipite et bibite ex
eo omnes: hic est enim calix sanguinis mei noui et aeterni
testamenti, mysterium fidei, qui pro uobis et pro multis
effundetur in remissionem peccatorum. Haec quotiescumque
feceritis, in mei memoriam facietis. Unde et memores sumus,
Domine, nos tui serui sed et plebs tua sancta, Christi Filii tui
Domini dei nostri tam beatae passionis, necnon et ab inferis
resurrectionis, sed et in caelos gloriosae ascensionis, offerimus
praeclarae maiestati tuae de tuis, donis ac datis hostiam puram,
hostiam sanctam, hostiam inmaculatam, panem sanctum uitae
aeternae et calicem salutis perpetuae; supra quae propitio ac
sereno uultu respicere digneris et accepta habere, sicuti accepta
habere dignatus es munera pueri tui iusti Abel, et sacrificium
patriarchae nostri Abrahae, et quod tibi obtulit summus sacerdos
tuus Melchisedech, sanctum sacrificium, inmaculatam hostiam.
Supplices te rogamus, omnipotens Deus, iube haec perferri per
manus Angeli tui in sublime altare tuum, in conspectu diuinae
maiestatis tuae, nobis quoque peccatoribus famulis tuis de
multitudine miserationum tuarum sperantibus, partem aliquam et
societatem donare digneris cum tuis sanctis Apostolis et martyr-
ibus . . . et omnibus sanctis tuis, intra quorum nos consortium,
non aestimator meriti sed ueniae, quaesumus largitor admitte, per
Christum Dominum nostrum.

It is generally agreed that the Canon ends with the doxology before
Pater noster. But where may it be said to begin? Printed missals have
always placed the title *Canon Missae* before *Te igitur*, and in this
position many medieval missals had a title *Incipit Canon actionis.*

Nobody looking at a printed missal or a manuscript missal of the Middle Ages would dream that the Canon had anything to do with the Preface or *Sanctus*. In the Old Gelasian Sacramentary (Vaticanus Reginensis 316), written about 750, *Te igitur* does not have a title, a capital *T*, or a new line; but runs straight on from the end of the *Sanctus*. But in many medieval missals, as in printed editions, *Te igitur* begins a new page, the *T* being a great illuminated letter, which in medieval iconography developed into a picture of the crucifixion, and was then transferred to occupy the whole of the previous page on its own. It thus looked as if the Preface and *Sanctus* had nothing whatever to do with the eucharistic prayer or Canon; nor, for centuries, did it sound as though it had. For the Preface was sung out loud and was heard by all, but the Canon was said inaudibly by the celebrant, while at a sung mass the singers went on with the music of the *Sanctus*, and at a low mass the people occupied themselves with their private devotions. In fact the Preface and Canon were originally continuous, and it was much easier to perceive this when both were said aloud.

So long as the prayer was said silently, it was difficult to see what *igitur* could mean at the beginning of a new sentence and a new section, and Botte and Mohrmann do not even render it in their French translation of the Canon. Professor N. M. Denis-Boulet maintains that '*igitur* n'a guère qu'une valeur explétive', and that it was as weak as the Greek δὲ in the early centuries.[57] This interpretation is so untrue that Botte and Mohrmann are unable to cite any parallel to *igitur* with this enfeebled meaning, and in fact its meaning was always 'therefore', referring to something which went before it. In the earliest state of the Canon this would be the Preface.

The Roman Canon has two offerings, joined by *Qui pridie*; the first is the offering of the gifts of the Church, bread and wine. These are offered in *Te igitur*, in *Hanc igitur oblationem*, and in *Quam oblationem*. The gifts are then consecrated by the recital over them of the Lord's Institution, in virtue of the priest imitating the words and acts of Christ. Then the consecrated gifts are offered in *Unde et memores*: 'offerimus praeclarae maiestati tuae de tuis donis ac datis hostiam puram, hostiam sanctam, hostiam inmaculatam, panem sanctum uitae aeternae et calicem salutis perpetuae.'

In *Te igitur*, therefore, the unconsecrated gifts are offered to the Father on behalf of the Catholic Church, and for its peace and unity,

---

[57] See A. G. Martimort, *L'église en prière* (Paris, 1961), p. 392.

and this offering is made by offerers in communion with their Father, or bishop – a sign of the unity of the Church for which they pray – and at certain seasons, such as Christmas and Easter, celebrating the most holy day of the Nativity, or Resurrection, or as it may be, and venerating the memory of certain saints, the protection of whose merits and prayers they entreat. There are three parallel present participles, the first of which, *communicantes*, is invariable, and the other two variable and used on particular occasions: *diem sacratissimum celebrantes* on one or two great feasts, and *memoriam uenerantes* on the feasts of martyrs. The original practice was to insert the name of the saint or martyr in whose tomb or on whose feast the mass was being celebrated; and it had become by St Gregory's time a generalized list, originally probably very short, then much longer, and finally reduced by St Gregory or about his time to its present proportions. Because of the variability of its form, the names wre omitted in the reconstruction of the Canon printed above. Fr V. L. Kennedy has demonstrated that the saints in *Communicantes* and in *Nobis quoque* are chosen because they were Roman, or had a cult at Rome: they are a local, that is, and not an universal list.[58] Four variable *Communicantes* clauses are to be found in the *Sacramentarium Veronense*, two each for Ascension and Pentecost.[59]

It has been shown that the word *communicantes*, like the other two participles, is connected with *Te igitur*.[60] We offer 'in communion with our father N'. The word *papa* is the Greek πάπας, 'father', and at the time it entered the Canon it referred to the bishop of the diocese where mass was being said. It was not till after the sixth century that the word *papa* was restricted to the bishop of Rome: when it was, other dioceses began to add the name of their own bishop, and so the addition *et antistite nostro N.* appeared, and then the remaining bishops of the Church acquired a mention, and the words *et omnibus orthodoxis atque catholicae et apostolicae fidei cultoribus* were added. The rightly believing defenders of the Catholic and Apostolic Faith are not the faithful in general, who are prayed for in the first part of this prayer, but the bishops in particular.[61]

---

58 V. L. Kennedy, *The Saints of the Canon of the Mass* (Vatican City, 1938).

59 *Sacramentarium Veronense*, ed. Mohlberg, nos. 178, 186, 204, 224.

60 See L. Eizenhöfer, 'Te igitur und Communicantes im römischen Messkanon', *Sacris Erudiri* VIII (1956), 14-75; also A. Paladini, 'Quaestiones de Communicantes', *Ephemerides Liturgicae* LXVIII (1954), 155-6.

61 P. de Labriolle, 'Une esquisse de l'histoire du mot *Papa*', *Bulletin d'ancienne littérature et d'archéologie chrétienne* I (1911), 215-20; B. Cappelle, 'Et omnibus

Hanc igitur was part of the Canon before *Memento Domine* was transferred from the deacon to the celebrant, and it was the original place for intercession in the Canon, certainly from the sixth, and probably from the fifth century. Before St Gregory the section consisted of the words, 'Hanc igitur oblationem seruitutis nostrae sed et cunctae familiae tuae, quaesumus Domine, ut placatus accipias'. The celebrant originally supplied at this point a mention of any persons who specially deserved mention, particularly the offerers or those on whose behalf they offered, and these included both living and departed persons.[62] St Gregory is known to have generalized this prayer, and to have added the words *diesque nostros*, etc.[63] After his time none of the particular intercessions survived except at solemn baptisms, when, at Easter and Whitsun Day vigils, the neophytes and their sponsors are still mentioned at this point.[64] This practice has gone on since the *Sacramentarium Veronense* or Leonine Sacramentary.

It is probable that *Hanc igitur* was in the Canon by the time of Pope Innocent I, since it is compatible with his words to Decentius in *Ep.* XXV, of 19 March 416, about the gifts being offered, doubtless in *Te igitur*, before the offerers are commended to God, presumably in *Hanc igitur*.

Quam oblationem

We reach the point now at which St Ambrose begins his citation of the Canon. Later, when *Te igitur* and *Hanc igitur* were introduced, with *Communicantes*, the abrupt beginning of St Ambrose's Canon, *Fac nobis hanc oblationem* was smoothed out and related to *Hanc igitur* by a relative clause, beginning *Quam oblationem*. The wording was also made slightly more formal by the addition of the adjectives and of the redundant but stylistic phrase *in omnibus*: 'in every respect'. The section is also a prayer for the consecration of the gifts – 'ut nobis

orthodoxis atque apostolicae fidei cultoribus', *Travaux Liturgiques* II (Louvain, 1962), pp. 258-68; G. G. Willis, *Essays*, pp. 125-7.

[62] Examples: *Sacramentarium Veronense* nos. 1012, for living bishops; 1107 for a bride; 1140 for the departed; *Gelasianum* no. 1631, for a dead priest. On the whole question of intercession for the living and departed within the Canon, see E. C. Ratcliff and A. H. Couratin, 'The Early Roman *Canon Missae*', *JEH* XX (1969), 211-24.

[63] *Liber Pontificalis*, ed. Duchesne, I, 312; Bede, *Historia Ecclesiastica*, II.1.

[64] E.g., *Veronense* 203: 'Hanc igitur oblationem, quam tibi offerimus pro his, quos ex aqua et spiritu sancto regenerare dignatus es, tribuens eis remissionem omnium peccatorum, quaesumus, placatus accipias, eorumque nomina ascribi iubeas in libro viventium'.

corpus et sanguis fiat dilectissimi Filii tui Domini dei nostri Iesu Christi, qui pridie quam pateretur' – carefully dovetailed into the Institution narrative by the relative pronoun *qui*.

Qui pridie

The absence of rhythmical endings in this section, noted above (p. 33), indicates that this is the oldest part of the Canon, and that which was the least revised in the three hundred years between 400 and 700. The Institution narrative[65] is characteristically Roman, and distinct from any other surviving Institution narrative. It is related to those cited by St Cyprian (*Ep.* LXIII) and St Ambrose (*De sacramentis* IV.21-7), and is less florid and more biblical than the narratives contained in Eastern eucharistic rites. It rests upon a strongly biblical base, derived from the narrative in St Matthew's Gospel (Matt. XXVI.26-8), supplemented from the Pauline account in I Cor. XI.23-6, with features derived from other places of Scripture. There is a tendency, extremely restrained by comparison with that manifested by Eastern liturgies, to embroider the biblical base with pious phrases from outside Scripture. There is also a proclivity to conform the first part of the narrative, referring to the Bread, and the second part, referring to the Cup, with one another, and to harmonize them and make them parallel. All these characteristics will be illustrated in the consideration, phrase by phrase, of the Roman narrative as it is seen in its final form at the beginning of the eighth century.

INSTITUTION NARRATIVE

Qui pridie quam pateretur	
Accepit panem	Vg. Matt., Marc., Cor. accipiens pane *d* Matt., *a,d* Marc. accepto pane Luc. Vg. accipiens panem *d* Luc.
In sanctas ac uenerabiles manus suas	
Elevatis oculis in caelum ad te deum patrem suum omnipotentem	cf. Matt. XIV.19, Marc. VI.41, VII.34, Luc. IX.16 Vg. and OL Ambr. respexit in caelum.

---

[65] For a detailed consideration of the Roman Institution narrative, see E. C. Ratcliff, 'The Roman Institution Narrative; its Beginnings and Early Background', *Studia Patristica* I (Berlin 1957), 64-82.

Tibi gratias agens	gratias egit Luc. Vg. et gratias agens Cor. Vg. agens *c* Luc.
Benedixit	OL and Vg. Matt. benedicens Vg. Marc. benedixit *d* Luc. benedixit *a d l* Marc.
Fregit	Vg. OL Matt., Marc, Luc, Cor. only variant: confregit *a* Luc.
Dedit discipulis suis dicens	Vg. Matt. deditque . . . et ait dedit eis et ait Vg. Marc. et dedit DL; dedit T dedit eis dicens Vg. Luc dicens LQR Illis OL Marc. (eis *aur f i l q r* Vg.) et dedit OL Matt. c c f ff² q dedit illis dicens OL Luc (deditque *aur b ff¹ g¹ l Vg*: dedit *h*; et dans *d*) (eis *aur c d* Vg discipulis suis *f*)
Accipite et manducate ex hoc omnes	accipite et comedite Vg. Matt. accipite et manducate. Cor. BKTVWZ² vg *c t*. Ambr. manducate LR; ex hoc omnes Q *cum b* accipite et manducate *tantum*: OL Matt. + ex hoc omnes *b* Matt.
Hoc est enim corpus meum	hoc est corpus meum Vg. Matt, Marc, + quod pro uobis tradetur, Cor. hoc est corpus meum, OL Matt. (est enim *a b f r¹* enim est *h*, meum corpus *d*, + quod pro uobis tradetur *ff¹*. cf. hoc est corpus meum, OL Marc. (enim *c f* + quod pro multis confringitur in remissione peccatorum *a*). hoc est corpus meum. OL Luc (*tantum: a d ff² i l*;) + quod pro uobis tradetur, hoc facite *t¹* quod pro uobis datur, hoc facite *aur c f g* Vg. + in (ad: *q*) meam commemorationem *aur c f r¹* Vg.
Simili modo posteaquam caenatum est	Similiter et calicem postquam cenavit Vg. Luc, Cor. Similiter et calicem, *aur c f q* Vg; postquam cenavit, *aur c* Vg. (cenaverunt *f*)
Accipiens et . . . calicem	et accipiens, Vg Matt. OL et accipiens calicem *d* Luc et accepit calicem et *c* Luc.; et adcepit calicem et Marc. *ff²* et accipiens calicem *d*
Hunc	
praeclarum	ex Ps. XXII.5 Vg.
In sanctas ac uenerabiles manus suas	
Item tibi gratias agens benedixit	gratias egit et benedixit, Matt. *F* Matt. OL, gratias egit; et (*d*) gratias agens, Matt. (*d,g*) benedixit et gratias egit, Matt. *a*
Dedit discipulis suis dicens	et dedit illis dicens, Matt. Vg., OL (eis *a d*). et dedit discipulis suis, *ff¹*

Accipite et bibite ex eo omnes	bibite ex hoc omnes, Vg. Matt., OL (eo-*d ff²*) *b g¹ h*: accipite et bibite ex hoc omnes (om. *a b c*)
Hic est enim calix sanguinis mei noui et aeterni testamenti	hic est enim sanguis meus noui testamenti, Vg. OL Matt. hic est sanguis meus noui (+ aeterni L Q) testamenti, Vg. OL Mar. hic est calix nouum testamentum in sanguine meo, Vg. Luc (noui testamenti *E, O*) hic calix nouum testamentum est in meo sanguine, Vg. Cor. (noui testamenti *D, K*) calix sanguinis mei, Matt. et aeterni, Matt. *b* Hic calix et noui testamenti, Luc *r¹* Hic est calix noui testamenti, Luc *aur c*. Hic calix nouum testamentum est, Luc *f* Hic est calix nouum testamentum, Luc *q, Vg.*
Mysterium fidei	ex. I Tim. III.9.
Qui pro uobis et pro multis effundetur in remissionem peccatorum	qui pro multis effunditur in remissionem peccatorum, Vg. Matt. (+pro uobis et Q) qui pro multis effunditur (+ in remissionem peccatorum Q), Vg. Marc. qui pro multis effundetur (effunditur *a d ff²* Vg.) in rem. pec. OL Matt. qui pro multis effundetur (-ditur *aur d l* (Vg.)) (+ in rem. pec. *a*) OL Marc. qui pro uobis fundetur, Vg. Luc qui pro uobis effundetur, Luc, *c f r¹* quod pro uobis effundetur, *q*, Luc. qui pro uobis funditur (-etur corr.) *aur* Luc.
Haec quotiescumque feceritis in mei memoriam facietis	hoc facite quotienscumque bibetis in meam commemorationem, Vg. Cor.

All eastern Institution narratives begin with the phrase from I Cor. XI.23, ἐν τῇ νυκτὶ ᾗ παρεδίδετο: 'in the night in which he was betrayed'. The Roman opening *qui pridie quam pateretur*, with which should be compared St Cyprian's opening of the second part, concerning the Cup, *sub die passionis*, connects the eucharist with the Passion as a whole and not with the Betrayal in particular. The Pauline phrase is Jewish. It regards the day as running from sunset to sunset, and therefore the Last Supper, and the Crucifixion and Death of the Lord belong to the same day. But the Roman reckoning is like ours, and in it the Supper belongs to the day before the Crucifixion, to Thursday and not to Friday. In connecting the Mass with the Passion in general, the whole Roman Narrative is related to the thought of St Cyprian in *Ep.* LXIII and it represents the close connection seen in that Epistle between the Supper, the Passion and the mass, which St Cyprian regards as three closely related parts of the unique sacrifice by which

Christ redeemed the world. *Qui pridie quam pateretur* is therefore to be seen as a phrase having profound theological significance. Such a doctrine requires a strongly scriptural narrative of the Institution of the eucharist, and accordingly we find that both in Cyprian and in the Roman books the narrative is closer to Scripture than the narratives in the Eastern rites. It is in fact more scriptural than the narrative in St Ambrose's Canon.

In general the Roman narrative is not a conflation of the four New Testament narratives, but is closer to the Matthaean narrative, supplemented from the Pauline source.

accepit panem: Mt. XXVI.26.

in sanctas ac uenerabiles manus suas: an addition from Eastern liturgical sources (cf. the Liturgy of St James, λαβὼν τὸν ἄρτον ἐπὶ τῶν ἁγίων καὶ ἀχράντων καὶ ἀμωμων καὶ ἀθανάτων αὐτοῦ χειρῶν).[66]

eleuatis oculis suis in caelum ad te Deum Patrem suum omnipotentem: cf. Mt. XIV.19. Mc. VI.41. Lc. IX.16, the Feeding of the Multitude, and John XVII.1. This phrase does not occur in the New Testament Institution narratives (but cf. the Liturgy of St James, *ibid.*: ἀναβλέψας εἰς τὸν οὐρανὸν).

tibi gratias agens (*egit* in some sources): cf. Liturgy of St James, *ibid.*: εὐχαριστήσας.

Is this parallelism with the narrative of the Cup?

benedixit fregit: cf. Liturgy of St James, *ibid.*: ἁγιάσας κλάσας.

dedit discipulis suis dicens: cf. Liturgy of St James, *ibid.*: ἔδωκε τοῖς ἁγίοις αὐτοῦ μαθηταῖς καὶ ἀποστόλοις εἰπὼν.

accipite et manducate ex hoc omnes: cf. Liturgy of St James, *ibid.*: Λάβετε φάγετε.

Ex hoc omnes is a parallelism from the narrative of the Cup.

hoc est enim corpus meum: Mt.

The narrative concerning the Cup is united to the narrative concerning the Bread by the words *simili modo*. The fact that the Cup was administered to the disciples by our Lord after supper is still commemorated by the words *postquam cenatum est* (cf. Liturgy of St James, *ibid.*: ὡσαύτως μετὰ τὸ δειπνῆσαι), which recalls the fact that at the Last Supper the Bread was broken and given at the beginning

[66] Brightman, *Liturgies Eastern and Western*, pp. 51-2.

of the meal, and the Cup was distributed at the end of it, as in the usual Jewish meal tradition. In the eucharist the two actions had coalesced by the middle of the second century (cf. Justin Martyr, *Apol*, ch. 66, cited above p. 8), and it is probable that this coalition had taken place before the end of the first century, but there is no certain evidence of this.

accepit: cf. Liturgy of St James, *ibid.*: λαβὼν.

hunc is a significant theological addition in the Roman Canon, identifying the Chalice of each mass with the Lord's chalice at the Supper, in other words identifying the eucharistic action with the Lord's eucharistic institution, and suggesting that the Lord is the true celebrant of every mass.

praeclarum is a scriptural addition not derived from the Institution narrative in the gospels, but from Ps. XXII.5: *calix tuus inebrians quam praeclarus est*.

in sanctas ac uenerabiles manus suas is an addition to the biblical narrative repeated from the Institution of the Bread in the interests of parallelism.

item tibi gratias agens is likewise harmonistic, and so is *benedixit* and *dedit discipulis suis*: cf. Liturgy of St James, *ibid.*: εὐχαριστήσας ἁγιάσας εὐλογήσας . . . ἔδωκε τοῖς ἁγίοις καὶ μακαρίοις αὐτοῦ μαθηταῖς.

accipite et bibite ex hoc omnes: cf. Liturgy of St James, *ibid.*: Πίετε ἐξ αὐτοῦ πάντες.

hic est enim calix sanguinis mei: cf. Table I, below, p. 149.

Bobbio and Stowe add *sancti* before *sanguinis*, but no other manuscript does, and this is an Hibernicism.

et aeterni is an addition from Hebr. XIII.20: for the rest, see Table I, below, p. 149.

For the whole phrase, cf. Liturgy of St James, *ibid.*: τοῦτό μου ἐστὶ τὸ αἷμα τὸ τῆς καινῆς διαθήκης.

mysterium fidei is derived from I Tim. III.9.

qui pro uobis et pro multis effundetur (-itur) in remissionem peccatorum: cf. Liturgy of St James, *ibid.*: τὸ ὑπὲρ ὑμῶν καὶ πολλῶν ἐκχεόμενον καὶ διαδιδόμενον εἰς ἄφεσιν ἁμαρτιῶν .

haec quotienscumque feceritis in mei memoriam facietis: cf. I Cor. XI.25 and Liturgy of St James, *ibid.*: τοῦτο ποιεῖτε εἰς τὴν ἐμὴν ἀνάμνησιν. ὁσάκις γὰρ ἂν ἐσθίητε τὸν ἄρτον τοῦτον καὶ τὸ ποτήριον τοῦτο πίνητε. τὸν θάνατον τοῦ υἱοῦ τοῦ ἀνθρώπου καταγγέλλετε καὶ τὴν ἀνάστασιν αὐτοῦ ὁμολογεῖτε ἄχρις οὗ ἔλθῃ.

The Roman narrative, deriving principally from Matthew, never had this command to perform the eucharistic action in memory of Christ after the consecration of the bread. Had the original Pauline form, therefore, been added after the consecration of the Cup, it would have had the effect of suggesting that the consecration of the Cup was more important than, or at any rate different from, the consecration of the Bread. On the other hand, to have left it out at the end of the Institution narrative would have spoiled the close connection which exists between *in mei memoriam facietis* and the words which immediately follow, *unde et memores*. So the Roman liturgists as early as the fourth century recast the Pauline phrase to include both bread and cup, and thereby showed themselves infinitely more sagacious than the Greek liturgists who ruined this connection by interpolating an acclamation of the people at this point (e.g., Liturgy of St James, *ibid.*, p. 52, lines 23-7).

Unde et memores

If the Roman Canon is reduced to the simpler form which it had in the sixth century, by the omission of certain accretions, its pattern becomes much clearer. We come now, after the Institution, to the third part of the Canon. This is the offering to the Father of the consecrated gifts, an offering joined to the offering of the unconsecrated gifts which opens the Canon by the Consecration, which comes in between. The pattern of the second offering may be thus summarised:

'. . . Ye shall do this in memory of me. Having therefore in remembrance his blessed Passion, and his Resurrection from the dead and his glorious Ascension into heaven, we . . . offer unto thy glorious Majesty the holy Bread of eternal life and the Cup of everlasting salvation, beseeching thee to look upon them, and to accept them . . . We pray thee to command them to be borne by thy holy Angel to thine Altar on high in the presence of thy Divine Majesty, and to grant to us sinners, who trust in the multitude of thy mercies, to have some part and fellowship with thy holy Apostles and Martyrs and with all thy saints.'

This reconstruction omits the *Memento* of the departed and the final clause of the paragraph *Supplices te rogamus*, which are intrusions into the earlier prayer.

The Anamnesis is in accordance with a common pattern in many parts of the Church, and the Oblation phrase which follows it is a development and formalization of what stands here in the rite of Ambrose. Ambrose reads *hunc panem sanctum et calicem vitae aeternae* and the developed Roman form is *panem sanctum uitae aeternae et calicem salutis perpetuae*. Both are elaborations of the simple form of the *Apostolic Tradition*, of which the Latin version reads *offerimus tibi panem et calicem*.

Supra quae and *Supplices te rogamus*

Between St Ambrose and St Gregory these two sections were developed and re-arranged. In *De sacramentis* they form one conflate section, which Professor Ratcliff believes may have been the original order at Rome. The final phrase of *Supplices*, 'ut quotquot ex hac altaris participatione sacrosanctum filii tui corpus et sanguinem sumpserimus omni benedictione caelesti et gratia repleamur', is not quoted by St Ambrose but is an addition, probably of the sixth century, when prayers for the fruits of communion were becoming fashionable. *Supra quae* asks for the acceptance of the gifts, and *Supplices* for their carrying to the heavenly altar. These sections contain two of the most ancient clauses of the Canon, namely, the prayer that God would accept the gifts as he accepted the sacrifices of Abel, Abraham and Melchisedech, and the theme of the lifting up of the gifts to the heavenly Altar in the presence of the Divine Majesty. The names of Abel, Abraham and Melchisedech were in the Canon in the time of St Ambrose at the end of the fourth century, but they are very likely to be as old as the second century, for these three offerers are all pre-Mosaic. In the fourth and fifth centuries it would have been quite possible for the Levitical sacrifices to be cited as prototypes of the eucharist, in some such way as the Roman ordination prayers from Pope Leo onwards use the Levitical priesthood as the prototype of the Christian ministry, citing the ordination of Aaron, and of his sons Eleazar and Ithamar. Both St Cyprian and St Ambrose often call deacons Levites. But these things would have been impossible in the second century, when the Church was in acute controversy with the Jews, and Christian theologians were teaching that God had rejected the sacrifices of the Jews, and only accepted the 'pure offering' of the Gentiles, foretold in Malachi I.11, and realized in the Christian eucharist. Of this Christian sacrifice the offerings of Abel, Abraham and Melchisedech were fitting prototypes, for Abel offered lambs, as Christians offer the Lamb of God; Abraham his only son, as Christians offer the only Son of God; and Melchisedech brought forth bread and wine, the elements of the Christian Eucharist.

The petition to the Father to direct the holy Angel to carry the oblation up to the heavenly altar is also very primitive.[67] In the second century, as we see from St Justin Martyr at Rome,[68] and from St Irenaeus in the south of Gaul,[69] it was possible to call the Son the 'angel' of the Father, and to conceive his ministry as carried out in the heavens. This latter notion can be traced back to St Clement of Rome at the end of the first century,[70] but the identification is made in the text of Isaiah IX.5 in the Septuagint, and in the pre-Vulgate Latin translations of that verse: μεγάλης βουλῆς ἄγγελος, *magni consilii angelus*, as may be seen in the Introit of the third mass of Christmas Day. In many of the Greek liturgies of the fourth and fifth centuries, though not in all, this tradition became confused, as it did in Ambrose, and the prayer speaks of 'angels' in the plural, and even of 'archangels'. The identification with Christ has thus been lost. In some Eastern sources, especially Egyptian, the notion of the angel or angels has been mixed up with the epiclesis, so that some rites ask for the gifts to be taken up to the heavenly altar, and for the Holy Spirit to be sent down in exchange to sanctify the gifts upon the earthly altar.[71] But the Roman rite never made this mistake, for the epiclesis did not find a place in it, and is indeed foreign to its structure and to its theory of consecration. It had instead, perhaps from the second century onwards, while it was still in Greek, the primitive theme of the heavenly altar.[72]

Nobis quoque peccatoribus

This appears to be the original ending of the Canon, and it runs on smoothly from the petition for the carrying up of the gifts to heaven,

---

[67] See G. G. Willis, 'God's Altar on High', *Downside Review* XC (1972), 245-50.

[68] Justin Martyr, *I Apol.*, ch. 63; *Dialogue*, ch. 93.

[69] Irenaeus, *Adv. Haer.* IV.18: 'est ergo altare in caelis: illuc enim orationes nostrae et oblationes nostrae diriguntur'; cf. Augustine, *Enarr. in ps.* XXV.10 (PL XXXVI, 193): 'auia est et altare coram oculis Dei . . . est coeleste altare.'

[70] I Clement XXXV.12; XXXVI.1.

[71] See Willis, 'God's Altar on High', p. 249, and H. W. Codrington, 'The Heavenly Altar and the Epiclesis in Egypt', *JTS* XXXIX (1938), 141-50.

[72] Willis, *ibid.*

since it requests that we, who have offered them, may likewise be exalted to the company of the saints. It should be noted that this reconstruction means that there is no intercession in the second part of the Canon: all the intercession is concentrated in the first part and is connected with the theme of offering. It is thus much better integrated with the Canon than in many Eastern rites, which added intercession at the end of the anaphora, after the epiclesis, which was regarded as providing conditions ideally suited to intercession.[73]

The list of saints now in *Nobis quoque* has, like that in *Communicantes*, been variable. Originally it was probably very short, then lengthened, and finally by the time of St Gregory reduced to its present size.[74] Like the list in *Communicantes* it contains saints buried in Rome or having a cult there.

The section *Per quem haec omnia* was interpolated at an early date, before the time of St Gregory, for the purpose of blessing any offerings other than bread and wine which required to be blessed, such as the oils for the neophytes' baptism, blessed on Maundy Thursday,[75] milk and honey at the Whitsun vigil,[76] the beans of Ascension Day,[77] and the first grapes on the feast of St Sixtus (6 August).[78]

Then finally comes the Trinitarian doxology, and the great AMEN, which is the people's response to the Eucharistic Prayer, attested as early as St Justin Martyr.[79]

The Lord's Prayer[80]

Since the time of St Gregory the Roman Canon has been immediately followed by the Lord's Prayer, with its introduction and embolism. It is well known that it was St Gregory himself who made some change in the arrangement of the Roman mass at this point. He himself says that

---

[73] See St Cyril of Jerusalem, *Myst. Cat.* V.9 (ed. Cross, pp. 33 [Greek] and 74 [English]).

[74] See Kennedy, *The Saints of the Canon of the Mass.*

[75] *Gelasianum*, no. 382.

[76] *Veronense*, no. 205.

[77] *Gelasianum*, no. 577.

[78] *Gregorianum*, no. 138.

[79] Justin Martyr, *Apol.*, ch. 67.

[80] I. Furberg, *Das Pater noster in der Messe*, Bibliotheca Theologiae Practicae XXI (Lund, 1968); G. G. Willis, 'St Gregory the Great and the Lord's Prayer in the Roman Mass', in *Further Essays*, pp. 175-88.

he did so in his letter of October 598 to John of Syracuse,[81] and this statement was copied by his ninth-century biographer, John the Deacon.[82]

There is no doubt about the text of St Gregory's letter, but there has never been agreement about its precise meaning, nor is it agreed what St Gregory found in the mass at this point, and what exactly was the change which he made. We begin by citing the text of his letter:

> orationem vero dominicam idcirco mox post precem dicimus, quia mos apostolorum fuit ut ad ipsam solummodo orationem oblationis hostiam consecrarent, et ualde mihi inconueniens uisum est ut precem quam scholasticus composuerat super oblationem diceremus, et ipsam traditionem quam Redemptor noster composuit super eius corpus et sanguinem non diceremus.

In the first sentence of this passage scholars from Amalarius onwards have taken the words *oblationis hostiam* together, as meaning 'the victim of the oblation', and have therefore interpreted St Gregory as meaning that it was the custom of the Apostles to consecrate the eucharist to the accompaniment of (*ad*) the Lord's Prayer (*ipsam orationem*) and of nothing else.

In the nineteenth century Probst perceived that it is much more natural to take the words *orationem oblationis* together, and *hostiam* separately. This would then mean that Gregory says that it was the custom of the Apostles to consecrate the Host to the accompaniment of the 'prayer of oblation' only. This view has been followed by Cabrol and Batiffol, among other modern scholars, and it is now probably the accepted view. It gives much better sense, and Brightman's interpretation of the whole passage is by far the most satisfactory.[83] St Gregory says that we say the Lord's prayer immediately after the Canon, because it was the practice of the Apostles to consecrate the sacrament with the Canon, or eucharistic prayer, and it therefore appeared unseemly to St Gregory that we should say over the oblation a prayer composed by some *scholasticus* and should not say over the Lord's Body the prayer which the Lord himself taught. Brightman was the first to make the likely suggestion that the prayer of human composition said over the oblations was the *oratio super oblata*, the Roman title of the prayer which the Gallicans call *Secreta*. If this prayer, of human

---

81 Gregory, *Ep. Reg.* IX.26 (ed. Ewald-Hartmann, MGH, Ep. II, pp. 59-60).

82 Iohannes Diaconus, *Vita Gregorii Magni* II.20 (PL LXXV, 94).

83 F. E. Brightman, 'S. Gregorii M., Ep. ix. 26', *JTS* XXIX (1928), 161-4.

composition, was recited over the unconsecrated oblations, St Gregory might well think it unfitting that the Lord's Prayer should not be said over the consecrated oblations. He therefore moved it to a position immediately following the Canon. Obviously St Gregory knew no better than we do what text the Apostles used in consecrating the eucharist: there is no record of this in the New Testament. But he may well have supposed that the Eucharistic Prayer in the *Apostolic Tradition* of St Hippolytus, or that in the eighth book of the *Apostolic Constitutions*, was of Apostolic derivation, and in fact neither of these has an *oratio super oblata* or the *Pater noster*.

The *oratio super oblata* was certainly said at the Offertory at Rome from the pontificate of Xystus III (432-40) or from that of Leo the Great (440-61),[84] so it would be familiar to St Gregory. In the letter to John of Syracuse, St Gregory says that he had received from Sicily a complaint that in four respects he was following Byzantine custom at Rome. Now Gregory had spent twelve years at Byzantium as *apocrisarius*, and was doubtless thoroughly familiar with the usage of the Church of that city. In all four cases he shows that he was reviving earlier Roman usage, and not imitating that of Byzantium. In regard to the Lord's Prayer he says that Roman use is for the priest to say it alone, but the Greek use is for the people to join with the celebrant in its recital. The use of Africa in Augustine's time was identical with that of Rome.[85] But this is a matter of comparatively small importance, which the Sicilians had not in fact raised. In placing the Lord's Prayer immediately after the Canon, instead of between the Fraction and Communion, St Gregory was undoubtedly following Byzantine use in opposition to the use, as it would appear, of the rest of Christendom.

It would appear, therefore, that St Gregory's innovation here consisted, not in introducing the Lord's Prayer into the Roman Mass, but in moving it back so that it immediately followed the Canon. His purpose in so doing was that it might be said over the Lord's Body and Blood. But, we may ask, would it not equally have been said over the Lord's Body if it had continued to be said before the Communion, when the Lord's Body was certainly lying on the altar? If the arrangement of the papal mass were the same in 598 as it was in 750, when *Ordo* I was

---

[84] See G. G. Willis, 'The Variable Prayers of the Roman Mass', in *Further Essays*, pp. 89-131.
[85] Augustine, *Sermo* LVIII.x.12 (PL XXXVIII, 399): 'in ecclesia enim ad altare Dei quotidie dicitur ista dominica oratio et augiunt illam fideles'.

written, the answer to the question just posed is negative. For in that *Ordo* the pope, having begun the Fraction, leaves it to be completed by the deacons, and retires from the altar to his throne, where he is communicated by the archdeacon. If in St Gregory's early years this procedure was as in the *Ordo*, but the Lord's Prayer was said after the Fraction, immediately before the Communion, it would have been said by the Pope at the throne, but the sacrament would have been on the altar. There is no evidence that this was the case in 598, but the mass was fairly static during the seventh century, and it may well have been the case when St Gregory ascended the throne of St Peter on 3 September 590. If so, it is easy to see why he moved the *Pater noster* to its position immediately after the Canon, so that the pope might say it over the consecrated oblation at the altar before going to his throne, just as he said the *oratio super oblata* at the altar over the unconsecrated elements.[86]

It has been assumed, for the purpose of this argument, that the Lord's Prayer was said at mass at Rome before St Gregory, but in a different position. This assumption is probably correct, but not certainly, for there is no explicit evidence before St Gregory that it was said at Rome. It is possible that he introduced it there. But this also is uncertain. Before the middle of the fourth century there is no evidence anywhere in Christendom that the Lord's Prayer was used at mass. After that time evidence for its use is abundant, and St Augustine states that all, or nearly all, the church so used it.[87] Evidently he knew of one or two exceptions to the rule, and it may be that Rome is one of the exceptions. This is not very likely, since Africa certainly used the Lord's Prayer at that time, and Milan almost certainly so, and Roman liturgical use was allied to the use of Milan and Africa.

The *Pater Noster* is introduced by the words *Oremus. Praeceptis salutaribus moniti et diuina institutione formati, audemus dicere, Pater noster.* This appears to be older than St Gregory, for the words *diuina institutione formati* have parallels in Firmicus Maternus in the middle of the fourth century, and in Priscillian (d. 385-6),[88] and *audemus*

---

[86] Cf. *Ordo* I, chs. 97-8 and 100 (MS G).

[87] Augustine, *Ep*. CXLIX.16 (PL XXXIII, 636): '. . . quam totam petitionem fere omnis ecclesia dominica oratione concludit'; cf. *Sermo* CCXXVII (PL XXXVIII, 1099): 'Ubi peracta est sanctificatio dicimus orationem dominicam'.

[88] Firmicus Maternus, *Mathesis* V.vii.4: 'animum tuum divina institutione formatum sollerti coniectura debes instruere'; Priscillian, *Tract.* 4: 'divinae institutionis praecepta servare.'

dicere in Gregory of Nyssa, Augustine and Jerome.[89] But there are strong indications in the text of the embolism that it is Roman and may come from the hand of St Gregory himself. The phrase *da propitius pacem in diebus nostris* recalls the words added to *Hanc igitur oblationem* by Gregory himself: *diesque nostros in tua pace disponas.* The choice of the saints mentioned in the embolism may be significant. The Blessed Virgin Mary was by the end of the sixth century apt to be mentioned in Roman prayer forms: SS Peter and Paul, the Apostolic founders of the Roman Church, are naturally named; and Gregory is known to have had a special devotion to St Andrew, for he dedicated a monastery which he founded on the Caelian Hill, on his father's patrimony, to St Andrew, and brought from Byzantium an arm of St Andrew to deposit in that foundation.

The Fraction

In moving the Lord's Prayer back to a position after the Canon, St Gregory left a hiatus immediately before the Communion, and disturbed the order of the actions between the Canon and the Communion. The history of these rites is discussed by Dom B. Capelle in his article 'Le rite de la fraction dans la messe romaine'.[90]

The situation was further complicated by revisions in the eighth and ninth centuries and later, but that is outside our period, and what we need to discover, if possible, is what was happening about the time of St Gregory. The most important act betwen the eucharistic prayer and the Communion is the Fraction. It is one of the acts of the Lord at the Supper: 'he brake it'. As the Lord's taking of the bread was an act preparatory to giving thanks over it, so the breaking was a preliminary to the giving of it to the disciples: 'He brake it, and gave it to his disciples.' As St Augustine says, *ad distribuendum comminuitur.* The Fraction therefore goes right back to the Lord's action at the Supper, and all the other elements of this section of the mass are subsequent additions: Lord's Prayer, *Pax*, Commixture, and the texts which accompany these actions. In later times symbolic and mystical interpretations were attached to the act of Breaking the Bread: perhaps

---

[89] Gregory of Nyssa, *De orat. dom.* (PG XLIV, 1140C and 1141D); Augustine, *Sermo* CL.5 (PL XXXVIII, 641); Jerome, *Con. Pelag.* III.15, (PL XXIII, 585).
[90] *Revue Bénédictine* LIII (1941), 5-40, reprinted in his *Travaux liturgiques* II (Louvain, 1962), pp. 287-318.

the first is that of Pope Sergius I (687-701), who ordred *Agnus Dei* to be sung at this point.[91] But originally the Fraction was simply an imitation of the Lord's recorded action, and was necessary as a preliminary to communion. The *Pax*, comprising a verbal greeting (*Pax Domini sit semper uobiscum*) and a greeting of the people by the celebrant, was originally placed before the Offertory, where it has ever since remained in Eastern rites, but in the West, except in Gaul and Spain, it had before St Gregory been moved to a position close to the Fraction. This had clearly happened in Africa by the beginning of the fifth century.[92] By St Gregory's time the *Pax* had been integrated with the Fraction and the Commixture.

The earliest detailed description of the rites at this point of the mass is to be found in *Ordo Romanus* I. The date of this is as much as 150 years after St Gregory, but, except for the introduction of *Agnus Dei* at the end of the seventh century, there was probably not much change between St Gregory and the earliest form of the *Ordo*, which is to be seen in Codex Sangallensis 614 (G). This describes the papal rite on Easter Day, and it should be borne in mind that the rite for a mass celebrated by somebody else may not have had the same ceremonies.

In *Ordo* I, and probably earlier, the elevation of the Host and chalice at the end of the Canon, later called the Little Elevation, but in the early Middle Ages being the sole elevation, was practised, but it had already lost its original connection, seen in many Eastern Rites, with the text τὰ ἄγια τοῖς ἀγίοις, *Sancta sanctis*.

In *Ordo* I the Little Elevation is shared by the pope and the archdeacon and takes place at the doxology which concludes the Canon. After the Lord's Prayer, with its embolism, at the end of which the pope's Host is broken in two, there are differences between the long recension and the short and earlier recension contained in MS G alone. The long recension states that the pope, after breaking his host, puts a piece of it into the chalice: *mittit in calicem de sancta*.[93] Immediately after this commixture he breaks on the altar one of his two hosts, and takes a piece from its right side, which he does not put into the chalice, but leaves on the altar. The remainder of his oblations are taken with him to the throne. There is then a fraction for the general communion,

---

[91] *Liber Pontificalis*, ed. Duchesne, I, p. 376: 'Hic statuit ut tempore confractionis dominici corporis *Agnus Dei qui tollis peccata mundi, miserere nobis* a clero et populo decantetur.'
[92] Cf. Augustine, *Sermo* ccxxvii.
[93] *Ordo* I. 95.

but the pope has no part in this. It takes place on the altar, and is performed by two deacons, to whom the oblations are handed by two subdeacons. The pope then communicates at his throne and drops into the chalice another fragment of the host, saying, *Fiat commixtio et consecratio corporis et sanguinis*, etc. The fraction by the deacons on the altar is functional: it is a general breaking up of the bread preparatory to communion. It is less easy to discern the purpose of the earlier fraction, when the piece detached is left on the altar. The shorter recension, in G, states that the purpose of this is that the altar shall not be without the sacrifice while the holy mysteries are being celebrated:

> praeter particulam quam pontifex de propria oblatione confracta super altare reliqui, quia ita observant, ut, dum missarum solemnia peraguntur, altare sine sacrificio non sit.[94]

The long recension has none of these words, and even in G it appears to be an addition, since the remark *ita observant* was obviously written outside Rome. In general, however, the short recension of the first *Ordo* is a thoroughly Roman document, and Dom Capelle is almost certainly right in suggesting that the fragment left on the altar is the *fermentum* to be sent to the *tituli*.[95] It is detached from the pope's host at the *Pax*, and it is at the *Pax* in the *titulus* that each priest will put it into his chalice, thus in a sense uniting his mass with that of the pope. But, if this guess is right, it needs to be remembered that there were at this time twenty-five *tituli* in the city of Rome, so that the piece detached from the pope's oblation would require division into twenty-five portions. It has to be borne in mind that the oblations are in the form of small loaves, and not in the form of the flat discs or wafers which we now use. It is for this reason, too, that the general fraction into pieces to be given to the communicants is such a long and elaborate process in the *Ordo*. As to the first fraction, it is not stated in the *Ordo* where the fragment used in the first commixture came from. If the pope had just broken it off, we have two fractions. But it may have been brought to him, and if so, it seems likely that it was brought from the *sancta* which in this *Ordo* is exhibited to the pope when he first arrives at the altar.[96]

If this conjecture is right, it will be significant that the fragment is called *sancta*: it is not a piece consecrated at this mass, but the piece reserved from the previous mass. Its commixture in the chalice now

---

[94] *Ordo* I. 105.
[95] See G. G. Willis, 'Roman Stational Liturgy', in *Further Essays*, pp. 5-7.
[96] *Ordo* I. 48.

unites this mass with the pope's last mass, just as the *fermentum* unites the pope's mass with the masses in the *tituli*. Both ceremonies are designed to emphasise the unity of the Roman Church. Mabillon first made this suggestion, but Capelle suggests that *mittit in calicem de sancta* may be an interpolation. If it is, then the text of G at this point would read, 'cum dixerit, Pax Domini sit semper uobiscum, archidiaconus dat pacem priori episcopo deinde ceteri per ordinem et populus similiter', which gives good sense, for it unites the words *Pax Domini* and the kiss of peace. *Ordo* VII, though it is of the ninth century, gives a pure and Roman recension of the Canon, free from the influence of the Alcuinian revision in the ninth century.[97] This *Ordo* distinguishes between the action of the pope as celebrant at this point, and that of other celebrants, thus: 'dum uero Dominus Papa dixit, Pax uobiscum, non mittit partem de Sancta in calicem, sicut ceteris sacerdotibus mos est.' This supports the view of Capelle that the papal mass in the eighth century did not have a commixture at the altar, and if so *mittit in calicem de sancta* will be an interpolation in *Ordo* I.

The pope said *Pax uobiscum*, but does not appear to have transmitted the kiss himself to anyone, though his pronouncing of the greeting was the signal that the kiss should be exchanged among other persons present. He breaks off the piece of his own host, leaves it on the altar, and goes to his throne, where he communicates, and the general fraction takes place on the altar. Before communicating he makes a commixture in his own chalice, and this act is without words at the time of St Gregory, but in the eighth or ninth century it is supplied with the words it still has, *Fiat commixtio*, etc. Then the pope receives the chalice from the archdeacon's hands.

When the mass is not celebrated by the pope, the arrangements are different. The *sancta* reserved at the pope's last mass is brought to the celebrant before the *Pax Domini*, and at this point he immerses it in his chalice, with three signs of the cross. The action is not after, but during the *Pax Domini*. When there was no *fermentum* the celebrant broke off a fragment of the host consecrated at this mass, and put it into his own chalice, and this has remained the basis of the acts of fraction and commixture in the Roman rite since that time.

---

[97] See Botte, *Le canon*, pp. 22-3. The text is in Andrieu (*Ordo* VII. 21-4).

The variable prayers and chants

The eucharistic prayer, which has been our main concern hitherto, is comparatively fixed, and subject to variation only in the Preface and in the intercessory paragraphs, beginning *Memento* and *Hanc igitur*. It appears that at the time of Justin Martyr and Hippolytus the eucharistic prayer was the only prayer in the rite, but after the Peace of the Church this ceased to be the case, and one of the first additions was that of variable prayers at certain points of the rite. Those which had appeared by the time of St Gregory were the Collect, or First Prayer, *Oratio prima*; the second collect, which in Roman books has no title, but at Milan was called *oratio super sindonem*, the Prayer over the Corporal; the prayer usually called by its Gallican name *Secreta*, but known in the roman rite as *oratio super oblata*, the Prayer over the Oblations; the *Oratio ad complendum*, or Concluding Prayer, which the Gallicans called *Postcommunio*; and the *Oratio super populum*. Of these the Collect, Prayer over the Oblations and Concluding Prayer have remained in all masses to the present day; the Prayer over the People was obsolescent in the time of St Gregory, and has remained only on ferias in Lent, and the Prayer over the Corporal was extinct by the middle of the eighth century, and was in any case only provided in some masses.

Collects, Secrets and Postcommunions are well established in the Roman rite before the accession of St Gregory, for they are provided in every complete mass in the Verona or Leonine Sacramentary, which dates from the pontificate of Vigilius (537-55), and in the early stratum of the Old Gelasian Sacramentary some twenty or thirty years later. They are prayers of a similar style and rhythm, which cannot have been composed before that style and rhythm were fully developed, and that was not the case at the beginning of the fifth century, but rather towards the middle of that century. The Collect had not appeared in Africa before the death of St Augustine, for his account of a miracle of healing which took place in church at Hippo just before mass began on Easter Day 426 shows that the mass began after the entry of the bishop and his attendants, with the bishop's salutation, doubtless *Pax uobis*, and the reading of the lessons.

The synaxis of Good Friday at Rome, preserved in the Old Gelasian and in the Gregorian sacramentaries, is a thoroughly primitive rite. It begins, as the African mass did in 426, with the lessons, though without any greeting by the celebrant. In the first quarter of the fifth century Rome had nothing before the lessons. Pope Celestine (422-32) is said to have added the Introit, to cover the entry of the ministers; the *Kyrie eleison* was brought in by Pope Gelasius (492-6) as part of the *Deprecatio*, and remained as a vestige when, one hundred years later, Gregory the Great removed the Litany or *Deprecatio* to save time; *Gloria in excelsis* was first used in the mass of Christmas Day, and in the time of Symmachus (498-514) its use was extended to most Sundays and the feasts of martyrs.

The *Liber pontificalis* unfortunately does not tell us who prefixed the Collect to the lessons. There is no sign of its presence under Celestine: it is there, as we have seen, by the middle of the sixth century. But we can take it further back by a hundred years, that is, into the middle of the fifth century. Probst and others have been inclined to attribute the development of the collect form and of the insertion of a first collect before the lessons to the pontificate of Damasus (366-84), but the development of the *orationes sollemnes* of Good Friday shows clearly that the collect form is not so early as Damasus, and the primitive Canon, as seen in *De sacramentis*, which may very well have been composed under Damasus, is quite different in style and rhythm from the collects.[98]

Capelle has shown that an Ascension mass in the Verona or Leonine Sacramentary may be attributed to Pope Leo.[99] This mass has a collect in the usual form. Professor F. L. Cross has similarly demonstrated that an Embertide mass is used by Pope Leo in a sermon.[100] These prayers, which include three first collects for the Pentecost Embertide, cannot be later than Leo, who died in 461, but Cross thinks they are probably before his pontificate, i.e., before 440, in which year Leo succeeded Xystus III. Since there was no collect at all in the pontificate of Celestine, we are forced back to the pontificate of Xystus III, 432-440. The solemn prayers of Good Friday consist of biddings which are not rhythmic, and may well date from the early fourth century, or even the end of the third, and of collects in the developed form and rhythm of which we have been speaking. The biddings and collects are known to

---

[98] See the discussions of the Solemn prayers in Willis, *Essays*, pp. 1-48, and of the origins of the collects in *Further Essays*, pp. 103-21; also *idem*, 'The Variable Prayers of the Roman Mass', in *Further Essays*, pp. 89-131.

[99] B. Capelle, 'Une messe de S. Léon pour l'Ascension', in *Travaux liturgiques*, II, pp. 71-8.

[100] 'Pre-Leonine Elements in the Proper of the Roman Mass', *JTS* L (1949), 191-7.

have been joined together by the time of Prosper of Aquitaine, who quotes from both forms in the *Auctoritates de gratia Dei*, which he wrote, probably at Rome, between 435 and 442, and also in *De vocatione gentium*, written about 450.[101] By the time of Pope Leo the collect had become a variable prayer, related to the day or to its lessons, or both. It has always remained so. But there is a possibiity that it was derived from some Eastern form. Dom Gregory Dix thought that it originated in the first prayer of the Sacramentary of Sarapion, bishop of Thmuis in the Delta of the Nile in the middle of the fourth century.[102] This is a fixed prayer, and prays that we may profitably hear the lessons which are to follow. None of the Roman collects which have survived do this; but the position of the Roman collect is the same as that of the prayer in Sarapion's liturgy.

Collects, secrets and postcommunions are prayers in collect form, in the same rhythmical style, with observance of the *cursus* rules, and they all seem to have originated at the same time. The Secret and the Postcommunion are prayers said aloud – the Secret went silent only at some time after Gregory – and they are prayers said by the celebrant in the name of all the people present. Each of them concludes and sums up an action which is covered by a chant sung by the *schola*; the Secret coming after the Offertory chant, and being itself a prayer offering the gifts to God; the Postcommunion coming after the Communion, and giving thanks for the gifts received and praying for the grace of perseverance to derive spiritual benefit from their reception.

A good case has been made out by Professor Jungmann for thinking that as the Secret and the Postcommunion conclude actions covered by chants, so the collect is designed to follow a chant.[103] If this is so, the chant in question must be the Introit, which occupies the *schola* and the people while the ministers enter the church and take their places near the altar. This theory would make the function of the collect identical with the function of the Secret and Postcommunion. It is furthermore reasonable to think that all the three chants were in their present position before the Collect, Secret and Postcommunion appeared in the middle of the fifth century. The oldest chant in the Roman rite is the chant between the lessons, whether it be Gradual, Tract or Alleluia. This chant is too long to cover the only action which it could cover, the

---

[101] See Willis, *Further Essays*, p. 115.
[102] Dix, *Shape of the Liturgy*, pp. 446-7.
[103] J. A. Jungmann, *The Mass of the Roman Rite* (London, 1961), pp. 190-2 and 240.

movement of the book and the reader from the altar to the ambo, and indeed it is integral to the structure of the mass in a way that the other three chants are not. It expands and interprets the lessons. But if the Gradual is the most ancient chant, the other three seem to have been in position before the time of Pope Xystus. There was certainly no collect at Rome when Celestine (422-32) introduced the Introit. The Offertory and Communion chants are attested by St Augustine for Africa, and were doubtless in use in his day at Rome. His notice in the *Retractationes* of his work against Hilarus in 397 shows that in 397 the Offertory and Communion chants had recently been introduced in Africa, and that Hilarus took exception to the innovation.[104] Doubtless they came into use at Rome about the same time, and at any rate before Celestine. Since these chants were apparently in the Roman rite twenty years or so before the variable prayers, there is nothing intrinsically impossible about Professor Jungmann's theory. If it is true, the Collect will have no relation to the lessons. Dom Gregory Dix, however, suggested that the Collect was not transferred, as some have suggested, from after the first lesson to before it, but was always in its present position, and that it was derived from Alexandria, since we see that Sarapion has a fixed prayer in this position. In Sarapion's *Euchologion* the prayer is entitled 'First Prayer of the Lord's Day', and there may be some connection between the words 'First Prayer' and the identical *oratio prima* of Latin sources.[105]

Dix points out that the greeting *Dominus uobiscum*, which in Africa, and perhaps at Rome, was immediately before the lessons when there was yet no collect, was transferred to precede the Collect after that had been introduced. This transfer tended to unite the Collect with the lessons which follow, and to separate it from the Introit which preceded it.

In Syria about 375 we find that the ordination rites of the *Apostolic Constitutions* have a prayer before the lessons, differing in the case of each order of the ministry. The form of these variable prayers, Collect, Secret and Postcommunion, is characteristically Roman, and distinct from other forms of liturgical composition, for example the Canon, or eucharistic prayer, or the Preface. These forms are much longer and more rhetorical, with a liking for amplitude, hendiadys and pleonasm. The Collect is restrained in style, severe, economical of words, and very

---

[104] Augustine, *Retractationes* II.2 (PL XXXII, 364; CSEL XXXVI, 144).
[105] E.g., *Ordo.* I, 53.

Latin in its concinnity, and therefore impossible to translate satisfactorily into any other language. In many ways it is the ideal form of Christian prayer.

The Roman rule, to which before the year 1000 there are hardly any exceptions, is that liturgical prayer, including the Canon, and the collect type of prayer, is addressed to the Father, through the mediation of the Son. Elsewhere there are examples of prayers addressed to the Son. For instance, the original form of the Liturgy of SS Addai and Mari in Edessa was addressed to the Son.[106]

The Councils of Hippo (393) and of Carthage (397) legislated that prayer at the altar should always be addressed to the Father, so that the African Church was evidently aware of the practice of addressing prayer to the Son. Till about 1000 the Roman church rigidly observed the rule of addressing the Father, and even then only admitted occasional exceptions in collect-type prayers, but prayers addressed to the Son were more common in Gallican liturgy, where they were regarded as an antidote to Arianism.

The structure of collects is regular. Their pattern consists almost always of (1) an address to the Father; (2) a relative clause or a participial phrase qualifying the invocation or address; (3) the petition, usually in the imperative mood, but sometimes in the subjunctive; (4) a final clause defining the object or the expected result of the petition; (5) the conclusion, *Per Christum Dominum*, etc. Sections 2 and 4 may be dispensed with, leaving the essential parts 1, 3 and 5; 2, 3 and 4 may be duplicated; and the order of 1, 3 and 4 may be inverted or rearranged. Examples of such inversion and rearrangement may be cited.

3 Pateant aures misericordiae tuae

1 Domine

3 precibus supplicantium

4 et ut petita consequantur

3 fac eos quae tibi placita sunt postulare

5 per Christum etc.

3 Illumina

1 quaesumus Domine

---

[106] See E. C. Ratcliff, 'The Original Form of the *Anaphora* of Addai and Mari: a Suggestion', *JTS* XXX (1929), 23-32.

3 tenebras nostras et totius huius noctis insidias tu a nobis repelle
   propitius

5 per etc.

Such short collects are not common as First Collects, or collects of the
day, but occur more frequently as Secrets or Postcommunions. Prayers
of this type collected in the three great sacramentaries of the early
Roman tradition, between the fifth and seventh centuries, namely the
Leonine, Gelasian and Gregorian, are almost all written with regard to
the *cursus*.

The prayer which Roman liturgy knows as *AD POPULUM* or
SUPER POPULUM is similar to Roman collects in all literary respects,
form, language, rhythm, construction. It differs, however, from
Collects, Secrets and Postcommunions in that it is not a prayer of the
celebrant said by him in the name of all the people, but a blessing
addressed by the priest to the people, who are regarded as separate from
him and standing over against him. Its position was originally at the
very end of the mass, after the communion, and it served to dismiss the
people. At various times there have been four methods of dismissing
the people after mass: (1) *Oratio ad populum*, the earliest, attested from
the Leonine Sacramentary onwards; (2) The form *Ite missa est*, attested
from *Ordo* I onwards, that is from the middle of the eighth century; (3)
A silent blessing of the people by the pope as he leaves the church at the
end of mass, attested in the same *Ordo* I; and (4) The form *Benedicat
uos omnipotens Deus*, attested first in Mabillon's *Ordo* XIV, in the
fourteenth century. It is probable that the first three of these were in use
by the time of St Gregory, and therefore concern us in this enquiry.

Of forms 2 and 3 there is nothing to be said except that they have a
place in the Roman stational mass of the early eighth century, which we
have reason to believe represents the use of St Gregory's time. Of the
oratio super populum it may be said that it was obsolescent after
Gregory. It occurs at the end of every complete mass formulary in the
Leonine Sacramentary, so that in the pontificate of Vigilius, during
which this book was put together (537-55), it was evidently the regular
custom to conclude mass with it. Indeed the pontificate of Vigilius itself
provides a story which illustrates this usage. Vigilius was arrested in
church on the orders of the emperor, and transported to Byzantium.
This happened on St Cecilia's Day, 22 November 538, when he was
celebrating the stational mass beyond Tiber, on the west bank of the
river, in Region VII, at St Cecilia's church. He was hustled off by the

police at the end of the communion of the people, and before he could pronounce the *Super populum* blessing. The people followed him to the wharf of the Tiber, and asked that they might receive this blessing, which he imparted to them from the deck of the ship as it set sail.[107] Evidently they regarded the blessing as customary and indeed essential. In the Old Gelasian (MS Vat. Reg. 316), an *oratio super populum* is not provided for every mass, but for all Sundays and weekdays in Lent, Christmas and its Octave, the Epiphany, the three Sundays next before Lent, Ascensiontide, Whitsuntide, Embertides and for the Dedication of a Church. This represents a restriction by comparison with the Leonine Sacramentary. In the Gregorian tradition in the next century, the seventh, there has been further restriction and the position in *Hadrianum* and *Paduense* D. 47 is about the same as in the Missal of Pius V in 1570, namely a *super populum* prayer for the ferias of Lent only, from Ash Wednesday to the Wednesday before Easter inclusive. In these books there are no such prayers on Sundays, even in Lent.

The survival of this prayer in Lent is typical of the conservatism of Lenten liturgy. It is not known why the *Super populum* went out of use. Professor Jungmann suggests that St Gregory transformed the prayer from being a blessing on all the communicants to being a blessing on the public penitents. As public penance disappeared during the seventh century, the blessing disappeared with it, except on the ferias of Lent. To this it may be objected that public penitents were excluded from mass during Lent, and readmitted on Maundy Thursday, so that the *super populum* prayer was retained just for the period when it would be useless for blessing penitents. Moreover, public penance disappeared before the seventh century at Rome, for the oath that the candidate for ordination was required to make that he was not guilty of the *quattuor capitula* was not required when public penitence was a living institution, but only when it became obsolete.[108] Yet this oath was imposed before the time of St Gregory. The other hypothesis urged to explain the disappearance of the *super populum* prayer is that of Professor Chavasse, and is preferable. He takes the prayer as still being a blessing on the communicants, and holds that during the seventh century it was replaced by the two forms mentioned in *Ordo Romanus* I,[109] except on ferias of Lent.

[107] *Liber Pontificalis*, ed. Duchesne, I, p. 297.
[108] See below, p. 142.
[109] See A. Chavasse, *Le sacramentaire gélasien* (Tournai, 1958), pp. 188-9.

Roman stational liturgy

The Roman Church, like other city churches in the early days of Christianity, began as a small compact body able to assemble for worship in one building under the presidency of its bishop. As it expanded and became more numerous, this unity became a practical impossibility. Yet Rome continued for centuries to lay great store by the principle of unity, of the one family of God in the City under the presidency of its one bishop, or father, *papa*. Therefore, when the Church became too large to assemble in one building for its regular worship, it sought means by which this unity might be expressed in a liturgical form. The two principal methods of setting forth this unity in worship were the stational mass, and the practice of *fermentum*.[110]

The definitive description of this practice is contained in the decretal letter of Pope Innocent I to the bishop of *Eugubinum*, or Gubbio, in Umbria, of March 416. The letter answers several questions which Decentius had asked, and one of these concerns *fermentum*. Innocent's words are:

> De fermento uero quod die dominica per titulos mittimus, superflue nos consulere uoluisti, cum omnes ecclesiae nostrae sint intra ciuitatem constitutae. quarum presbyteri quia die ipso propter plebem sibi creditam nobiscum conuenire non possunt, idcirco fermentum a nobis confectum per acolythos accipiunt, ut se a nostra communione, maxime illa die, non iudicent separatos. quod per parrochias fieri debere non puto quia nec longe portanda sunt sacramenta, nec nos per coemeteria diuersa constitutis presbyteris destinamus, et presbyteri eorum conficiendorum ius habeant et licentiam.[111]

Beside the pope's own mass, there were other masses celebrated by priests in other churches within the city, and in cemetery chapels in the *parrochia*, which is the region outside the city wall, in which are the churches in the cemeteries along the roads leading out of Rome. There are times when the priests attached to the basilicas and titles (*tituli*) come to the papal mass and attend there upon the pope. There are times when they cannot do this, because of their duties in their own churches at the same time. In this case the pope sends the *fermentum* to the priests

---

[110] See Willis, 'Roman Stational Liturgy', in *Further Essays*, pp. 1-87.
[111] Innocent, *Epistula ad Decentium Eugubinum*, ch. 5 (PL LVI, 516-17).

who celebrate mass in the titles at a slightly later hour than that of the papal mass. At the *Pax* the pope performs the fraction, and detaches from his oblation portions for as many priests as will receive the *fermentum*, twenty-five normally for the *tituli*, plus a few more, if necessary, for the patriarchal basilicas. Acolytes receive these fragments in linen bags, and carry them to the priests in the titles, and each priest, having received the consecrated fragment, places it in his chalice when he makes the usual commixture at the *Pax*. This unites his mass with that of the pope. Innocent adds that there is something to be said against carrying the reserved sacrament about for considerable distances, and that for this reason the *fermentum* is not sent to the churches outside the city, but only to those within it. The priests who celebrate in the cemetery churches outside the walls have authority to celebrate a mass completely independent of that of the Pope, and they are not united with him through the practice of *fermentum*, as are the priests of the titles. *Fermentum* disappeared in the seventh century, surviving only in the case of a stational mass celebrated in the absence of a pope by a priest or bishop, and for the mass celebrated by priests in their own churches on Holy Saturday.[112]

The passage quoted from Innocent sets forth clearly the types of churches and of services which exist in the diocese of Rome. There are the great basilicas, such as St John Lateran, hard by which the pope lives in the Lateran Palace, or *episcopium*, in the south-eastern part of the city; St Paul without the Walls, St Peter in the Vatican, St Mary Major, and so on. These churches are served by priests, and sometimes by monastic priests. In the time of Pope Simplicius (468-83) the basilicas of St Peter, St Paul and St Laurence were in the hands of the central administration of the Roman church, and he assigned duties in them to the priests of the *tituli* in regions VII, I and III.[113] Later on, St Mary Major was similarly provided for, and from the eighth century the Lateran was served by suburbicarian bishops.

The *tituli* were smaller churches served by priests, and answering in some respects to parish churches in modern Europe, in the sense that

---

112 For the first of these, see *Ordo* II. 6. Cf. the gloss on the letter of Innocent quoted in Andrieu II, 62. In the same passage is the mention of the second case.
113 *Liber Pontificalis*, ed. Duchesne, I, p. 249: 'Hic constituit ad sanctum Petrum apostolum et ad sanctum Paulum apostolum et ad sanctum Laurentium martyrem ebdomadas ut presbyteri manerent propter penitentes et regio tertia ad sanctum Laurentium, regio prima ad sanctum Paulum, regio sexta vel septima ad sanctum Petrum.'

they serve the people and have resident clergymen responsible for the services in a particular church. Until long after St Gregory these numbered twenty-five. The cemetery churches in the suburbs were also served by priests. At a date later than Pope Innocent, indeed later than Gregory, there sprang up in the city, especially in the poorer parts near the Tiber docks and wharves, the deaconries, from which deacons administered poor relief, and to which churches were attached. Naturally, they are not mentioned in Innocent's letter. *Titulus* originally means the documentary evidence of possessing an immovable piece of property, the title-deeds, as we still say in English. It is then transferred to mean the property itself. In ante-Nicene days, before the Church began to erect permanent buildings appropriated to divine worship, Christians met in private houses, especially in the large mansions of affluent Christians, which could provide a room or hall large enough to accommodate the Church. These were the first *tituli*, and at Rome they were often called by the names of their owners, e.g., *titulus* Gaii, *titulus* Pammachii, or *titulus* Caeciliae, for some of the owners were women. After the Peace of the Church they tended to be rebuilt, extended or modified.

It has been seen that *fermentum* is intimately connected with the pope's stational mass. The pope did not always celebrate mass in his own cathedral, which in the period we are discussing, and for long afterwards, was St John Lateran. He went, on certain days at least, to other churches in the city, attended by the papal court, and by the deacons of the seven ecclesiastical regions into which the city was divided, by the subdeacons and acolytes of those regions, and by priests from the regions. This stational system was flourishing in the fifth century, and continued for many centuries: indeed it was only finally extinguished by the exile of the popes to Avignon in the early fourteenth century. But the earliest detailed description of it is contained in *Ordo* I, which may be dated about 750, and represents the state of things about 700, a century later than St Gregory. There seems to have been very small modification of it in the course of the seventh century, so it may reasonably be accepted as giving a fair picture of what was happening in Gregory's own time. There were two types of stational masses. In the simpler type, described in *Ordo* I, the pope rides to the church where the station is held, and is received there by the clergy. The more elaborate form is that preceded by a *collecta*. In this arrangement the pope meets the attendants who will assist him at the stational mass at a church which is different from that where the mass is to be celebrated.

This is the church of the *collecta*, or gathering of the papal court. Thence the papal procession, after saying a preliminary prayer (*oratio ad collectam*), proceeds to the stational church, and there the mass is celebrated in the usual papal form. In Gregory's time there appear to have been only three days with a *collecta*: Ash Wednesday, *collecta ad S. Anastasiam, Statio ad S. Sabinam*; the *Litania Maior*, or Greater Rogation on 25 April, *Collecta ad S. Laurentium in Lucina, Statio ad S. Petrum*; on the feast of St Caesarius, 1 November, *Collecta ad SS. Cosmam et Damianum*. The sources do not state where the station was, but it must have been at St Caesarius, who had ony one church in Rome, on the Palatine.

At the end of the seventh century the Syrian pope, Sergius I, added *collectae* on the four feasts of the Blessed Virgin which had been instituted at Rome since St Gregory: the Purification, 2 February; the Annunciation, 25 March; the *Dormitio*, 15 August; and the Nativity, 8 September. On all these days the *collecta* was at St Hadrian in the Forum, and the station at St Mary Major. These four feasts were adopted from the East during the seventh century: there is no trace of them in the time of St Gregory, and the *Liber pontificalis* implies that Sergius did not introduce these four feasts, but supplied them with a *collecta*, thereby making their observance more solemn.

The Gregorian Sacramentary (MS Padua D. 47) has an *oratio ad collectam* on certain Wednesdays in fasting weeks, those after the first Sunday in Lent (Ember Day), the fourth Sunday in Lent (*In Mediana*), the sixth Sunday in Lent, Whitsun Wednesday, and the Wednesdays in the Ember Weeks in September and December. The seventh century must therefore have seen a considerable augmentation of the days which had a *collecta*.

The *collecta* church is not named in *Paduense*, but the stational churches of these days are mentioned in this sacramentary, and in all the others which have station notes.

The stational system printed in the *Missale Romanum* of 1570 can be traced back to the *Comes* of Würzburg, dated about 625, which may very well represent the arrangements of St Gregory. Mabillon credits St Gregory with arranging the system as it has since continued, and this may well be correct, since Gregory, a Roman by birth, would be likely to have an interest in an institution so characteristically Roman. The stational procession was preceded by the cross of the region which was in course on that day, and these crosses were stored at St Anastasia, which is convenient by reason of its central position in the City. Psalms

71

and litanies were sung in the procession, and it may be that when St Augustine of Canterbury and his monks sang litanies as they approached the city of Canterbury, they were imitating a custom which they had learned in the stational liturgy of their native Rome.

Ordo Romanus I is an almost purely Roman document, describing the papal liturgy of Easter Day at St Mary Major. It survives in two recensions, of which the first, MS Sangallensis 614 (G), dating from the ninth century, is the sole surviving witness, and contains a shorter text than all the other manuscripts, which have the long recension. Both recensions are Roman, and therefore bear witness to Roman and not to Gallican tradition. It is a tradition belonging to a date much earlier than the date of G; in fact the *Ordo* must have been complete by 750, but it is later than 701, for it contains *Agnus dei*, the *confractorium* chant which was introduced by Sergius I (687-701). However, apart from the introduction of *Agnus dei*, and possibly of some modification at the Fraction, *Pax* and Commixture, the rite had probably changed very little since St Gregory's time.

The contents of the *Ordo* are adequately described by its title: 'Incipit ordo ecclesiastici ministerii Romanae ecclesiae, vel qualiter missa celebratur'. The *ordo* begins with a summary description of the liturgical administration of the city (1-6).[114] The clergy in all its ranks is divided among the seven ecclesiastical regions, each region having a deacon (1), and subdeacons with acolytes (2). In Easter Week one of the regions is responsible for the performance of the papal station for one day. Sunday is the turn of Region III, Monday of Region IV, Tuesday of Region V, Wednesday of Region VI, Thursday of Region VII, Friday of Region I and Saturday of Region II. This applies to the procession if there is a *collecta*, as well as to the mass. On solemn days, with or without a *collecta*, the acolytes of the region in course, and the *defensores* of all seven regions, assemble early at the *patriarchium*, or papal residence, ready to conduct the pope to the stational church (7). A groom (*strator*) walks on either side of the pope's horse in case it slips (8). Before the pope certain officials ride in the procession, including the regionary deacons, subdeacons, notaries and *defensores* (9). Certain other officials follow the pope (10). Immediately before the pope walks an acolyte carrying the chrism in an *ampulla* wrapped in a linen cloth (11). Since not all the people are mounted, the procession

---

[114] The numbers in round brackets in the text refer to the paragraphs of the text of *Ordo Romanus* I in Andrieu's edition.

must advance at walking pace. On Easter Day there is a special ceremony on the way, at the place called *Merulana* where the pope is met by the notary of the region, who announces to him the number of candidates, male and female, who have been baptized at the Easter Vigil during the night at St Mary Major. The pope himself was administering baptism at St John Lateran, and the baptisms at St Mary Major, and at other basilicas, were adminstered by priests (15). The books and vessels needed at the papal mass are carried in the procession, and we infer that the books were carried in cases, to keep the rain off them, for during the service, when they are required, they are taken out of the cases, and later put back into them (19-23).

On arrival at the station church the pope is received (25-8) and proceeds to the sacristy (*secretarium*), supported by the deacons (29). The first business is to take the gospelbook out of its case and to place it upon the altar (30-1). The pontiff then vests in the sacristy, with the assistance of the subdeacons (32-6). The regionary subdeacon meantime puts the singers in order and gives them their instructions, and reports to the pope when he has done so (37-9). All is now ready for a start, and the procession enters the church, headed by lights and incense. During the entry the entry chant (*Introitus*) is sung (44). The pope, as he enters, gives his right hand to the archdeacon, and his left to a second deacon (45). The pope never seems to have carried a pastoral staff, and no such instrument is handed to him in *Ordo* XLA either.

In the procession the pope is preceded by a subdeacon with incense, and by seven acolytes of the region which is in course, on Easter Day Region III. These carry tapers (46). When the pope arrives at the altar, two acolytes hold open pyxes containing the *Sancta* reserved from a previous mass, and the subdeacon shows this to the pope or to the deacon. He adores the sacrament and, if there is too much, orders the surplus to be reserved (48). It is not explained by the *ordo* what the *Sancta* is intended for, or how there can be too much, but the most likely explanation is that it is required for placing in the chalice at the commixture (95), to unite the last papal mass with the present mass. For this purpose only a small fragment would be required, and so the rest might be reserved for future use, though it is not easy to see why at the last mass any more than necessary should have been reserved, unless it were that it was required for purposes other than the commixture, for example for communion of the sick.

The seven taperers, when they reach the place where the *schola* are singing the Introit, divide, four on one side and three on the other, and allow the pope to pass between their ranks and those of the *schola*, and to reach the altar, where he gives the peace to one of the hebdomadary bishops, and to the archpriest, and to all the deacons (49). He then signals to the singers to break off the Introit psalm and to sing *Gloria patri* and the antiphon (50). At this period the psalm had not been reduced, as it was in the Middle Ages, to one verse: it was sung as long as might be needed for the action which it was designed to cover, and when this action was completed a signal was given to the choir to conclude. The tyranny of musicians prolonging services at their own whim had not yet been invented. The pope then kisses the gospelbook and the altar and retires to his throne, where he stands facing east (51). The *schola*, having now completed the final antiphon of the Introit, immediately begins the *Kyrie eleison* (52), unless there has been a *collecta* and the litany, which is full of *Kyries*, has been sung on the way to the stational church. The pope, turning to the people, intones *Gloria in excelsis Deo*, and then turns to the east while it is sung out by the *schola*, and then he turns once more to greet the people *Pax uobiscum*, then, turning east, he says *Oremus* and the first collect (*prima oratio*). At the end of this he sits down, and so do all the bishops and priests (53), while the epistle is read by a subdeacon from the *ambo* (56). The response is sung by one cantor, and the *Alleluia* verse by another (57). During this singing the deacon who is to read the gospel kisses the gospelbook and carries it from the altar to the *ambo*, preceded by two subdeacons with incense and two acolytes with candles (59). The deacon who reads ascends the steps of the *ambo*, and the attendants stand at floor level below the steps. At the end of the gospel the pontiff says to the reader, *Pax tecum*, and to the whole people, *Dominus uobiscum* (63). The deacon who has been gospeller descends the steps of the *ambo*, hands the gospelbook to the subdeacon who found him the place (61), and he in turn hands it to the other subdeacon, who holds it before his breast and offers it to be kissed by all in order (64). The gospelbook was always regarded as a symbol of Christ's Presence in his Church. The book is then put back into its case, and taken away by an acolyte belonging to the same region as the subdeacon who has been holding it (65).

The mass in this *Ordo* has of course no creed, for that was not introduced at Rome till the eleventh century, nor has it a sermon. Some popes, for example Leo and Gregory, preached frequently at mass, as did Ambrose at Milan and Augustine in Africa, but there was no rule requiring preaching of sermons, and for very long periods the Roman rite was without them. In the interests of orthodoxy this is just as well. There being therefore no diversions at this point, the gospel is immediately followed by the Offertory. On Good Friday the *orationes sollemnes* are still said after the gospel, and were so said at every mass until the time of Gelasius I (492-6), but he removed them from regular use, and therefore they do not appear in *Ordo* I.

The Offertory is the most important action which has so far taken place. The deacon of the third region goes to the altar, and an acolyte brings to him the chalice, covered with a corporal. He hands the corporal to the deacon, who, with the help of another deacon, spreads it upon the altar (67). The pope then receives the offerings of the notables (69), and the archdeacon, following the pope, receives the offerings of wine in small vessels (*amulae*). He pours the contents of these, when full, into a large chalice held by the regionary subdeacon. An acolyte follows with a still larger chalice (*scyphus*), into which he pours the contents of the archdeacon's chalice each time it is filled (70). The oblations of bread received by the pope are taken from him by the regionary subdeacon, and handed to another subdeacon, who puts them into a linen corporal (*sindon*) held by two acolytes (71). The hebdomadary bishop receives offerings not received by the pontiff, and places them in the corporal (72). The pope then descends before the *confessio* into the nave to receive the offerings of certain officials of the papal court, and then he receives oblations from the women in their part of the church (74-5).

This is the last collection of bread performed by the pope, so he returns to his throne and washes his hands. The archdeacon washes his own hands before the altar. He greets the pope, and then disposes the oblations on the altar: they are brought to him by the subdeacons (78). He prepares the chalice by pouring water into the wine which it contains in the form of a cross (80). The deacons then come to the pope at his throne, and he rises and comes to the altar, where he receives oblations from the hebdomadary priest and the deacons (82). The archdeacon thereupon receives the pope's own oblations, which consist of three hosts, from the hands of the oblationary, who is usually a deacon or subdeacon, and hands them to the pope (83). The pope having placed these three hosts on the altar, the archdeacon takes the chalice from the regionary subdeacon, and sets it upon the altar to the right of the pontiff's oblation (84). These actions conclude the Offertory, and therefore the pope signals to the *schola* to interrupt the

Offertory chant and, all the ministers having taken their places, the Canon opens with the singing of the Preface by the pope (86-8).

The pope waits till the *Sanctus* is completed before beginning the eucharistic prayer. It is the view of the long recension that the Canon begins at *Te igitur*, but the short recension in MS G takes the older view, that it begins with *Dominus uobiscum* and *Sursum corda* before the Preface.[115]

The *Ordo* describes no further action by anybody until the pope in the silent recitation of the Canon reaches the beginning of *Nobis quoque peccatoribus*: here warning is given by the *ecphonesis* to the subdeacons, who rise. At the words *Per quem haec omnia*, the archdeacon rises, and at the words *per ipsum et cum ipso*, he elevates the chalice, holding it by the handles wrapped in the veil. He holds it elevated by the celebrant's side (89). This is what was later termed the little elevation, when the great elevation at the words of consecration had been introduced in the later Middle Ages. But at this time the little elevation is the only elevation in the rite. The pope then consigns the chalice with the host (90). The *Pater noster* is then said by the pope alone, who adds the embolism, *Libera nos* (94).

At the words *Pax domini sit semper uobiscum*, pronounced by the pontiff, all manuscripts except G mention a commixture (95).[116] In all sources the *Pax* is then given by the archdeacon to the first hebdomadary bishop, and then to others in order (96). The pope gives the *Pax* to nobody, but proceeds immediately to the fraction, breaking his host on the right side, and leaves the fragment on the altar, but his other oblations he places on a paten held by the archdeacon (97). The pope immediately returns to his throne (98). The archdeacon then takes the chalice from the altar, and hands it to the regionary subdeacon, who stands by the right side of the altar holding it (100). The subdeacons and acolytes approach the altar from both ends, carrying bags to receive the oblations from the archdeacon (101). These oblations are fragments of bread which will be carried in the linen bags as *fermentum* to the titles. The deacons then complete the fraction which the pope began before retiring to his throne (102-4). When all the bread has been broken up and removed from the altar, leaving the particle first broken off by the pope, the archdeacon signals to the *schola* to begin *Agnus Dei*, and joins the other ministers who hold the paten (105). After the fraction the

---

[115] See above, pp. 41-2.
[116] See above, pp. 57-60.

deacon takes the paten to the throne for the pope's communion (106). The pope takes the host from the paten and bites a piece off it and, making a triple sign of the cross, puts the fragment into the chalice held before him by the archdeacon. (107). This is the second commixture, accompanied, according to the manuscripts of the long recension, by the formula *Fiat commixtio et consecratio corporis et sanguinis domini nostri Iesu Christi accipientibus nobis in vitam aeternam. Amen. Pax tecum. Et cum spiritu tuo* (107). The chalice is then administered to the pope by the archdeacon (107), who carries the chalice back to the altar, and announces the place and day of the next stational mass. MS W is the only one which gives the form of this announcement: *Illo die veniente, statio erit ad sanctum Illum, foras aut intus civitate.* The acolyte holds the *scyphus*, or large ministerial chalice, and the archdeacon pours into it a little of the consecrated wine from the pope's chalice to consecrate it. The bishops then come to the throne to be communicated by the pope (108), but the priests communicate at the altar (109). The first bishop stands at the end of the altar, having received the chalice from the archdeacon, and communicates the members of the various orders, down to the *primicerius defensorum* (110). After this is completed, the archdeacon takes the chalice from him and pours its contents into the *scyphus* for the general communion (111-12). After this the pope comes down from his throne, and communicates the notables, from whom he had received oblations at the offertory. They receive the chalice from the archdeacon (113). The priests assist in communicating the people (116). As soon as the pope begins to communicate the notables the *schola* intones the communion chant, *antiphona ad communionem*, and continues until the pope, having finished administering the communion, signals them to break off (117). The pope, having communicated the women, who receive after the men in the congregation have been communicated, returns to his throne, and there communicates the regionaries, who receive the chalice from the archdeacon (118). At the end of the communion, as at the end of the offertory, the pope sits down on this throne and washes his hands. Finally he goes to the altar and says the *oratio ad complendum* (123), and dismisses the people: *Ite, missa est* (124). The *oratio super populum* having become obsolete at Rome outside Lent, there is nothing further to be said at the altar, and the pope returns to the sacristy, preceded by lights and incense, as he came in (125). He is followed by all the ministers (126).

77

III

The Kalendar and Lectionary

During the first six centuries the *Temporale* of the Roman Kalendar reached its full development, and remained thenceforward until 1970 unchanged in essentials. But by the time of St Gregory the *Sanctorale*, though it had developed from nothing, was still relatively simple, and had a long way to develop before it reached the complexity which it was to attain in the Tridentine Missal of 1570.

At the beginning there was one feast, the Christian *Pascha*, the Day of the Lord's Resurrection, celebrated each year, indeed each week, for its establishment made every Sunday holy, as the circle of seven days revolved on itself and brought round again the octave, the eighth day, symbolizing eternity as it returns to the beginning of the circle, in the same way as the wedding ring symbolizes eternity by its perfect roundness. This concept has a parallel in Judaism, where the annual Feast of the Passover, commemorating the greatest deliverance of Jewish history, the Exodus from Egyptian captivity, has its weekly counterpart in the weekly feast of the Sabbath. So Christians have always celebrated weekly the greater Redemption from sin and death wrought by the Lord's Resurrection 'early in the morning, on the first day of the week'.[1]

On the evening of the Sunday when this mighty event had happened, the disciples of Christ were gathered in private, behind locked doors, and 'Jesus came and stood in the midst of them and said, "Peace be unto you".'[2] It is the normal Jewish greeting, 'Good evening', and one which they must often have heard from his lips, '*Shalom*'. But on Easter Day it had a deeper significance, for it was the greeting of the Risen Lord to his flock gathered together on the first Christian Sunday. It can hardly have been accidental that at the same time the next week, on Sunday evening, the same disciples, plus St Thomas, were

[1] Mark XVI.2.
[2] John XX.19.

78

assembled in the same place, and that the Lord came again, with the same greeting, 'Shalom'.[3] The assembling of the Church of Christ on the Lord's Day, as it was soon to be called, was already established, and it has remained the basis of the Christian year ever since. Twenty years later St Paul tells the Corinthian Christians to collect money each week for charitable purposes, and suggests that this be done 'on the first day of the week',[4] because on Sunday this will be convenient, when the faithful are gathered for worship. At the end of the century the visionary on the island of Patmos in the Aegean, in exile from the churches of Asia Minor which he has served, and to whom his visions are to be addressed, receives the visions from God when he is 'in the Spirit upon the Lord's Day'.[5] At the end of the first century the governor of Bithynia in Asia Minor, Pliny, likewise reports that the Christians in his province are accustomed to meet for religious purposes on a fixed day, *statuto die*, which it seems safe to assume to be Sunday.

The earliest detailed description which we have of Christian worship in any part of Christendom is the *First Apology* of Justin Martyr, sent to the Emperor Antoninus Pius about 155. In it the two feasts of the Resurrection, the annual *Pascha* and the weekly *Pascha*, are described, and described in such a way that it is clear that the celebration of the Lord's service, the eucharist, which is characteristic of every Sunday, is precisely the same rite which takes place on the annual Resurrection Feast of Easter Day, though on that day only it is preceded by the baptism of converts.[6] Baptism and eucharist are described in the next important liturgical document to proceed from the Roman Church, which is the *Apostolic Tradition* of Hippolytus, and in this work there is also a description of the rites of ordination, which take place on Sunday.[7]

At Rome, as everywhere else in Christendom, there is no sign before the Peace of the Church in 313 of any development of this very simple kalendar, of Easter Day and all Sundays in the year. Not until after this date does Pentecost become a special Sunday with baptisms as on Easter Day. Nor is there any mention of Christmas, the Epiphany, the Ascension Day, the Octave of Pentecost, or any feasts of martyrs. All

[3] *Ibid.* 26.
[4] I Cor. XVI.2.
[5] Rev. I.9-10.
[6] *I. Apol.*, chs. 65-7.
[7] *Ap. Trad.*, 3: *die dominica*.

these, and certain other days, appeared before the end of the sixth century. It is possible, however, that there are one or two fasts on weekdays which were observed before the age of persecution had passed. Tertullian about the end of the second century speaks of *stationes*[8] which are fasts and occasions of liturgical assemblies, and take place on Wednesday and Friday. Wednesday and Friday are days, *feriae*, which have always had special significance in liturgy. For instance, they were Ember Days at Rome in the Ember Weeks, and Ember Weeks are basically an adaptation of pagan observances connected with the harvest, and it is not possible to be sure how far they go back in Roman liturgy. Certainly they originated as *tria tempora* and not as *quattuor tempora*: the fast of the first month, March, was the last to appear, and the three early fasts, of the fourth, seventh and tenth months, June, September and December were connected with the Roman harvests of corn (June), wine (September), and oil (December). The names of the fasts of the fourth, seventh and tenth months also point to their origin in times before the fourth century when the Roman Church still began its liturgical year on 1 March, and not, as it was doing by the sixth century and probably by the fifth or even the fourth, on Christmas Day.[9]

THE POST-NICENE DEVELOPMENT OF THE KALENDAR

Christmas and Epiphany

In Africa the Donatists always refused to observe the feast of Christmas, because at the time of their schism in 312, it was not observed by the African church, and hence they considered it, when it was introduced by the Catholics, as a celebration of the *traditores*, and an innovation. If it was not observed in Africa in 312, it was probably not observed at Rome either at that date. But it must have appeared at Rome soon afterwards, for the Chronographer of 354 supplies a Roman list of commemorations which is from the year 336, and this begins with the entry of Christ's birth: 'viii *Kal Ian*. Natus Christus in

---

[8] Tertullian, *De orat.* 23 (CSEL XX, 197); cf. *Ad uxorem* II. 4 (CSEL LXX, 116); *De fuga* I. 6 (CSEL LXXVI, 19); *De orat.* XIX.1 (CSEL XX, 192); *De ieiunio* I. 4 (CSEL XX, 275 bis); *De corona* XI. 3 (CSEL LXX, 176).
[9] On Ember Days, see Willis, *Essays in Early Roman Liturgy*, pp. 49-98.

Bethleem Iudeae'.[10] This is the earliest mention anywhere of the feast of Christmas; it is the earliest mention of its Western date, 25 December; and, since in the Chronography it stands in the first place at the head of the commemorations, it provides the earliest evidence for the Roman habit of beginning the Christian Year on Christmas Day, as later documents often do, e.g., the Gelasian Sacramentary, the Gregorian Sacramentary, and the earliest lectionaries in the seventh century. It is not certain why this date was fixed. There were primitive notions floating about that the Crucifixion was on 25 March, the old first day of spring, and that, since our Lord must have lived a complete number of years, his conception must be celebrated on 25 March, and his Nativity will therefore be celebrated on 25 December, the winter solstice. Perhaps it was fixed then because it could not be celebrated in the spring anywhere near Easter, and the old Roman Feast of *Natalis Solis Inuicti* on 25 December was thought to be an admirable date for the birthday of him who is the Sun of Righteousness, whom death and darkness cannot conquer. Perhaps this is the more likely explanation, since Christmas is a Western feast, probably Roman, and Rome had a tendency to Christianize pagan observances, as we have noted above in connection with Ember Days, and which occurs again in the adoption of 25 April, as the day of the Greater Rogation, when prayer was offered and litanies were said in procession for God's blessing on the crops, on the day when the pagans kept the *Robigalia*, and besought the gods to remove blight *robigo* from their crops.

Christmas Day at Rome originally had one mass, of which the station was at St Peter's. This station is attested in the pontificate of Anastasius I (399-401), by Arnobius Junior.[11] The station remained there for centuries. St Gregory is the first witness of the system of three stations on this day.[12] The stations were at midnight on the vigil at St Mary Major, the dawn mass at St Anastasia and the day mass at St Peter. St Anastasia's was a title in memory of the martyr of Sirmium, who had a cult at Rome, and whose feast was on 25 December. Accordingly she had commemorations in the Collect, Secret and Postcommunion until

[10] *Chronica Minora*, ed. T. Mommsen, MGH, AA IX (Berlin, 1892), p. 70.

[11] Arnobius, *Praedestinatus*, 82 (PL LIII, 615 B): 'Quo lecto in media Romana id est ecclesia Lateranensi . . . in ipso initio Quadragesimae, sancto Anastasio episcopo antistite'.

[12] Gregory, *Hom.* I.8 (PL LXXVI, 1113): 'missarum sollemnia ter hodie celebraturi sumus'.

these were abolished, together with the stational notes and other characteristically Roman features, in the revised Missal of 1970.

The feast of Christmas was later taken over by the East, and the original Eastern feast of the Nativity, called Epiphania, or Theophania, was adopted at Rome. It seems that the original Christmas gospel at Rome was Matt. II.1-12, the Visit of the Magi, but that when the Epiphany came in this gospel was at Rome transferred to 6 January, and Luke II.1-20 was substituted on Christmas Day. When in the late sixth century three masses were arranged for Christmas Day, Luke II was divided into two gospels, II.1-14 at midnight, and II.15-20 at dawn, and John I.1-14 was appointed for the day mass. Matt. II on the Epiphany was used at Rome and in Africa, but in other churches John II.1-11 and Luke III.21-2, the Lord's Baptism, were commonly used for the Epiphany.[13] The station of the Epiphany has always been at St Peter.

Pre-Lent

Between the Epiphany and Lent there is a maximum of nine Sundays, of which six are numbered after Epiphany, and three, originally reckoned after Epiphany, had by the time of St Gregory come to be entitled Septuagesima Sunday, Sexagesima Sunday, and Quinquagesima Sunday; names based upon the old name for Lent, Quadragesima, and signifying roughly the fortieth, fiftieth, sixtieth and seventieth days before Easter. The three pre-Lent Sundays were not organized at one and the same time: they came in at different dates in different churches as extensions backwards of the penitential period which preceded Easter. And they emerged in reverse order: first Quinquagesima, which appears at Rome about 520, probably in the pontificate of Hormisdas (514-23), since the earliest mention of it is in *Liber Pontificalis*, compiled originally in his time.[14]

Sexagesima appeared next, about 550, and both these Sundays are in the *Temporale* of Book I of the Old Gelasian Sacramentary, originating about 560, and Septuagesima Sunday is first attested in the headings of the Homilies of St Gregory the Great. Homily XIX is headed, *Habita ad populum in basilica beati Laurentii Martyris dominica in*

---

[13] See B. Botte, *Les origines de Noel et de l'Epiphanie* (Louvain, 1932) and G. G. Willis, *St Augustine's Lectionary*, Alcuin Club Collections XLIV (London, 1962), pp. 58-62.

[14] *Liber Pontificalis*, ed. Duchesne, I, p. 129: 'hic [Telesphorus] constituit ut septem ebdomadas ante Pascha ieiunium celebraretur'.

Septuagesima. Professor A. Chavasse has argued that this sermon was delivered on St Laurence's day, 10 August, on the ground that it refers to *mense Iulio nuper elapso.* But it has been established by Dom Henry Ashworth and Fr L. J. Crampton, that *nuper* can refer to a much longer period than ten days or a fortnight, and that the gospel on which this homily comments is the parable of the Labourers in the Vineyard (Matt. XX), which has ever since St Gregory been the gospel of Septuagesima Sunday, of which the station has always been at St Laurence. The choice of this lesson may well be connected with the Roman habit of engaging agricultural labourers at the beginning of February. Indeed there are many signs that the liturgy of these three Sundays was drawn up at one time and that this was done at Rome. Dom Henry Ashworth suggests that Gregory's Homily XIX was preached on Septuagesima Sunday 11 February 591.[15] The collects and the chants of these masses may very well have been compiled by St Gregory himself. The stations of the three masses are at St Laurence, St Paul and St Peter, in that order. These are the churches of the three patrons of the city of Rome, all of whom suffered martyrdom in the city. All the masses are concerned with troubles which beset the Church, wars, famine, pestilence, earthquake. What is more likely than that they were compiled by St Gregory, himself a citizen of Rome, to implore the divine protection for his own city, over which he presided as bishop? His predecessor Pelagius II died of the plague which infected the city after the river Tiber burst its banks, and his pontificate of fourteen years was overshadowed by natural calamities and the threats of the Lombard invasion, which interrupted the roads of northern and central Italy, and constantly threatened the peace of the Romans. Consider the collects of these Sundays:

Septuagesima

Preces populi tui quaesumus domine clementer exaudi, ut qui iuste pro peccatis nostris affligimur, pro tui nominis gloria misericorditer liberemur: per.

Sexagesima

Deus qui conspicias quia ex nulla nostra actione confidimus: concede propitius, ut contra adversa omnia doctoris gentium protectione muniamur: per.

---

[15] H. Ashworth, 'The Influence of the Lombard Invasions on the Gregorian Sacramentary', *Bulletin of the John Rylands Library* XXXVI (1954), 305-27.

Quinquagesima

Preces nostras quaesumus domine clementer exaudi, atque a peccatorum vinculis absolutos ab omni nos adversitate custodi: per.[16]

Read the plaintive petitions of the prayers, and recall the references contained in the chants of these days which the antiphonaries have preserved, and which, according to a tradition as old as the eighth century, showed the influence of St Gregory's revising hand. So on Septuagesima Sunday we have

circumdederunt me gemitus mortis, dolores inferni circumdederunt me et in tribulatione mea invocavi Dominum.
Adiutor in oportunitatibus in tribulatione.
exsurge, Domine. non praeualeat homo.
de profundis clamaui ad te, Domine.
inimici tui, Domine, peribunt, et dispergentur.

From Sexagesima Sunday:

Exsurge, quare obdormis, Domine? . . . obliuisceris tribulationem nostram.
sciant gentes quoniam nomen tibi Deus.
pone illos ut rotam et sicut stipulam ante faciem uenti.
commouisti Domine terram et conturbasti eam (on earthquakes).
Sana contritiones eius, quia mota est.

Quinquagesima, on famine:

esto mihi in Deum protectorem . . . dux mihi eris et enutries me.
aufer a plebe tua opprobrium et contemptum.
manducaverunt et saturati sunt nimis.[17]

Lent

Lent began everywhere as a short but strict fast before Easter, covering only Good Friday and Easter Even, and many churches, including that of Africa, were doing this in the third century, or even at the end of the second.[18] Some Eastern churches then extended it backwards to a length of six days, beginning on the Monday before Easter. The first evidence about Lent at Rome is the fifth Festal Letter of St Athanasius for 340, written from Rome, which shows that Rome

[16] *Das Sacramentarium Gregorianum*, ed. Lietzmann, pp. 24-5.
[17] G. Morin, 'La part des papes du sixième siècle dans le développement de l'année liturgique', *Revue Bénédictine* LII (1940), 3-14; J. Froget 'Les anticipations du jeûne quadragésimale', *Mélanges de science religieuse* III (1946), 207-34.
[18] Tertullian, *De ieiunio* II. 13-14: 'dies quibus ablatus est sponsus'.

then had a fast of six weeks. Lent began on the sixth Sunday before Easter, and ended on Thursday before Easter, making a length of forty days, plus Good Friday and Easter Even, which were observed at an earlier period than Lent, and in the fourth century were regarded as falling outside Lent. Professor A. Chavasse maintains that before the Lenten fast at Rome developed into six weeks, Rome had a three weeks' continuous fast, beginning on Monday after the third Sunday before Easter, and continuing till Easter Even. He is followed in this opinion by Vogel.[19]

The only evidence which Chavasse produces in favour of his thesis is that the gospels for these three weeks are from the seventh century onwards taken from St John's Gospel, and that the Greek ecclesiastical historian Socrates states that Rome had a three-week Lent. As to the former point, it may be urged that Rome had a six-week Lent three hundred years before the earliest surviving Roman lectionary system, and that at the beginning of the fourth century, when, according to Chavasse, the three-week Lent was provided with lessons from St John, in fact there were no lectionary tables at all: the celebrant still had complete discretion as to the choice of lessons. Moreover, Socrates is not a trustworthy witness for Roman liturgy, and in any case was writing in 439, almost exactly a hundred years later than the date at which we know that Rome had a six-week Lent. There is in fact a perfectly good explanation of the words of Socrates. He says that there were three continuous (συνήμμενοι) weeks of fasting in Rome. Now three weeks of fasting in Lent could not be continuous with one another, since they would be periods from Monday to Saturday, each separated from the others by Sunday, which is never a fast. What he means is that the weeks were each continuous within itself, that is, fasting extended from Monday to Saturday. This was true of Rome in the fourth century, and in the fifth, for Rome, unlike many other churches, always fasted on Saturday. They were not weeks like the week of Quinquagesima Sunday until the sixth century, which only had fasts on Wednesday and Friday, like other weeks in the year, or like the Ember Weeks, which had fasting on Wednesday, Friday and Saturday. These were discontinuous weeks of fasting, but the weeks in Lent were continuous fasts. Mgr Callewaert has urged the most plausible explanation of Socrates's mistake, which is that the weeks were weeks

---

[19] C. Vogel, *Introduction aux sources du culte chrétien au moyen âge* (Spoleto, 1966), pp. 271-2.

with six fast days, but of special strictness, and that they are the weeks of the First Sunday in Lent, which from Pope Leo's time was an Ember Week, of the Fourth Sunday in Lent, which was *Mediana* Week from at least the time of Gelasius (492-6), and Holy Week, *Hebdomada maior*, which was from its beginning a fast of special importance and solemnity. All three weeks had in the time of Gelasius ordinations at the Saturday vigil which concluded them.[20]

To sum up, there is no evidence, apart from that urged by Chavasse, for thinking that Lent at Rome, or anywhere else, ever had a length of three weeks.

When the total length of Lent was thirty-six days, the weekdays between the sixth Sunday before Easter and Easter Day, it is seen by several of the Fathers as being a tithe or tenth of the year, for example by John Cassian,[21] Gregory the Great,[22] and Isidore of Seville.[23] The four days at the beginning, Wednesday, Thursday, Friday and Saturday after Quinquagesima Sunday were added in the latter half of the sixth century, to make up forty days of fasting, in imitition of the forty days of fasting of Our Lord, Moses and Elijah.

The fast of Christ (Matt. IV.1-11) was read in the gospel of the First Sunday in Lent from the fourth century onwards, and those of Moses (Exod. XXIV) and Elijah (III Kings XIX.3-8) read on the first Wednesday in Lent.

St Augustine calls the Easter Vigil the 'mother of all holy vigils'. It was an all-night vigil, according to Tertullian[24] and included the celebration of baptism.[25] Canon 5 of the Council of Nicaea in 325 is the earliest Eastern evidence for a six-week Lent. This canon orders that two synods of bishops shall be held in the year, one in the season of τεσσαρακόστη which equals the Latin *quadragesima* and of course implies a length of forty days.

A letter from St Athanasius to his friend Sarapion, bishop of Thmuis in the Egyptian Delta, in 331, six years after the Council of Nicaea, speaks of a six-week Lent as an established custom in Egypt. Augustine

---

[20] Gelasius, *Ep*. XIV (*ad universos episcopos per Lucaniam*), ch. 11, ed. Thiel, *Ep. Rom. Pontif.* (Braunsberg, 1868), I, pp. 368-9; *Liber Diurnus* in PL CV, 75-6; G. G. Willis, *Essays*, pp. 101-4 and *idem*, 'Mediana Week', *Downside Review* LXXXVI (1969), 50-3.

[21] *Conlationes* XXI, 25 and 28.

[22] *Hom. XVI in Euang.* 5.

[23] *De officiis* I.37.

[24] *Ad uxorem* II.4.

[25] Tertullian, *De bapt.* II.19.

asserts that a six-week Lent was universally observed.[26] It was also universally called *Quadragesima*.[27] He says that it was connected with the fasts of Christ, Moses and Elijah.[28] For him, it is an image of the Israelites' forty years of wandering in the desert.[29] By contrast, the fifty days of Eastertide which follow represent the joys of eternal life,[30] for it is seven times seven, equalling forty-nine, plus one, bringing us back to the original, and is therefore a symbol of perfect glory.[31]

In Africa the only Saturday in Lent which was a fast was Easter Eve, but at Rome all the Saturdays were fasts. At Rome, as in Africa, however, Good Friday and Easter Even were not regarded as being in Lent. Lent finished on Maundy Thursday, and was followed by the *Pascha*. This is very clear in Pope Leo's sermons on the First Sunday in Lent. Twelve sermons[32] tell us of the liturgy of this Sunday. He is one of those who think that the forty days is the imitation of the Temptation Fast of Our Lord. Lent terminates for him, as for the Africans, on Maundy Thursday, and Leo calls the First Sunday *initium Quadragesimae* or *caput Quadragesimae*, and the same terminology is seen in the *Gelasianum*. Leo speaks of fasting, mortification and penance, and Lent is a *quadraginta dierum exercitatio*.[33] In his time the station is already at the Basilica of St John Lateran. According to Arnobius Junior, this was the practice at the end of the fourth century.[34] The gospel Matt. IV.1-11 was used in Gaul and at Naples and Milan as well as at Rome. Psalm XC is quoted in the gospel, and is used in the chants of this day in the antiphonary from the eighth century onwards, but probably it goes back to 400 and possibly earlier. It is still recited in full as the Tract, and this itself is a sign of antiquity, for originally the text of chants consisted of full psalms, and later these came to be abbreviated to one or two verses.[35]

The arrangement of masses in Lent from the Wednesday after Quinquagesima Sunday to Maundy Thursday was not complete until the eighth century, when the Thursdays were provided with a mass and a

---

[26] *Serm.* CCIX.1; CCX.8.
[27] *Ibid.* CCLXX.3.
[28] *Ibid.* CCV.1, CCX.9, CCLII.10; *Ep.* LV.28.
[29] *Serm.* CCLII.11.
[30] *Ep.* LV *passim*; *Serm.* CCX.8.
[31] *Ep.* LV.28.
[32] PL LIV, 264-308.
[33] *Serm.* IV.1.
[34] See above, n. 11.
[35] On the Lenten stational scheme, see Willis, *Further Essays*, pp. 44-9.

station by Gregory II (715-31) – before that time only Maundy Thursday had had a mass; the four *Vacat* Sundays after the Ember Weeks were provided with a mass, and the Saturday before Palm Sunday, on which day the pope had not celebrated mass, but had distributed alms, had previously been vacant, and the Thursday and Saturday before the First Sunday. All these were still vacant at the time of Gregory. The day before Palm Sunday was six days before Good Friday, the ancient *Pascha*, and six days before he suffered Christ had his feet anointed by the woman at Bethany, and said, 'Pauperes habetis semper uobiscum, me autem non semper habetis'.[36] In the Würzburg Gospelbook, which dates from about 650, this gospel as in *Missale Romanum*, is appointed for the Monday before Easter, six days before the *Pascha Resurrectionis*.

The masses of the greatest days in Lent, when the largest congregations were to be expected, were in the principal basilicas, which had the largest accommodation. These days, with their stations, are:

Dominica Prima	ad Lateranis	
Feria IV	ad S. Mariam	Q.T.
Feria VI	ad Apostolos	Q.T.
Feria VII	ad S. Petrum	Q.T.
Dominica Secunda		vacat
Dominica Tertia	ad S. Laurentium	
Dominica Quarta	ad Hierusalem	
Feria IV	ad S. Paulum	Mediana
Feria VII	ad S. Laurentium	Mediana
Dominica Quinta	ad S. Petrum	Mediana
Feria VII	ad S. Petrum	
Dominica Sexta	ad Lateranis	
Feria IV	ad S. Mariam	
Feria V	ad Lateranis	
Feria VI	ad Hierusalem	
Sabbato Sancto	ad Lateranis	

Holy Week, or *Hebdomada Maior*, was not organized liturgically at any one time. The *Pascha*, comprising Good Friday, Easter Eve and

---

[36] John XII.8.

Easter Day, was the first part of it to appear, and was there by the beginning of the third century. Originally Monday, Tuesday and Saturday were aliturgical, and Saturday has remained so, except that, like the Saturdays in Ember Weeks from early times, and like the Vigil of Pentecost at a later date, it was the occasion of a night vigil service, and had no mass in the morning. The Vigil was the most important one of the year, and will be treated here under the heading of Eastertide. Good Friday had its station at the Basilica of the Holy cross in Jerusalem (Santa Croce in Gerusalemme), and the station was in the afternoon, in accordance with the usual practice on fast days. It seems probable that it originally resembled other station days which were fasts, in having no mass, but just a synaxis, or first part, without consecration or communion. Then before the sixth century it developed to the extent of having a communion from the reserved sacrament, which had been consecrated on the previous day, Maundy Thursday. Reservation was in the species of bread, as usual, and on Good Friday the chalice was consecrated by Commixture of a particle of the Host, together with the recital of the Lord's Prayer. At some times and places there was a general communion from the Reserved Sacrament by all the people, but this disappeared in the early Middle Ages, and has been revived only in the recent revisions. The structure of the Good Friday rite is archaic, both in respect of the absence of consecration and the manner of communion, which are a survival of an early practice applied originally to all fast days. It is also archaic in respect to the beginning of the synaxis, which shows none of the items added later, such as Introit and *Kyrie*, but begins with the lessons, as mass always did in Augustine's day. It has also preserved to the present day the *orationes sollemnes*, the Roman form of the *Oratio fidelium*, which occupied this position in the mass, and were used daily during the fifth century, until Pope Gelasius (492-6) replaced them except on Good Friday, by the litany which came to be known as *Deprecatio Gelasii*. He inserted this before the lessons and the collect, and when St Gregory the Great, a century later, removed the litany, he left its vestigial response, *Kyrie*, in the same position at the beginning.[37]

Wednesday and Thursday, as we have seen, were provided with masses and stations earlier than Monday and Tuesday, which, when the stational list was completed, were always observed at less important churches than Wednesday and Thursday. The *oratio ad populum* which

[37] See Willis, *Essays*, pp. 10-28.

survived in Lent after the time of Gregory, finishes on the Wednesday. The mass of Maundy Thursday, in pre-Gregorian times, was an evening mass, in commemoration of the Institution of the eucharist at the Last Supper in the evening. The Old Gelasian Sacramentary has three masses for this day: one is the evening mass, which was characteristic of the Roman rite up to and after the time of Gregory, and which had no synaxis, but began at the Offertory; the others were morning masses, one for the blessing of the chrism, and the second for the reconciliation of penitents, who had been excluded from the mass, after the manner of catechumens, during Lent.

Eastertide

In Africa from the beginning of the third century, as it is testified by Tertullian, and at Rome from about the same time, as we see from the *Apostolic Tradition* of Hippolytus, the Easter season of fifty days began with the great and long vigil of the *Pascha*, at which Holy Baptism was administered, and at which the neophytes joined with the faithful in receiving the Holy Communion.[38] At Rome the pope baptized at the Lateran, but the numbers of candidates were by the time of St Gregory too large to be accommodated in one church, and certain other churches in the city had baptisteries, in which priests administered baptism at Easter and Pentecost. The numbers of the candidates, male and female, were certified to the pope at the place called Merulana as he rode from the *episcopium*, or papal palace, to St Mary Major on Easter morning for the day mass.[39]

The baptismal liturgy of the Old Gelasian (Vaticanus Reginensis 316), is not a papal liturgy, but is for priests celebrating baptism in the titles. The papal rite of baptism is described in *Ordo* XI, which dates from half a century after Gregory. There is a second mass on Easter Day, the morning or day mass, celebrated about 9 a.m. at St Mary Major. The pope is here attended by the officials and clergymen of the third region. During Easter Week there was a stational mass daily (Thursday being originally excepted), which was attended by the newly

---

[38] See below, pp. 116-36.

[39] *Ordo* I.15: 'Die autem resurrectionis dominicae, procedente eo ad Sanctam Mariam, notarius regionarius stat in loco qui dicitur Merolanas et, salutato pontifice, dicit: *In nomine domini nostri Iesu Christi, baptizati sunt hesterna nocte in sancta Dei genetrice Maria infantes masculi numero tanti, feminae tantae.* Respondit pontifex: *Deo gratias.* Et accepit a sacellario solidum unum; pontifex autem pergit ad stationem.'

baptized, and at which they heard instruction from the bishop about the sacraments.[40] On Easter Saturday, the octave of their baptism, the station was again at St John Lateran, and the neophytes wore their white robes for the last time. It thus acquired the name of *Sabbatum in albis depositis*. The stations are at important basilicas, as is usual on important days, and the basilicas of the three city patrons are used on Monday, Tuesday and Wednesday.

Four days between Easter Saturday and Pentecost have special solemnity in Rome.

(i)   *Pascha Annotina*. By the time of St Gregory this day is observed.[41] It is the anniversary of Easter Day in the previous year, and therefore of the baptisms which had taken place the previous Easter. Obviously it might fall as easily in Lent as in Eastertide, but we cannot say whether it was transferred or suppressed if it fell on an important day. Clearly it could never fall on a Sunday.[42]

(ii)   *The Greater Rogation*. This fell on 25 April, and was intended to replace the pagan *Robigalia*. Like *Pascha Annotina*, it was characteristically Roman, and did not take root elsewhere.

(iii)   A feast of less solemnity was that called Mid-Pentecost. This was half way between Easter and Pentecost, and therefore the twenty-fifth day after Easter, that is, Wednesday after the Third Sunday after Easter.[43]

(iv)   *The Ascension Day*. The Lord's Ascension was originally commemorated as part of the mystery of redemption at Easter, and indeed Luke (XXIV.50-3), and John (*passim*), give the impression that the Resurrection and the Ascension of Christ are inseparable parts of the process by which He returns to His Father. But, as is well known, already in the first century the *Acts of the Apostles*[44] suggest that the Ascension is a separate historical event which can be dated at forty days after Easter, and therefore ten days before Pentecost. So on this fortieth day the Ascension Day was fixed when it began to have a commemoration separate from Easter. As with all the feasts commemorating the acts of Christ and the events recorded in the gospel we look to Jerusalem, and we look in the fourth century, and accordingly

---

[40] See below, pp. 122-5.
[41] See, e.g., *Gel*. I. liii; *Pad*. 84.
[42] See below, pp. 101-2.
[43] C. Callewaert, 'Notes sur les origines de la Mi-Carême', *Revue Bénédictine* XXXVIII (1926), 60-9.
[44] Acts I.3.

are not surprised to find that indefatigable lady tourist from Spain, Etheria, or Egeria, recording the celebration of a feast on the fortieth day after Easter. But she does not state that it commemorated the Ascension. This is towards the end of the fourth century. The Feast soon spread to the West, and by the end of the fourth century was firmly established there, as we gather from the many sermons of Augustine which were preached on this day. At Rome there are sermons for the day by Pope Leo, and in the sixth century the day appears in the Leonine[45] and Gelasian[46] Sacramentaries. So it was well established before Gregory.

It was the practice of the primitive Church to forbid the people to kneel in church during Eastertide, as a symbol of joy. Nor were there any fasts in this joyful time of fifty days. *Alleluia* was a chant proper to this season, and originally confined to this season. Gregory extended its use outside Pentecost, and this was one of the four innovations for which he was criticized by those whom John of Syracuse reports to him.[47] Before very long it was extended to cover the whole year, except the period from Septuagesima to Easter.

Pentecost

The Sunday called Pentecost was not originally of great importance. It merely concluded the glorious fifty days of Eastertide. It then came to be treated as a lesser kind of Easter Day. Baptism came to be administered at its vigil, as at Easter, and at this time it acquired two masses, like Easter Day, a vigil baptismal mass and an ordinary Sunday morning mass. It was probably the institution of baptisms at this feast which led to the development of an Octave of Pentecost. During this week the neophytes would come to church daily, as during Easter week. Again, Thursday was the last day to be provided with a station and mass, and this not till the seventh or eighth century. By the time of Gregory it had become an Ember Week, the fast of the fourth month. Probably this was found to be inconvenient, since in the papal mass stations it would involve instructing the neophytes and examining the candidates for holy orders on Wednesday and Friday, and this would involve two masses on those days, or else a very crowded programme.

---

[45] *Leon*. IX.
[46] *Gel*. I. lxiii.
[47] Gregory, *Ep*. IX.26.

Ordinations would of course not affect the service in baptismal churches except the papal stational church and St Mary Major on Wednesday and SS. Philip and James on Friday, since these were the stational churches on Ember Days, at which the candidates were examined by the pope. In about half of the years the so-called fast of the fourth month would have been observed in the third month (May) had it fallen in Pentecost week. So soon after Gregory the fast was kept in June, after Pentecost, and accordingly we find Leo II (682-3) ordaining on Sunday 27 June 683, which was the Third Sunday after Pentecost. England followed the earlier rule, which Egbert of York in the eighth century claims that we had received from our teacher and apostle St Gregory, and kept Embertide in Whitsun week. But the rest of the Western Church tended to keep Ember Week out of Pentecost until Gregory VII finally fixed it in the Octave of Pentecost,[48] and there it has remained.

The period from Pentecost to Christmas

The first half of the year being thus occupied by the feasts of Redemption and the great fast of Lent, six months and more of the year remain until the Redemption cycle begins again at Christmas, in fact somewhere between twenty-eight and thirty-two Sundays and the weeks following them. With one or two exceptions, such as days in the *Sanctorale* and the Ember Weeks, there are no papal stations in this half of the year, until Advent begins, and in Advent no stations until probably after St Gregory. The Sundays did not acquire their own masses until after St Gregory. But before his time, sixteen masses which begin Book III of Vaticanus Reginensis 316 seem likely, by reason of their number, to have been intended to be used twice through in a year with an early Easter and thirty-two Sundays between Pentecost and Christmas. Similarly, provision of sixteen chants is made in the antiphonary, which may be traced back to 740, and might very well preserve some of the work of Gregory, to whom an ancient tradition assigns an interest in Roman chant.[49]

---

[48] Bernold of Constance, *Micrologus* 25 (PL CLI, 997).
[49] Paulus Diaconus, *Vita Sancti Gregorii Magni* II.6 (PL LXXV, 90): 'Deinde in domo Domini more sapientissimi Salomonis propter musicae compunctionem dulcedinis Antiphonarium centonem cantorum studiosissimus nimis utiliter compilavit; scholam quoque cantorum quae hactenus eisdem institutionibus in sancta Romana Ecclesia modulatur, constituit'.

Advent in Gaul, and in certain other places, had five or six Sundays before Christmas. Rome seems to have started with five or six, including the Sunday next before Advent, which was at Rome, but not elsewhere, the *Dominica uacat* after Ember week. Long before St Gregory these Sundays had been reduced to three or four. The first Sunday was the Sunday following the feast of St Andrew on 30 November. This might leave only three Sundays before Christmas, all in December, and by the time of Gregory the number was fixed at four, the first of these being the Sunday nearest to St Andrew, either the day of his feast, or the Sunday preceding or following, and thus falling between 27 November and 3 December, as at present. In Gregory's time the liturgical year began on Christmas Eve, with the morning mass, and not for a long time was the first Sunday in Advent regarded as being the start of a new liturgical year. In the time of Gregory, and for long after, the Roman civil year began on 1 March, but the consuls entered upon their office on 1 January, a date marked in some seventh-century lectionaries with the words, *In aduentu iudicum*.

In the arrangements of the Sundays after Pentecost there is a clear distinction between books of the Gelasian and of the Gregorian tradition. The Old Gelasian book has no masses assigned to any particular Sunday after Pentecost. The Eighth-Century Gelasians have the provision for the Sundays in one continuous series. In all Gelasian books the *Sanctorale* is in a separate collection. But in all the Gregorian books the *Sanctorale* is mingled with the *Temporale*, as it is in the Leonine Sacramentary fifty years before Gregory. This is true for the whole year. The Sundays after Pentecost are not arranged, as in the Gelasian tradition, in one continuous series, but in five blocks – Sundays after Pentecost; Sundays after the Apostles (*post Apostolos*, i.e., after SS. Peter and Paul on 29 June); Sundays after St Laurence (10 August, *post Laurentii*); Sundays after St Cyprian (14 September, *post Cypriani*); and Sundays after the Angel (Michaelmas Day, 29 September, *post Angeli*).

THE CHRISTIAN YEAR AT THE END OF THE SIXTH CENTURY

The earliest Kalendar of the Roman Church is that simple one seen in the Chronography of 354. It is short, is purely Roman, and is a list of persons, mainly martyrs, commemorated at Rome. Most of them were buried there, and the commemorations are localized by the addition to the saint's name of the place of his deposition. This method of listing saints is continued in later Roman books, and is a sign of Roman origin. The Roman base of later kalendars is discernible by the preservation of the notes of the Roman cemeteries where the saints' bodies reposed, and where they were originally commemorated.

The next list, a fuller one, is that seen in the headings of masses in the so-called Leonine or Verona Sacramentary. It is a Roman list, without any later additions from outside Rome, and it was compiled during the pontificate of Vigilius (537-55). Shortly afterwards, say about 560, comes the original stratum of the Old Gelasian sacramentary (Vaticanus Reginensis 316). This originated about 560-70, but the sole manuscript which preserved it was written near Paris about 750, and so its kalendar, like its prayers, contains many Gallican elements. But the basis, which has many agreements with the Leonine kalendar, is a Roman document. Certain Roman features, such as the stations, and the places of deposition of the saints commemorated, have been removed, as being of no interest to persons living miles away from Rome.

These are the only three lists available before the time of St Gregory, but it will be legitimate to take into consideration certain other documents later than his pontificate, which preserve older features, such as are likely to be older than Gregory, or the product of the liturgical revisions of the sacramentary, lectionary and antiphonary which have from about the eighth century been attributed to his hand. The earliest of these are the three lectionary tables which will here be referred to as the Würzburg Epistolary, a list of epistles contained in MS. 62 of the University Library at Würzburg,[50] and which is dated about 625; the Würzburg Gospel list, a list of gospels from the same manuscript, but not contemporary with the Epistle list: the date of this is about 650;[51] and the Lectionary of Alcuin, of which the base is a document coming from about 626-7, soon after the Würzburg Epistle list. This last table was published, with a critical commentary, by Dom A. Wilmart.[52] The latest manuscripts we shall use are two of the Gregorian Sacramentary: both are of the ninth century, but both contain elements which are as old as the time of Gregory, and some are even

[50] G. Morin, 'Le plus ancient Comes ou Lectionnaire de l'église romaine', *Revue Bénédictine* XXVII (1910), 41-74.

[51] G. Morin, 'Liturgie et basiliques de Rome au milieu du VIIe siècle, d'après les listes d'Evangiles du Würzburg', *Revue Bénédictine* XXVIII (1911), 296-330.

[52] A. Wilmart, *Le Lectionnaire d'Alcuin* (Rome, 1937).

older. These are the *Hadrianum*, the copy of the book sent by Pope Hadrian to Charles the Great at the end of the eighth century,[53] and the *Paduanum*, or MS. D.47 of the Chapter Library at Padua.[54] In spite of the lateness of these manuscripts, the earliest elements are discernible, and will be seen to show considerable agreement with the earliest sources which are here used, despite the presence in them of many later elements.

Christmas

As we have seen, the only commemoration noted in the Chronography of 354 which is not that of a saint or martyr is that of Christmas Day: 'viii Kal. Ian. Natus Iesus in Bethleem Iudeae.' After that it appears in all Roman Kalendars. Originally it had one mass, the day mass, probably at 9 a.m., at St Peter's, but by the time of St Gregory it had the three masses, at midnight, dawn and in the morning, which it has retained ever since. In all the sources we are here considering, from the Gelasian Sacramentary onwards, Christmas has a mass on the Vigil, celebrated at 3 p.m. as was customary on fast days, and the three masses on Christmas Day. These same sources all have the three feasts in the Octave, St Stephen the Protomartyr on 26 December, St John Evangelist on 27 December, and the Innocents on 28 December. In the Gelasian tradition these are embedded in the *Temporale* and are not in the *Sanctorale* in Book II, as are other saints' days. The characteristic of all Gregorian books is that the saints' days are embedded in the *Temporale*, until the plenary missals, which emerged much later, separated the *Sanctorale* from the *Temporale*, as the Gelasian tradition had always done. But the festivals in Christmas week have always remained the exception to this rule, and stayed embedded in the *Temporale*. St Silvester, pope from 314 to 335, occurs on 31 December in all these sources except the Leonine, where he occurs in October, and in the Gelasian, which omits him. The Octave Day of Christmas is 1 January except in the Würzburg Epistle list and in Alcuin's Lectionary. It is probable that this day appeared after St Gregory. When it did appear it was the Octave Day simply; only later did it become a feast of Our Lady,[55] and well on in the Middle Ages the commemor-

[53] Ed. H. Lietzmann, *Das Sacramentarium Gregorianum* (Münster, 1921).

[54] Ed. L. C. Mohlberg, *Die älteste erreichbare Gestalt des Liber Sacramentorum Anni Circuli der römischen Kirche* (Münster, 1927).

[55] See B. Botte, 'La première fête mariale de la liturgie romaine', *Ephemerides Liturgicae* XLVII (1933), 425-30.

ation of the Circumcision of Christ. In some of our sources there is a mass entitled *In aduentu iudicum*[56] for use on this day, and this refers to the fact that in Rome the consuls assumed office on 1 January. *Hadrianum* provides a mass for one Sunday after Christmas, and so does *Paduense*, and Alcuin's table provides one Sunday.

Epiphany

In the early Roman tradition this is commemorated on 6 January, and in most lists has an octave. Alcuin has two Sundays after Christmas. There is a vigil of Epiphany in the Old Gelasian, but *Hadrianum* and *Paduense* have no vigil, nor is there a vigil in the Würzburg Epistolary, but the Gospel list in this manuscript has a vigil, with station at St Peter's, though it does not specify a station for the day. There is some variation in the number of Sundays after Epiphany. The Old Gelasian and the *Hadrianum* provide no masses for the Sundays after Epiphany. In the case of the Old Gelasian this is because the celebrant is supposed to use the masses from the collection of sixteen masses which are placed at the beginning of Book III. The maximum number of Sundays which can occur between Pentecost and Christmas is thirty-two, so that in a year with an early Easter it would be possible to read these masses twice through on Sundays, and the Sundays after Epiphany could be supplied from the same collection. The explanation of the absence of these Sundays from *Hadrianum* is that this book is a papal sacramentary, which provides only for those days when the pope has a stational mass, and these ferial Sundays are not among stational days. But the other Gregorian mass book, *Paduense*, has supplied five Sundays after Epiphany. The Würzburg Epistle book has eight Sundays at this point, which in a year with a late Easter would go down to Sexagesima inclusive; but the gospelbook of this manuscript has ten Sundays, which is too many, especially as it has the three pre-Lent Sundays. The Alcuin Lectionary has five Sundays after Epiphany. There are no Sundays at all in the Chronography, and the Leonine Sacramentary is deficient till Ascension Day.

The Würzburg Gospelbook stands alone in providing for every Wednesday and Friday, and for some Saturdays, after Epiphany.

---

[56] E.g. Alcuin 225 (Epistle I Tim. II.1-7).

97

Pre-Lent Sundays

We have seen that the three Sundays called Septuagesima, Sexagesima and Quinquagesima were in the kalendar by the time of St Gregory, and that the Communion anthems from the Psalms I-XXVI in order, beginning on the Wednesday after Quinquagesima, were all established before St Gregory. This is on the whole the position recorded in the books which we are now considering, but there is some variation in the details. In the Old Gelasian the mass for Septuagesima Sunday is the next mass after the Epiphany. It then has a mass for Sexagesima Sunday, but none for Quinquagesima, but the Wednesday following is the first service in the fast, and there are masses for Friday and Saturday, but not for Thursday. The Wednesday and Friday, for which provision is made in this week in most of the books, were the normal weekly stational masses, and it was long after St Gregory before the four days before the first Sunday in Lent were regarded as part of Lent. *Hadrianum* has the three Sundays. It provides for Wednesday, Thursday and Friday in Quinquagesima week, and it is surprising to find that provision is made for this Thursday: certainly it was not filled until the pontificate of Gregory II, who also filled the Thursdays in Lent. *Paduense* represents an earlier state of affairs: it provides for three Sundays and Wednesday and Friday after Quinquagesima. The same is true of the Würzburg Epistle Book, and this happens also in the Würzburg Gospelbook and in Alcuin's Lectionary.

Lent

There are no Lenten masses in the Leonine or Verona Sacramentary, since the first three and a half months of the year are missing from the unique manuscript. The other sources which we are using represent various stages in the process of filling up the days of Lent, which was not completed till the eighth century, when Gregory II (715-31) filled up the Thursdays. In the pontificate of Gregory the Great none of the Thursdays had a mass except the last, Maundy Thursday, which was anciently observed, and was an important mass, in an important basilica, St John Lateran in which Lent ended, as it had begun in the same church on the first Sunday of Lent, the sixth Sunday before Easter.

In the Gelasian Sacramentary this Sunday has the sub-title, 'in Quadragesima incoantis inicium'. Naturally there are no station notes in this sacramentary, which was written in Gaul. But the station was at

St John Lateran by the pontificate of Anastasius (399-401), and thus formed an exception to the general rule that the Sunday before the Ember Days at the four seasons was at St Peter's. This may be explained by the fact that the station of the first Sunday in Lent was fixed by about 400, whereas the earliest attestation of the Lent Embertide is by Gelasius, who was pope 492-6. All the sources have these arrangements for the first Sunday.

There was no station on Thursday till the eighth century, but the day is noted in some sources, among them the Würzburg Epistolary, which even has a station 'ad S. Mariam', and similarly in Alcuin's Lectionary it has lessons but no station. The Old Gelasian has masses for weekdays in this week, except Thursday, but they are not masses of the fast of the first month. These follow the masses of Monday, Tuesday, Wednesday, Friday and Saturday, and are themselves followed by the ordination rites, which in the Gregorian tradition are usually placed in December, which was for long at Rome the most usual time for ordinations. All the other books we are considering have the Ember Days in the first week of Lent. They have also the usual *Vacat* Sunday which follows the Ember Days in the Roman traditon, but the Gelasian has filled this Sunday. The Third Sunday in Lent is noted in the Gelasian as the day of the first Scrutiny: 'Tertia Dominica quae pro scrutiniis electorum celebratur.' This is from the sixth-century stratum of the book, and the final form of the book as all the other sources in this chapter, is designed for a system of seven scrutinies.[57] The other books have a normal week, with stations except on Thursday.

The Fourth Sunday in Lent, *Dominica in Vicesima*, is Mid- Lent, and under the old arrangements before St Gregory is the day of the second of the three baptismal scrutinies. This is noted in the Gelasian Sacramentary, as is the case with the first scrutiny on the preceding Sunday, and of the third scrutiny on the succeeding Sunday. The station of this day is at the Church of the Holy Cross in Jerusalem (Santa Croce in Gerusalemme). Thursday in this week was vacant until the eighth century. All other days had masses, and in Roman sources it is usually entitled *Mediana* Week. The days described as being *in mediana* are Wednesday and Saturday, and these are the days which in the lectionaries have two lessons before the Gospel, a sign both of importance and antiquity.[58] The week *in mediana* runs from Monday to

---

[57] See below, pp. 119-22.
[58] See Willis, *Essays*, pp. 101-4.

the following Sunday. The Old Gelasian has no mention of *mediana*; but neither has *Hadrianum*, where mention might have been expected in a purely Roman and indeed papal book. Nor has *Paduense* any mention of it, during the week or on the fifth Sunday in Lent. The Würzburg Gospelbook does not mention *mediana* but it occurs in the Epistle Book in the same manuscript and in the Alcuin Lectionary. The fifth Sunday in Lent is marked in the Old Gelasian as the day of the third and last scrutiny, and the Würzburg Epistle list describes it as *in mediana*, but no other source mentions that this is the Sunday *in mediana*. Thursday in the fifth week was vacant till the eighth century, and so was Saturday, when there was no station, but the pope distributed alms. In the Old Gelasian this day has been filled, and so it has in some of our Roman sources, but its vacancy is noted in *Paduense* and the Würzburg Epistolary.

The Sunday before Easter is entitled in *Hadrianum* as *Die Dominico in Palmas ad Sanctum Iohannem in Lateranis*, but the palm procession was an innovation from Jerusalem which did not come in till after St Gregory. Alcuin's Lectionary employs the title *Dominica in Indulgentia ad Lateranis*.

In this Great Week, *Hebdomada Maior*, or *Authentica*, the earliest days to be provided with a station and mass were Wednesday and Thursday, and then by the sixth century Monday and Tuesday had been filled, as they are in all our present sources. Maundy Thursday, originally the last day of Lent, before the *Pascha* of three days began, had at first one mass, and that probably in the evening, in commemoration of the Institution of the eucharist at the Last Supper. In some of these Roman sources it has three masses, one for the reconciliation of penitents who had been under discipline throughout Lent, one for the consecration of chrism, and one for the primitive evening mass. This is the situation to be seen in the Old Gelasian. *Hadrianum* has only one mass on this day; but *Paduense* has two masses, one in the morning and one in the evening. The Würzburg Epistolary has only one mass, and this is the chrismal mass: 'Feria v ad Lateranis quando crisma conficitur'. In the Gospelbook the situation is precisely the same, and this is true of Alcuin's Lectionary.

The station of Good Friday is at the Holy Cross in Jerusalem except in *Gelasianum*, which is without station notes, and books later than St Gregory suggest that it was observed at 3 p.m. On Saturday the vigil mass of Easter at night is attested in all these sources.

Eastertide

There is general agreement among the sources about the arrangements in Eastertide, that is in the fifty days between Easter and Pentecost. This period was one of unbroken joy, without fasts, and until the time of Gregory it appears to have been the only period when *Alleluia* was used. He extended its use outside the great fifty days. According to ancient tradition it was forbidden to kneel during this period.

The pattern of Eastertide is agreed among our authorities, but the arrangement of the masses tends to vary, as do the titles of the Sundays. The general shape of the period is that Easter has an octave, in which Thursday, unlike most Thursdays in Lent, has a station, and during this week the neophytes were accustomed to attend church daily, and often received instruction from the bishop about the eucharist. Easter Saturday was the last day when they appeared in baptismal robes: hence its title *Sabbatum in albis depositis*. Like the previous Saturday, when the baptisms had taken place, it had its station at the Lateran. There were then five Sundays before Ascension Day, placed on the fortieth day after Easter, as we have seen, during the latter half of the fourth century, and then there was one Sunday after Ascension, and at the seventh weekend the Paschal period concluded with the Vigil of Pentecost, when baptism was again administered, and with the Feast of Pentecost on the seventh Sunday after Easter Day.

Two characteristically Roman features occur in this period in nearly all our sources: the *Pascha Annotina*, the anniversary of the Easter Day of the previous year, and therefore of its baptisms; and the Greater Rogation, *Litania maior*, on 25 April.

The Old Gelasian has provision for all days in the octave of Easter and for *Pascha annotina*, but not for *Litania maior*. It has six Sundays *post octabas Paschae*, which is one too many, unless *octabas paschae* means the octave of the Saturday, Easter Eve, on which the baptism had taken place. In *Hadrianum* all the octave is filled, including Thursday; the *Sanctorale*, broken off for Lent at St Valentine on 14 February, resumes with St Tiburtius on 14 April. This book provides for the Greater Rogation, but not for *Pascha annotina*. *Paduense* has provision for the Octave, for *Pascha annotina* and *Litania maior*, and for five Sundays *post octauas Paschae*; the Würzburg Epistolary list for the Feast and its octave, for the Octave Sunday, and for nine Sundays after the Octave. This is much more than is needed. It has the *Litania maior*, but no *Pascha annotina*. Both these occasions are provided for in the Würzburg Gospel list, and it has masses for the octave of Easter, and for five Sundays after Easter. Alcuin's Lectionary list has a full octave of Easter, *Pascha annotina*, and *Laetania Maiore*, an octave Sunday, and four Sundays after the octave.

Ascension Day

Ascension Day comes in the Leonine and in all these other books, on the fortieth day after Easter. The Würzburg Epistle Book has Ascension Day but no vigil, and the Gospelbook likewise. The Leonine has no vigil; Gelasian Ascension Day and the Sunday after Ascension; *Hadrianum* Ascension Day; *Paduense* Ascension and the Sunday after; the Würzburg Epistolary has no vigil, but the Evangeliary has, being twenty-five years later. This vigil would not be observed in Gregory's day. *Ebd. VI* in the Gospelbook is the sixth Sunday after Easter, and therefore the Sunday after Ascension Day. There is also a vigil in Alcuin's Lectionary, and there is one Sunday after it.

Pentecost

Pentecost was originally the concluding day of the Paschal season, and it had, like the first day of that season, a vigil at which baptism was administered. The week following it was a ferial week, having the customary station days on Wednesday and Friday, which were originally without a mass. It developed gradually in two directions. It acquired an octave, with an octave Sunday, and all its days, including Thursday, were provided with a mass, so that it became very like Easter Week. But by the end of the fifth century it had also become an Ember Week, the fast of the fourth month. Between Gelasius and Gregory I this was the case, and therefore the stations on Wednesday, Friday and Saturday were those usual in Ember Weeks, St Mary Major on Wednesday, the Holy Apostles on Friday, and St Peter on Saturday for the vigil with the ordinations. After Gregory, during the seventh century, Ember Week was moved out of this week, and it was not restored to this week until the eleventh century, under Gregory VII. England, however, as distinct from the Continent, seems to have followed the practice of Gregory in observing Embertide in Whitsun Week.[59]

---

[59] Egbert, *De instit. cath.*, XVI. ii (PL LXXXIX, 440) and Willis, *Essays*, pp. 68-72.

Accordingly the sources we are at present considering, from the sixth and seventh centuries, show some variety in their treatment of the week of Pentecost. The arrangements in the Leonine or Verona Sacramentary are the most primitive in this group. It has a mass for the vigil and for the Sunday. It has the Ember Days in this week, with masses for Wednesday, Friday and Saturday; but there are no masses for Monday, Tuesday and Thursday, and none for the following Sunday, so that there is no sign of an octave. The Old Gelasian has provision for the Vigil and the Feast, and an octave has now appeared, and the Ember Days are placed in this week. After the Octave Sunday are placed masses for the reconciliation of heretics and for the dedication of churches. *Hadrianum* has the vigil service, with baptisms, and the mass on the Sunday morning. The Ember Days are observed in this week, but there is no Thursday station as there is in Easter Week, and as we find in the Old Gelasian in this week. The Octave Sunday is observed. The Gregorian Sacramentary of Padua has the vigil baptismal mass and that of the Sunday, and it observed the octave, except Thursday; and this is an Ember Week, followed by the usual *Vacat* Sunday.

The Würzburg Epistolary, the nearest document to the pontificate of Gregory, has the vigil and feast of Pentecost; a complete octave including Thursday, and Ember Week is in the week after Pentecost, and Pentecost week has the non-Ember lessons. The *Sanctorale* then continues after the Ember Week. The Sunday after Whitsun Week is not, however, the octave day of Pentecost, nor the vacant Sunday, since it does not follow the Ember Days, but is a primitive kind of 'All Saints Day', listed as *Dominica in nat. sanctorum*. All Saints' Day on 1 November is a later and Gallican innovation.

The Gospelbook in the same manuscript differs from the Epistle Book. It places Ember Week in Whitsun Week, and Thursday is a vacant day. Alcuin has a full octave, with Thursday and the following Sunday filled. But it is not Ember Week: this follows the feast of SS. Marcellinus and Peter on 2 June. After the Ember Days is *Dominica ut supra*, and then *Dominica III post Pentecosten*. With this should be compared the ordination by Leo II (682-3) held on 27 June 683.[60]

---

[60] See *Liber Pontificalis*, ed. Duchesne, I, pp. 360 and 362, n. 11; and Willis, *Essays*, p. 70.

Sundays from Pentecost to Christmas

After Pentecost there were at the time of St Gregory no papal stations on Sundays until Christmas, except on the Sundays immediately preceding and following the fasts of the seventh and tenth months. Therefore the books before his time make no provision for the other Sundays. In the Old Gelasian, however, there are, as we have seen, sixteen masses at the beginning of Book III, after the Canon, and these could be used, twice each, on the Sundays in this period, which have a maximum of thirty-two. In all our books Advent comes at the end of the year. The antiphonary was the first book to begin the liturgical year at the beginning of Advent, but no manuscript of the antiphonary is earlier than the eighth century, so it is not possible to know when the plan of beginning at Advent emerged. It is clear from the sacramentaries and lectionaries that at the time of Gregory the year began with Christmas Eve. Curiously enough, the Leonine Sacramentary, the only document of this period to be arranged under months, places Christmas Day, with St John Evangelist and the Innocents' Day, in December at the end of the year. The Old Gelasian has no division into months, but Book II gives the feasts in chronological order in one series. The most characteristic distinction between Gelasian and Gregorian books is the separation in Gelasian books of the *Sanctorale* and *Temporale*. Naturally the Gregorian books differ from one another in the precise position which they allocate to Sundays or blocks of Sundays in relation to the saints' days, but they do not place the Sundays in one series: they divide the Sundays into groups, Sundays *post Pentecosten*; *post Apostolos* (i.e. after the feast of SS. Peter and Paul on 29 June); *post Laurentium* (i.e., after 10 August); *post Cyprianum* (i.e., 14 September) – this is not used by all Gregorian books; *post sancti Angeli* (i.e., after 29 September). In some books the Sundays in Advent are a separate block at the end of the half year.

The Gelasian, near the end of the *Sanctorale*, has a set of *Orationes de Adventu Domini*. *Hadrianum* has four Sundays in Advent: three followed by Ember Week, and then the fourth Sunday. *Paduense* has no Sundays after Cyprian: it has a *vacat* Sunday after the September Ember Days; and in Advent three Sundays, with a *vacat* Sunday afterwards. The third of its three Sundays in Advent which precede the Embertide is marked with its station at St Peter: this is the traditional Roman station on the Sunday preceding the Ember Week. The fourth Sunday, the one between the Ember Week and Christmas, is vacant.

The Würzburg Epistolary has some saints' days after Pentecost, but it has hardly any mention of Sundays in this period, apart from five Sundays in Advent, and it places the ordination masses after instead of before the Vigil of Christmas. There are, however, thirty sets, without numbers or titles, and these are presumably intended for the maximum of thirty-two Sundays between Pentecost and Christmas. After this follows a mass *In Aduentu Iudicum*, for the entering of the consuls into office on 1 January. The Würzburg Gospelbook, however, has no Ember Days in December, nor any Sundays in Advent: it has some Sundays during the half year, but nothing approaching a full provision. The Lectionary of Alcuin has fairly full provision for Sundays, and for the two Ember Weeks in this period. All the Sundays are in their groups, after Pentecost, the Apostles, the Angel, not interspersed with saints' days. The saints' days are placed between groups of Sundays. It has four Sundays in Advent, counted backwards, Dominica IV, III, II *ante natale Domini*, then Ember Days, then *Dominica I ante Natale Domini*. Then follows the mass at Nones on Christmas Eve, then the ordination rites, out of place as in the Würzburg Epistle Book; and at the end the mass for 1 January, *In Aduentu Iudicum*.

SANCTORALE

The earliest extant Roman Martyrology is the *Feriale Ecclesiae Romanae* in the Chronography of 354,[61] which gives a list of twenty-four commemorations of Roman saints, with a note of the place where they were buried, or where their cult was observed in their memorial or cemetery chapel.

viii Kal.Ian.	Natus Christus in Betleem Iudeae.
xiii Kal.Feb.	Fabiani in Callisti et Sebastiani in Catacumbas.
xii Kal.Feb.	Agnetis in Nomentana.
viii Kal.Martias.	Natale Petri de cathedra.
Non. Martias.	Perpetuae et Felicitatis, Africae.
xiv Kal.Iun.	Partheni et Caloceri in Callisti, Diocletiani VIIII et Maximiano VIII (304).

[61] Ed. T. Mommsen, *Chronica Minora*, MGH, AA IX (Berlin, 1892), p. 71.

iii Kal.Iul.	Petri in Catcumbas et Pauli Ostense, Tusco et Basso cons. (258)
vi Idus Iul.	Felicis et Filippi in Priscillae et in Iordanorum, Martialis Vitalis Alexandri et in Maximi Silani. hunc Silanum martirem Novati Furati sunt et in Praetextatae, Ianuari.
iii Kal.Aug.	Abdos et Semnes in Pontiani: quod est ad ursum piliatum.
viii Idus Aug.	Xysti in Callisti et in Praetextati Agapiti et Felicissimi.
vi Idus Aug.	Secundi Carpofori Victorini et Seueriani. Albano et Ostense VII ballistaria . . . Cyriaci Largi Crescentiani, Memmiae Iulianetis et Ixmaracdi.
iii Idus Aug.	Laurenti in Tiburtina.
Idus Aug.	Ypoliti in Tiburtina et Pontiani in Callisti.
xi Kal.Septemb.	Timotei Ostense.
v Kal.Sept.	Hermetis in Basillae Salaria vetere.
Non Sept.	Aconti, in Porto, et Nonni et Herculani et Taurini.
v Idus Sept.	Gorgoni, in Lavicana.
iii Idus Sept.	Proti et Iacinti, in Basillae.
xviii Kal.Octob.	Cypriani, Africae. Romae celebratur in Callisti.
x Kal. Octob.	Basillae, Salaria vetere, Diocletiano IX et Maximiano VIII Consul. (304)
Prid.Idus Octob.	Callisti in Via Aurelia miliario iii.
v Idus Nov.	Clementis Semproniani Clavi. Nicostrati in comitatum.
iii Kal.Dec.	Saturnini in Trasonis.
Idus Decem.	Ariston in Pontum.

The first item is the calendrical note on 25 December, recording the birth of Christ, to which reference has been made above,[62] but all the others are depositions of saints. They form the essential core of the Roman *sanctorale* from their own compilation to the recent revision of 1969. *Depositio Martyrum* is not entirely a list of martyrs, nor does it contain all the names of all the martyrs of the Roman Church. But nearly all the names in it persist in Roman kalendars, and the saints are either buried in the city or around it, or else like St Cyprian of

[62] See above, pp. 80-1.

Carthage, have a cult in Rome. In this they are similar to the saints listed in the Canon of the Mass.[63]

We are concerned in this section with commemorations round about the time of St Gregory, as they are to be seen in the documents we are considering, and which illustrate this period, not with all of them, but with a representative selection.[64]

The saints of the Octave of Christmas, who are unique in being embedded in all sources in the bosom of the *Temporale*, are biblical, except St Silvester, on 31 December, and he was pope (from 314 to 335), and is listed among the *Episcopi Romani* in the Chronography of 354.[65]

There is then a gap in these sixth-and seventh-century lists over Epiphany, and the *Sanctorale* generally resumed with St Felix on 14 January, but the Würzburg Epistle list resumes with St Sebastian on 20 January. St Prisca (18 January), and St Agnes, two commemorations on 21 and 28 January, are old Roman saints who were early in the kalendar. SS. Fabian and Sebastian occur in the Chronography: 'XIII Kal.Feb. Fabiani in Callisti et Sebastiani in Catacumba'. St Agnes follows: 'xii Kal.Feb. Agnetis in Nomentana'.

The kalendars of this early period show the development of the feast of Our Lady on 2 February. The kalendar of the Roman Church at the time of St Gregory had no feast whatever of the Blessed Virgin Mary. The *Liber pontificalis*[66] states that Pope Sergius I instituted *collectae* and processions to the stational church on four feasts of Our Lady, the Purification (2 February); the Annunciation (25 March), the Assumption or *Dormitio* (15 August), and the Nativity (8 September). It does not state that Sergius instituted these feasts, but that he provided them with a *collect*, a procession and station. They were presumably observed at Rome before his time (687-701). But not long before, since the earliest elements of the books here considered do not include mention of them. For instance, the Chronography includes none of them. And in some of the other sources only tentative mention is made. For example, *Hadrianum*, two hunded years after St Gregory's death, has 2 February, Ypapanti. This Greek title does not mention the Virgin,

[63] On this subject, see the important monographs by H. Delehaye, *Les origines du culte des martyrs* (Brussels, 1933); and V. L. Kennedy, *The Saints of the Canon of the Mass* (Vatican City, 1963).

[64] See W. H. Frere, *Studies in Early Roman Liturgy I. The Kalendar* (Oxford, 1930).

[65] Ed. Mommsen, *Chronica Minora*, pp. 73-6.

[66] Ed. Duchesne, I, p. 376.

even if it be held to imply her presence at the meeting of the Christ with Simeon and Anna. *Paduense* has a similar entry: '2 Feb., Ypapanti ad sanctam Mariam'. The Würzburg Gospel List has, 'die secundo mens. Feb.' and no other title. In Alcuin 2 February is marked as *in die qua beata Virgo offerebat Christum in templo*. The Old Gelasian has on 2 Feb. *Orationes in purificatione sanctae Mariae*, a more developed title than is found in the earlier Roman sacramentaries, and doubtless of Gallican origin. The same comment may be made of its entry for 25 March: *Adnuntiatio sanctae Dei genetricis et Passio eiusdem Domini*.

Most kalendars in the early days kept Lent clear of commemorations, and the usual custom in these early tables is to have a gap between St Valentine on 14 February and St Tiburtius on 14 April. However, the earliest source has one or two exceptions. It notes, *Natale Petri de cathedra*, the feast of St Peter's throne on 22 February, and then its list is interrupted from 7 March, *Perpetuae et Felicitatis Africae*. This is the African Felicity: the Roman virgin Felicity, the one who is mentioned in the Canon, is commemorated in Roman kalendars on 23 November, the same day as St Clement, who was pope at the end of the first century. The *Hadrianum* has two items in the Lenten blank, and both are later than the date of its original drafting. One is on 12 March, *Gregorii Papae*, the anniversary of the death of St Gregory the Great on 12 March 604; and the other is *Adnuntiatio sanctae Mariae* on 25 March. This is, like the Purification, an addition of the seventh century. In the Lectionary of Alcuin there is a mass in *adnuntiatione sanctae Mariae*.

After Easter the *Sanctorale* resumes, often with St Tiburtius on 14 April. In the Old Gelasian we have SS. Philip and James on 1 May: this is the Roman feast, being the dedication of the Basilica of the Apostles at Rome. But it is not in the earlier Roman sources. The Old Gelasian has the feast of the Invention of the Cross on 3 May and the Exaltation of the Cross on 14 September. These are late-comers into the Roman tradition, and were derived from Jerusalem or from the Gallican tradition. The early Roman rite, till after the pontificate of St Gregory, had no feasts of the Holy Cross any more than it had any feasts of the Virgin Mary. But the Invention of the Cross occurs in *Hadrianum* in which it is a later addition. On 6 May *S. Iohannes ante portam Latinam* is found in *Hadrianum*. On 13 May *Paduense* has *Natale sanctae Mariae ad Martyres*: this is one of the feasts which are not depositions of the relics of saints, but the feast of the dedication of a church, in this case of *S. Mariae ad Martyres*, a building which had been the

Pantheon, and was consecrated as a church by Pope Boniface IV (608-15). This was the first feast to be added to the kalendar after the death of St Gregory.

The Vigil and Feast of the Nativity of St John the Baptist (24 June) occurs in the Leonine, and in *Hadrianum* and *Paduense*, but it is absent from the early Roman list of A.D. 354. The feast and Vigil occur in all the Roman sources, the Würzburg Epistle and Gospelbooks, and Alcuin's Lectionary, and also in the Old Gelasian.

These sources also concur in the feast of the Apostles SS. Peter and Paul on 29 June. It has an octave in most of them, and certain books, e.g., The Gelasian, and *Hadrianum* and *Paduense*, provide for separate commemorations of St Peter on the 29th and St Paul on the 30th. Since both the Apostles suffered martyrdom and were buried at Rome, they appear in all Roman sources from the earliest lists available. In the Chronography of A.D. 354 they are entered as, *iii Kal.Iul. Petri in Catacumbas et Pauli Ostense Tusco et Basso cons*. 29 June is the feast of their translation after the end of the Decian persecution in 258, according to the consular date.

On iii Kal. Aug. (30 July), SS. Abdon and Sennes are one of the most ancient feasts at Rome, occurring in all these sources from the Chronography onwards. The same may be said of Pope Xystus, 6 August, a victim of the Decian persecution, and of his deacon St Laurence, who followed the footsteps of his martyred bishop four days later. St Laurence, with SS. Peter and Paul, was regarded as one of the patrons of the Church of Rome, and the feast of 10 August appears in all these sources, often with a vigil and sometimes with an octave, and is one of the days, like SS. Peter and Paul, from which the Sundays in the Roman *Temporale* are reckoned.

On 13 August the Chronography has *Idus Aug. ypoliti in Tiburtina et Pontiani in Callisti*. This entry continues in the later lists. Pontianus, who was pope from 230-5, and Hippolytus, a dissident priest of the Roman Church, both died in exile in the mines of Sardinia, and were brought back to Rome for burial. Pontianus the lawful bishop, was buried in the cemetery of Callistus, that is in the official cemetery of which Callistus, when archdeacon under Sephyrinus, before he himself succeeded Zephyrinus in the papal throne in 217, was in charge; and Hippolytus on the *Via Tiburtina*.

Hadrianum and *Paduense* have the Assumption of St Mary the Virgin on 15 August, and the Nativity on 8 September: but, like the feasts of 2 February and 25 March, these are not primitive, and were probably not introduced before the middle of the seventh century. The date of the Nativity was formerly occupied by St Hadrian, and his commemoration remained on that day in the kalendar, and its memory was preserved by the observance of the *collecta* of the Virgin's feast at the church of St Hadrian in the forum.

The Chronography list observes St Cyprian on 14 September: *xviii Kal. Octob. Cypriani Africae. Romae celebratur in Callisti*. St Cyprian, the most illustrious martyr of Africa, suffered at Carthage and was buried there. His entry in the Chronography is a good example of the method of commemorating at Rome a non-Roman saint. Usually Rome joins his name with that of Cornelius, pope from 251 to 253, who was Cyprian's friend and suffered also in the Decian persecution, but not in the same year. But in this, the earliest list, there is no mention of Cornelius. The Exaltation of the Holy Cross, an Hierosolymitan feast, was observed on the same day, 14 September, and in the Roman books of the Middle Ages replaced SS. Cyprian and Cornelius on the 14th, and they were moved to the 16th. But in the pontificate of Gregory, as we have noted, Rome observed no feasts of the Holy Cross. St Cyprian, like SS. Peter and Paul and St Laurence, was a date governing one division of the Sundays after Pentecost in some Roman books.

The feast *sancti Angeli*, Michaelmas Day (29 September), was significant in early Roman liturgy, being one of the feasts which head one of the groups of Sundays after Pentecost. This group is usually called *post sancti Angeli*. It is, like 13 May, the dedication feast of a Roman church, that of St Michael on the *Via Salaria*. It does not appear in the Chronography. The Leonine describes it as *Natale basilicae Angeli in Salaria*, but puts it erroneously on 30 September. The Würzburg Epistle list contains this day.

Only Alcuin' Lectionary denotes 1 November as All Saints' Day: in Roman use this day was the feast of St Caesarius, who was patron of a church in Rome; and this name is in most of the other kalendars. It was a day when there was a *collecta* and procession, and the station church was St Caesarius.

Many of these early kalendars have the Roman commemorations of St Cecilia on 22 November, which was observed in 538, as we learn from the arrest of Pope Vigilius on 22 November in St Cecilia *trans Tiberim* on the saint's feast.[67] St Clement and St Felicity, the Roman virgin of that name, both mentioned in the Canon, were observed from

---

[67] See above, p. 66.

early times on 23 November. The Gregorian books observe St Andrew on 30 November, usually with a vigil on 29 November: St Andrew had a church in Rome, St Andrew *in Catabarbara*, near St Mary Major, to which St Gregory brought a piece of Andrew's arm.[68] In view of Gregory's known devotion to St Andrew, it seems likely that he introduced this feast into the Roman kalendar.

In December the last Roman feasts before the end of the year, on Christmas Eve, are St Lucy (which is very common in the Roman books), also mentioned in the Canon, whose feast is on 13 December, and St Thomas the Apostle on 21 December, which occurs in the Old Gelasian.

THE LESSONS AT MASS

The earliest mass lectionaries of the Church of Rome are those contained in the Würzburg MS. Mp.th. 62 of which the Epistle list is dated about 625, and the Gospel list 650 or in the following decade. The original base of the Alcuin Lectionary has been dated about 626 or 627. All these lists are contained in manuscripts later than the seventh century, and therefore contain additions and features which are later than the seventh century, and later than St Gregory. But the main basis of these tables probably represents the state reached by the Roman Lectionary at the time of St Gregory, and it is generally accepted that the lessons were an aspect of the liturgy to which St Gregory gave attention.[69] The system of lessons underwent enrichment and development in later centuries, but very many lessons in use in the seventh century continued in use until the revision of 1970.

Before St Gregory, the lectionary system was largely undeveloped. The lessons continued to be at the discretion of the celebrant long after he had lost control of the content of the eucharistic prayer, and down to the end of the sixth century the celebrant retained the choice of the lessons. On the greater festivals the lessons must naturally reflect the subject of the day, and the number of passages suitable for use is therefore limited. Hence these days are the first days to have a fixed lesson. On other days the celebrant chooses the lessons, and he may do

[68] See above, p. 57.
[69] See W. H. Frere, *Studies in Early Roman Liturgy, II. The Roman Lectionary* (Oxford, 1934); and *III. The Roman Epistle-Lectionary* (Oxford, 1935).

this in a haphazard fashion, to suit the subject of his sermon, or systematically, so as to read a book of the Bible continuously. Until 1970 the Roman Missal retained survivals of this *lectio continua*, for example on the first four Sundays after Epiphany, with their Epistles drawn from Romans XII and XIII.[70]

Evidence concerning the lessons at Rome is very scarce indeed until the seventh century. No tables or lectionaries have survived, even if they existed, and the historian is therefore dependent upon incidental references, particularly those to be found in sermons. We know that St Gregory gave attention to the gospel lessons, since John the Deacon, in his *Vita* of Gregory, written between 873 and 875, says of him: 'sed et Gelasianum codicem de missarum sollemniis pro exponendis euangelicis lectionibus in unius libri uolumine coarctauit'.[71] It is possible to compile from references in the Homilies of Gregory on the gospels, forty in number, a list of gospels used at Rome in his pontificate.

LIST OF GOSPELS ATTESTED IN THE HOMILIES OF ST GREGORY THE GREAT

Temporale

Day	Homily	Gospel
Nat.Dni. nocte	VIII	Lc. II.1-14
Epiphania	X	Mt. II.1-12
Dominica in Septuagesima	XIX	Mt. XX.1-16
Dominica in Sexagesima	XV	Lc. VIII.4-15
Dominica in Quinquagesima	II	Lc. XVIII.31-44
Dominica I Quadragesimae	XVI	Mt. IV.1-11
Dominica V Quadragesimae	XVIII	Jn. VIII.45-69
Die Paschae	XXI	Mc. XVI.1-7
Feria II	XXIII	Lc. XXIV.13-35
Feria IV	XXIV	Jn. XXI.1-14
Feria V	XXV	Jn. XX.11-18
Sabbato	XXII	Jn. XX.1-9
Octaua Paschae	XXVI	Jn. XX.19-31
Dominica secunda post octauas Paschae	XIV	Jn. X.11-16
Ascensio Domini	XXIX	Mc. XVI.14-20

---

[70] Willis, *St Augustine's Lectionary*, pp. 5-9.
[71] *Vita S. Gregorii* II. 7 (PL LXXIV, 94A).

Day	Homily	Gospel
Dies Pentecostes	XXX	Jn. XIV.23-31
Ebdomada II post Pentecosten	XXXVI	Lc. XIV.16-24
Ebd. II post Pentecosten	XL	Lc. XVI.19-31
Ebd. III post Pentecosten	XXXIV	Lc. XV.1-10
Q.T. Sept. Feria VI	XXXIII	Lc. VII.36-50
Q.T. Sept. Sabbatum	XXXI	Lc. XIII.6-13
Dominica IV (?III) ante Nat. Dni.	I	Lc. XXI.25-42
Dom. III (?II) ante Nat. Dni.	VI	Mt. XI.2-10
Dom. II (?I) ante Nat. Dni.	VII	Jn. I.19-28
Sabbatum mensis decimi	XX	Lc. III.1-11

Sanctorale

Day	Homily	Gospel
Agnetis	XII	Mt. XXV.1-13
Agnetis	XI	Mt. XIII.44-52
Sebastiani	XXXVII	Lc. XIV.25-33
Pancratii	XXVII	Jn. XV.12-16
Nerei et Achillei	XXVIII	Jn. IV.46-53
Processi et Martiniani	XXXII	Lc. IX.23-7
Felicitatis	III	Mt. XII.46-50
Mennae	XXXV	Lc. XXI.9-19
Felicis	XIII	Lc. XII.35-40
Clementis	XXXVIII	Mt. XXII.1-13
Andreae	V	Mt. IV.18-22
Siluestri	IX	Mt. XXV.14-30
De apostolis	IV	Mt. X.5-10

The introduction of the feast of the Epiphany at Rome before 419[72] involved an adjustment of the lessons of Christmas and Epiphany.[73] At that period Rome had only one mass on Christmas Day. Christmas commemorated the birth, and the Epiphany, when it came in at Rome, had to be given a different theme from the Birth, which it had until then commemorated in Eastern Christendom. The theme was the manifestation of Christ to the Gentiles. In Africa this was the theme at the

---

[72] See above, p. 82.
[73] C. Coebergh, 'Les Pericopes d'évangiles de la fête de Noël à Rome', *Revue Bénédictine* LXXVII (1966), 128-33.

beginning of the fifth century, as we see from all the epiphany sermons of St Augustine.[74] The Bobbo Missal has two lessons for Christmas Day, Matt. I, the Nativity, and Matt. II, the Visit of the Magi, and this might be a relic of the original arrangements at Rome. If so, Matt. II will have been removed to 6 January when the Epiphany came in.[75] St Gregory, preaching at the midnight mass of Christmas in the Basilica of St Mary Major, states that the gospel was Luke II.1-14,[76] which has since then remained at this mass. The principal mass of Christmas, that of the day, was always celebrated at St Peter's, and the gospel at this mass was Matt. II. When this was transferred to Epiphany, John I.1-14 was substituted for it, and probably by the end of the fifth century. It appears in all the lists later than Gregory, but he himself has left no homily which attests the reading of John I on Christmas Day. The original gospel, Luke II.1-20, was divided when the three masses were instituted, before Gregory, and Luke II.1-14 was used at midnight, as Gregory attests, and Luke II.15-20 at the day mass. This has continued to the present, but again, there is no evidence in Gregory's sermons for the gospel at the dawn mass at St Anastasia, but only of the midnight mass, when the gospel ends at verse 14.

At Hippo, St Augustine read Luke II.1-39 on Christmas Day, and Matt. II.1-11 on the Epiphany. Africa in his day did not observe the three pre-Lent Sundays. These were only established at Rome during the sixth century, and by the end of that century St Gregory's Homilies show that their gospels were Matt. XX.1-16 on Septuagesima, the parable of the Labourers in the Vineyard, which, as was noted above, may have been connected with the practice of engaging agricultural labourers at Rome in early February; on Sexagesima Luke VIII.4-15, the Parable of the Sower, on Quinquagesima Luke XVIII.31-44, the Healing of the Blind Man, including the dominical saying, so well fitted for the Sunday before Lent, 'We go up to Jerusalem'. These gospels remained constant in all the later lists.

The gospel of the first Sunday in Lent, Matt. IV.1-11, the Temptation of Christ, was established by the time of St Gregory, and has continued to the present in all Roman sources. The use of this

---

[74] Willis, *St Augustine's Lectionary*, pp. 61-2.
[75] See C. Mohrmann, 'Epiphanie', in her *Etudes sur le latin des chrétiens* I (Rome, 1958), pp. 245-75.
[76] *Hom.* I (PL LXXVI, 1113).

pericope was also widespread. The gospel of the next Sunday, *Dominica quinta in mediana*, upon which St Gregory preached, has also continued down to modern times: John VIII.45-69. Roman use concerning the lessons of the Easter Octave was variable: the pericopae from the Gospels are of course drawn from the four accounts of the Resurrection appearances, but the order varies. The earliest account to be composed of the finding of the empty tomb by the women (Mc. XVI.1-7), is attested as the gospel of Easter morning by Gregory in Homily XXI. He says that the gospel for Easter Monday was Lc. XXIV.13-35, the appearance to Cleopas and his fellow disciple on the road to Emmaus. This has continued in all Roman sources.

Homily XXIV gives John XXI.1-14 on Wednesday. This is the appearance to seven disciples by the lake of Tiberias. This lection is not continued on Thursday, but this day has the Gospel Jn. XX.11-18, the appearance to Mary Magdalen on Easter morning. Homily XXII attests the use of Jn. XX.1-9 on Saturday. On Low Sunday it appears from Homily XXVI that Jn. XX.19-31 was read. This is a common choice for this day, since the lesson includes the appearance of the Lord to the Apostles minus St Thomas on Easter evening, and his appearance to St Thomas with the others on the following Sunday. St Gregory's Homilies supply no information as to what was read on Tuesday and Friday.

We find from Homily XIV that the lesson from John X.11-16, about the Good Shepherd, was used on the second Sunday after Easter; this is another lesson which has continued in Roman tables ever since.

The gospel on Ascension Day is Mc. XVI.14-20, a lesson characteristic of Roman use for many centuries, as is Jn. XIV.23-31 for Pentecost. This is not the lesson which Augustine gives for Pentecost, however.

On the second Sunday after Pentecost, Gregory's table has the Parable of the Great Supper, Lc. XIV.16-24. On the same day, apparently, it is stated in Homily XL that the gospel was the Parable of Dives and Lazarus (Lc. XVI.19-31). On the third Sunday after Pentecost we find Lc. XV.1-10.

In the September Embertide we find on Friday Lc. VII.36-50, and on the Ember Saturday Lc. XIII.6-13.

The three lessons which are mentioned for use in Advent in Gregory's Homilies, Lc. XXI.25-42; Matt. XI.2-10; and Jn. I.19-28, have all continued in use during Advent, though on different Sundays in various systems.

IV

The Rites of Initiation

The main sources of information concerning the rites by which
Christians at Rome were initiated in the first six centuries down to the
pontificate of St Gregory the Great (590-604) may be enumerated as
follows (and see Table II, below, pp. 150-1):

(i) The *First Apology* of Justin Martyr written about 155.[1] In chs. 61-6
this work gives some account of initiation, leading up to a description of
the baptismal eucharist. The rite which it describes is much less
elaborate than that outlined in any of the other sources, but this does not
imply that Justin's rite was as simple as a first reading might suggest.
For example, Justin gives an outline of the ceremonies of the eucharist,[2]
but he says nothing of what we now call confirmation, that is, the
imposition of the hand or the unction, with prayer for the gift of the
Holy Ghost. It is not likely, in view of the many references to this rite in
the New Testament, and of its constant re-appearance in all the later
Roman documents, that this rite was entirely absent from baptism at
Rome in the middle of the second century. A far more likely
explanation of Justin's silence is the operation of the *disciplina arcani*,
the secrecy by which Christians concealed from the knowledge of
pagans facts about Christian worship and practice which might have
been misunderstood or misinterpreted. Confirmation might well have
been one of these matters. We shall, however, find all the way through
our enquiry, down to St Gregory's time, that this reticence lingered
long after the age of persecution had passed. For example, even the
candidates themselves who were seeking baptism were not taught the
Creed or the Lord's Prayer until the last weeks of their preparation, nor
were they allowed to be present at the eucharistic prayer until they had
been baptized. It was the custom to explain the eucharist to them in

---

[1] Ed. J. K. T. Otto, *Iustini Opera*, 2nd ed., 3 vols. (Jena, 1846-9).
[2] *Ibid.* ch. 66.

Easter Week, after they had been admitted to communion at the vigil service of Easter Day. Although Justin's account in the *First Apology* is not a full one, there is much in it which re-appears in the later history of baptism at Rome.

(ii) The *Apostolic Tradition* of Hippolytus, about 215.[3] The detailed account of initiation in ch. 21 of this work[4] is the only considerable piece of evidence from pre-Nicene times coming from Rome. The most complete text of this chapter of the *Apostolic Tradition* is the Coptic version, and even here the Sahidic has a long lacuna, which can be supplied by a Bohairic translation of the original Sahidic, but this Bohairic is as late as the year 1804.[5] However, parts of the chapter are preserved in the Latin version in the Verona palimpsest, in the Arabic and Ethiopic versions, which ultimately derive drom the Sahidic;[6] so that a fairly complete view of the original Greek is probably attainable, though, since none of the versions is earlier than the Latin, which cannot have been made much before 400, it cannot be known with certainty how much is due to the hand of Hippolytus himself, and so dateable to about the year 215, and how much has been introduced or changed before the date of the various versions. On the other hand, as we shall see, several cardinal features of the later Roman rite, as it was in the sixth and seventh centuries, are already to be seen in the rite of *Apostolic Tradition*, and so it is reasonable to use this rite as part of the evidence for the Roman *ordo baptismi*.

(iii) *Tertullian and Cyprian*. Neither of these African writers of the third century worked in Rome, but, down to the disappearance of African Christianity in the Arab invasion of the seventh century, there were close connections between North Africa and Rome, and the liturgy of these two places was akin. No actual liturgical text from Africa has, however, survived; but the works of Tertullian at the end of the second and the beginning of the third century, and of Cyprian in the middle of the third century, will furnish some references to baptismal liturgy to set side by side with Roman evidence.

---

[3] Ed. G. Dix, *The Apostolic Tradition of St Hippolytus*, 2nd ed. rev. H. Chadwick (London, 1968); B. Botte, *La tradition apostolique de saint Hippolyte* (Münster in Westfalen, 1963).

[4] Ed. Dix, pp. 33-8; ed. Botte, pp. 44-59.

[5] Ed. W. C. Till and J. Leipoldt, *Der koptische Text der Kirchenordnung Hippolyts*, Texte und Untersuchungen LVIII (Berlin, 1954).

[6] See Botte's edition, cited above, n. 3.

(iv) *St Ambrose*. Nor did St Ambrose ever work at Rome, but Milan, like Africa, was closely associated with Rome in liturgy, and Ambrose states emphatically that he desires to follow Roman use in all things.[7] But in the case of baptism we shall see that in one cardinal ceremony, carrying theological implications, at least in the mind of Ambrose, he diverges from Rome, and thinks it necessary to justify his divergence at length.[8] Nevertheless, on the whole, it is reasonable to take his evidence as bearing on Rome as well as on Milan, and so his catechetical lectures on baptism will be cited here.[9]

(v) *The Letter of John the Deacon to Senarius*. This letter[10] may be dated about 500, and it was written at Rome by a Roman deacon, probably the one who was later to become Pope John I. It provides Roman evidence from Rome.

(vi) *The Old Gelasian Sacramentary*. The Old Gelasian Sacramentary, handed down in an unique manuscript, Vaticanus Reginensis 316, was not written till about the year 750, and then in France, probably in a nunnery at Chelles, near Paris. But, though compiled in Gaul, it has a thoroughly Roman base, which, if it can be detached, may be taken as evidence for Roman usage about 560, a generation before St Gregory.[11]

(vii) *Ordo Romanus XI*. The date of this *Ordo*[12] is about 650, and it is a purely Roman document. It may therefore be taken as showing the state of the rites of initiation at Rome forty to fifty years after St Gregory, and it provides evidence of one important change which had taken place at Rome since the death of Gregory in 604. This was the suppression of the old practice of three Scrutinies held on the third, fourth and fifth Sundays in Lent and the substitution of a series of seven Scrutinies, all held on weekdays between the third Sunday in Lent and Easter Even.

(viii) *The Gregorian Sacramentary*. Much of this sacramentary is later than Gregory, and thus falls, like *Ordo* XI, outside the period

---

[7] *De sacramentis* III.i.5 (CSEL LXXIII, 40): 'non ignoramus quod ecclesia romana hanc consuetudinem non habeat, cuius typum in omnibus sequimur et formam . . . in omnibus cupio sequi ecclesiam romanam.'

[8] *Ibid*. III.i.5-7.

[9] *Explanatio symboli*, *De sacramentis* and *De mysteriis*, all in CSEL LXXIII.

[10] Ed. A. Wilmart, *Analecta Reginensia*, Studi e Testi LIX (1932), pp. 170-9.

[11] Ed. L. C. Mohlberg, *Liber Sacramentorum Romanae Aeclesiae Ordinis Anni Circuli* (Rome, 1969); see also A. Chavasse, *Le sacramentaire gélasien* (Tournai, 1958).

[12] Ed. Andrieu II, 417-47.

which we are examining. Dom Henry Ashworth suggests that it may have been compiled in the pontificate of Honorius (625-38), but it contains earlier elements, which will be useful for illustrating our study of earlier books, and it is thoroughly Roman, at least in the uncontaminated form of the *Hadrianum*.[13]

Evidence for the rites of baptism, confirmation and first communion, as contained in the texts listed above, is set out in tabular for ease of consultation below, pp. 150-1.

PRELIMINARY CEREMONIES

It is clear from all the post-Nicene witnesses of roman liturgy that baptism, which was normally administered at the vigil service of the night between Easter Eve and Easter Day, was preceded by a number of preparatory sessions in the church at which, by exorcism, demons were cast out of the candidates, and instruction was given by which their minds were made ready for the reception of the sacrament of enlightenment. It is not possible to be sure how much of the *Apostolic Tradition* of Hippolytus belongs to the original work composed about 215; but its description of the preliminaries of baptism in ch. 20[14] is not very detailed or explicit. It is, however, not preserved in Latin, but only in the Sahidic version, supported by the Arabic and Ethiopic.[15]

Scrutinies

These rites were carried out at public masses during Lent, when baptism was to be administered at Easter, and during Eastertide when the candidates were to be baptized at Pentecost.[16] Notice was given of impending scrutinies.[17] The candidates were brought by their sponsors to church, and the scrutinies wre carried out after the gospel, and when

---

[13] Ed. H. Lietzmann, *Das Sacramentarium Gregorianum* (Münster in Westfalen, 1967); cf. J. Deshusses, *Les sacramentaires grégoriens* (Fribourg, 1971).

[14] *Apostolic Tradition*, ed. Dix, p. 30; ed. Botte, p. 42.

[15] For the text of the Sahidic, see Till and Leipoldt, *Der koptische Text*.

[16] For the text applying to Whitsuntide baptisms, see *Gelasianum* I. lxvi-lxxx, ed. Mohlberg, pp. 592-643.

[17] *Gel.* I. xxix, ed. Mohlberg, pp. 283-4.

they were concluded, the candidates were given a blessing,[18] and dismissed. Not until they had been baptised did they stay for the Canon of the Mass and receive their communion. Two great changes which took place during our period must be borne in mind throughout the consideration of baptism. The first was that the candidates in the first five centuries were normally adults, though whole families might be baptized together, and in that case would be likely to include children, whereas from about 500 candidates were almost exclusively the children of Christian parents, and the rites described by John the Deacon and those contained in the Gelasian Sacramentary, and in *Ordo XI*, and in the Gregorian Sacramentary, are all designed for children. The second change took place between the old stratum of the Gelasian, which is to be dated about 560, and *Ordo* XI, dated about 650. This is the development from three scrutinies to seven, a sacred number intended to signify the sevenfold gifts of the Holy Ghost. So the earliest description of the baptismal rites which we have from Rome, that of the *Gelasianum*, is designed for infants. After the scrutiny, the children are taken out of the church, and kept in custody by helpers until their parents, having heard mass, take them away home. Hippolytus mentions scrutinies, but does not specify their number.[19] The same may be said of John the Deacon.[20] In the original form of the Gelasian Sacramentary there are three scrutinies, which take place on the third, fourth and fifth Sundays in Lent.[21] In the notice (*denuntiatio*) of the scrutiny, the parents are instructed to bring the children on the appointed day, which in the later eighth-century form of this sacramentary, is a weekday, about noon. When the children arrive, their names are noted by an acolyte, and they are placed in order, the boys on the right and the girls on the left. The priest says the appointed prayer over them.[22] Examples of this prayer may be seen in the old Gelasian[23] and in *Hadrianum*.[24] The propers of the three original

---

[18] Examples of this can be found in *Hadrianum* 81-3.

[19] *Ap. Trad.* ch. 20, ed. Dix, p. 30; ed. Botte p. 42.

[20] Ed. Wilmart, *Analecta Reginensia*, pp. 171-3.

[21] Third Sunday, *Gel*.I.xxvi, 193-9; Fourth Sunday, *Gel*.I.xxvii, 225-8; Fifth Sunday, *Gel*.I.xxvii, 254-7.

[22] *Gel*.I.xxix, 283: 'Denuntiatio pro scrutinio quod tertia hebdomada in Quadragesima secunda feria initiarum (*1.* initiatur).' This mention of Monday in the third week of Lent indicates that this item belongs to the eighth-century stratum of the book, and not to the original sixth-century material, for at that time the scrutinies were still on Sundays.

[23] *Gel*.I.xxx, 285-7.

[24] *Hadr.* 81 equals *Gel.* 285.

scrutiny masses on the third, fourth and fifth Sundays in Lent are given by the Gelasian.[25] Between 560 and 650, as we have seen, the number of these scrutinies was increased from three to seven, and they were moved from Sundays to weekdays. The lessons originally used at mass on the three scrutiny Sundays[26] were now used on the third Friday, the fourth Wednesday and the fourth Friday, and in the Roman Missal they remained on these days till 1970. The new *ordo* is seen in *Ordo Romanus* XI.[27] Each scrutiny comprises exsufflation, blowing upon the candidate's face,[28] imposition of the hand with exorcism to cast out the demons, and imposition of salt on the candidate's tongue. The *ordo* begins with the *denuntiatio*, or announcment of the first scrutiny, and this scrutiny takes place on Monday after the third Sunday in Lent, the same day as in the later stratum of *Gelasianum*, but three hours earlier, namely at 9 a.m.[29] The arrangements for inscribing their names on a list, and segregating boys from girls, are the same as in *Gelasianum*.[30] The priest signs each with his thumb on the forehead[31] and lays his hand on their heads.[32] The names of the godparents are recited in the mass which follows at *Memento, Domine*.[33] At *Hanc igitur* the names of the candidates are recited.[34] At the end of the mass the priest announces the second scrutiny, which is held on Saturday in the third week.[35] At mass on that day the ceremonies performed at the first scrutiny on Monday are repeated.[36] At the conclusion of this scrutiny the day and place of the third scrutiny are published by the priest. The day is not here specified, but it is a weekday in the fourth week of Lent.[37] Procedure at the third scrutiny is identical with that at the first two.[38] This scrutiny,

---

[25] Third Sunday, first scrutiny, *Gel.*I.xxvi, 193-9; fourth Sunday, second scrutiny, *Gel.*I.xxvii, 225-8; Fifth Sunday, third scrutiny, *Gel.*I.xxviii, 254-7.

[26] John IV.6-32; IX.1-38; XI.1-45; Num. XXIX.1-13; Is.I.16-19; II Kings XVII.17-24.

[27] The first scrutiny is described in paragraphs 38 ff., with the scrutiny mass; the second scrutiny in 38; the third in 40, the fourth in 77, the fifth in 79, the sixth in 80; the seventh in 82 ff.

[28] *Ep. ad sen.*, 3.

[29] *Ordo* XI.1.

[30] *Ibid.* 2.

[31] *Ibid.* 3.

[32] *Ibid.* 4.

[33] *Ibid.* 34.

[34] *Ibid.* 35.

[35] *Ibid.* 37.

[36] *Ibid.* 38.

[37] *Ibid.* 40.

[38] *Ibid.* 41.

however, has the *traditio euangeliorum*.[39] The *traditio symboli* takes place at the same time.[40] The *traditio dominicae orationis* immediately follows.[41] At the end of this scrutiny[42] the priest announces the fourth scrutiny, to be held in the course of the fifth week.[43] The fifth scrutiny is then announced and it takes place later in the fifth week.[44] It is stated[45] to be the same as scrutinies one, two and four. The sixth scrutiny is then announced.[46] It takes place on a day to be announced in Holy Week. The seventh and final scrutiny is held on Easter Eve at 9 a.m. the priest begins by making the sign of the cross on the foreheads of the candidates.[47] The *Effeta* ceremony is then carried out, the priest touching the ears and nostrils of the candidates with spittle.[48] The Creed is then said[49] and after a blessing, the candidates are dismissed.[50]

Instruction

Mention has already been made, in dealing with the scrutinies, of the instruction given to the candidates during the time of their preparation in the course of Lent. Down to the seventh, and even the eighth, century, the rule of secrecy, *disciplina arcani*, was maintained, long after the dangers of persecution had passed. The candidates were admitted to the early part of the mass, and heard the lessons and the sermon, and on scrutiny days the instruction was specially designed for them. But they were sent out of the church before the Prayer of the Faithful (*oratio fidelium*), and so their first communion, after their baptism and confirmation, was also the first time that they heard mass, and they had received absolutely no instruction about it. This was generally imparted to them in lectures by the bishop delivered daily at mass during Easter Week. Every day the neophytes came to mass, still wearing the white robes which they had assumed on emerging from the baptismal font on Easter Eve. The day on which they last wore them,

[39] *Ibid*. 42-60.
[40] *Ibid*. 61-8.
[41] *Ibid*. 69-71.
[42] *Ibid*. 75.
[43] *Ibid*. 76-7.
[44] *Ibid*. 78.
[45] *Ibid*. 79.
[46] *Ibid*. 80.
[47] *Ibid*. 84.
[48] *Ibid*. 85.
[49] *Ibid*. 86.
[50] *Ibid*. 87-8.

Easter Saturday, came to be entitled 'the Saturday when the white garments were laid aside', *Sabbatum in albis depositis*. Examples of the instruction on the eucharist thus imparted in Easter Week may be seen in the *Mystagogical Catecheses* of Cyril of Jerusalem, the *De sacramentis* and *De mysteriis* of Ambrose of Milan, and the *Catecheses* of John Chrysostom and Theodore of Mopsuestia at Antioch in West Syria, and possibly some of the (Syriac) Homilies of Narsai may have been connected with this usage, though he was a priest and not a bishop.

It has been noted in the last section that the pre-Paschal instruction was centred on the exposition of the Gospels, the Creed, and the Lord's Prayer. Instruction is mentioned in the *Apostolic Tradition*[51] but is not there described in detail. The same may be said of John the Deacon's *Epistle to Senarius*.[52] From the early stratum of the *Gelasianum* in the middle of the sixth century to the *Hadrianum* in the eighth, the pattern of the instruction is fixed in its main outline, in spite of the change which took place during this period from three scrutinies to seven. In *Ordo* XI, the tradition of the four gospels takes place at the third scrutiny, which is held on a day in the fourth week of Lent which is announced at the second scrutiny on the Saturday in the third week.[53] The candidates, with their sponsors, come early to the church and the deacon calls out 'Let the catechumens stand forth'.[54] The acolyte then calls them out by name in order, and the scrutiny is performed in the same manner as on the two first occasions in the previous week.[55] Then the two lessons for the opening of the ears are read.[56] These two lessons are Isaiah LV.2-7, followed by the Responsory *Venite, filii*, and Colossians III.9, followed by the Responsory *Beata gens*.[57] Thereupon four deacons, preceded by lighted tapers and incense, enter from the sacristy, each bearing a copy of one of the four gospels, and they lay the four books on the four corners of the altar.[58] First of all, the priest gives an explanation of what a gospel is, why there are four gospels, and what is the meaning of the symbols of the four evangelists given in Ezekiel I.10.[59] The first deacon then carries the gospel of St Matthew from the

---

[51] *Apostolic Tradition*, ch. 20, ed. Dix, p. 30; ed. Botte, p. 42.
[52] Chs. 3 and 4, ed. Wilmart, *Analecta Reginensia*, pp. 171-3.
[53] *Ordo* XI.40.
[54] *Ibid.*: 'catechumeni procedant'.
[55] *Ibid.* 51.
[56] *Ibid.*: 'in aurium apertione'.
[57] *Ibid.* 43.
[58] *Ibid.* 44.
[59] *Ibid.* 45.

altar to the *ambo*, preceded by two candles and incense, and reads the opening passage of Matthew.[60] When this has been read, the subdeacon carries the gospelbook of Matthew back to the sacristy on a linen cloth.[61] The priest then expounds Matthew's gospel.[62] The same procedure is followed in the case of the other three evangelists.[63] The tradition of the gospels is later than the other two traditions because it replaced for infants the earlier form of instruction given to adults. For this reason it dos not appear in Africa in Augustine's time, when the majority of candidates were adults.

The second tradition is that of the Creed. There is a prefatory explanation by the priest,[64] and then an acolyte takes hold of one of the male candidates, and holds him in his left arm before the priest, who says, 'In what language do they confess our Lord Jesus Christ?' The acolyte, on behalf of the boys to be baptized, says, 'In Greek', and then recites the Creed in Greek.[65] The priest then repeats the question towards the female candidates,[66] and the acolyte answers similarly on their behalf. Another acolyte takes another boy in his left arm; the priest asks the same question, and this time the answer is 'In Latin'. The Creed is then repeated in Latin, and the procedure is reiterated for a girl.[67] The priest then gives an exposition of the Creed[68] of which the text is given. There was a change from the Apostles' to the Nicene Creed between 500 and 550.[69] The fact that in *Ordo* XI the tradition of the Creed has to be done in both Greek and Latin shows that it is within the Byzantine period, when both the languages were used by the faithful of the Church of Rome, that is between about 550 and about 750. In fact the date of the *Ordo* is about 650, the middle of this period.

The third tradition is that of the Lord's Prayer. The priest introduces it, and reads the text of the Prayer, a phrase at a time, interspersed with brief explanations.[70] At the end of all this instruction, the catechumens are dismissed, and the parents carry them out of the church, and leave

[60] Matt. I.1-22; *Ordo* XI.48.
[61] *Ordo* XI.49.
[62] *Ibid*. 50.
[63] *Ibid*. 51-60. The openings of the other three gospels are: Mark I.1-8; Luke I.1-17; John I.1-14.
[64] *Ordo* XI.61.
[65] *Ibid*. 62.
[66] *Ibid*. 63.
[67] *Ibid*. 64-6.
[68] *Ibid*. 67.
[69] *Gel*. I.xxxv, 312-14.
[70] *Ordo* XI.69.

them nearby in custody while they themselves return to hear the rest of mass.[71] The Old Gelasian describes a very similar tradition of the Gospels, the Creed, and the Lord's Prayer,[72] with rubrics similar to the descriptions in *Ordo* XI, the texts of the traditions, and the bases of the faith in very similar terms. The traditions of the Creed and the Lord's Prayer are attested by Augustine in Africa a hundred and fifty years before the date of the Old Gelasian.[73]

The Imposition of Hands and the Blessing

These acts are mentioned as early as the *Apostolic Tradition*, but Hippolytus does not state who performs them.[74] This is also the case with the Epistle of John the Deacon nearly three hundred years later.[75] Both in the Old Gelasian[76] and in *Ordo* XI,[77] hands are laid on the candidates by the acolytes, and then by the priest. The prayer used by the priest is the same in each case, *Aeternam ac iustissimam*, etc.

The Salt

There is no mention of this among the preliminaries described in the *Apostolic Tradition* but it was a regular practice at Rome and in Africa, and finds a place in all our sources other than Hippolytus.[78] The Gelasian has an exorcism by which the salt is exorcised and blessed,[79] a form for the imposition of the salt in the candidate's mouth,[80] and a prayer after the giving of the salt.[81] *Hadrianum*[82] has the form for blessing the salt, and so has *Ordo* XI.[83]

---

[71] *Ibid.* 73-4.
[72] *Gel.* I.xxxv-xxxvi.
[73] Aug. *Serm.* LVIII.
[74] *Ap. Trad.* ch. 20, ed. Dix, p. 30; ed. Botte, p. 42.
[75] *Ep. ad Sen.* 3.
[76] *Gel.* I.xxxiii, 291-8.
[77] *Ordo* XI.4, 18 ff.
[78] For example, John the Deacon, *Ep. ad Sen.* 3: 'accipit etiam catechumenus benedictum sal in quo signatur, quia, sicut omnis caro sale condita seruatur, ita sale spientiae et praedicationis uerbi Dei mens fluctibus saeculi madida et fluxa conditur, ut ad soliditatem stabilitatis atque permansionis digesto paenitus corruptionis humore diuini salis suauitate perueniat'.
[79] I.xxxi, 288.
[80] I.xxi, 289.
[81] I.xxi, 290.
[82] *Hadrianum*, 80.
[83] *Ordo* XI, 5 ff.

Blessing of the Oils

The Sahidic, Arabic and Ethiopic versions of the *Apostolic Tradition* mention the blessing of the oils.[84] These are described as the oil of exorcism and the oil of thanksgiving, and the former seems to be the pure olive oil used for the exorcism preliminary to baptism, and the latter a fragrant chrism, a mixture of oil and balsam used for the bestowal of the gift of the Spirit. In the *Apostolic Tradition* this blessing is mentioned at the beginning of the actual rite, but in all other Roman sources it comes at the end of the other preliminaries, and was carried out at the end of the chrismal mass on the morning of Maundy Thursday.[85] The Gelasian and Gregorian sacramentaries provide the prayers for the chrismal mass and for the exorcism and blessing of the oils which are performed during that mass. The *Apostolic Tradition* does not give the form, but states that the bishop gives thanks over the oil of exorcism and the oil of thanksgiving, and then hands them to the two deacons, who stand on either side of the priest, the deacon holding the oil of exorcism on the priest's left, and the one with the oil of thanksgiving on his right.

THE BAPTISM PROPER

The Effeta Ceremony

Whether in the course of the final scrutiny on the morning of Holy Saturday, or after the beginning of the baptismal rite on the night of Saturday to Sunday at Easter, the ceremony of the opening of the ears (*apertio aurium*, or *effeta*) was carried out. The basic ceremony was the touching of the ears and nostrils of the candidate, accompanied by the word *effeta*, that is 'Be opened', derived from the gospel account of the healing by our Lord of the deaf and dumb man.[86] It appears from Ambrose that the Marcan passage was read as a lesson before the candidates were touched.[87] In the *Apostolic Tradition* the celebrant,

---

[84] *Apostolic Tradition*, c. 21.

[85] See *Gel*. I.xi, 375-90 and *Hadr*. 78.

[86] Mark VII.32-7 and parallels.

[87] *De mysteriis* iii.4: 'quod uobis significauimus cum apertionis celebrantes mysterium diceremus, *Effeta*, quod est, adaperire, ut uenturus unusquisque ad gratiam quid interrogaretur cognosceret, quid responderet meminisse deberet. hoc mysterium celebrauit Christus in euangelio, sicut legimus cum mutum curaret et surdum.'

having concluded exorcisms, blows upon the candidate, and signs his forehead, nostrils and ears, but it is not stated that this is done with oil or spittle, as in some later sources, and it may be that it is done with the dry finger.[88] The same may be said of the references by Ambrose.[89] About 500 John the Deacon states that the candidates were touched with the oil of sanctification.[90] Fifty years later the earliest stratum of the Gelasian Sacramentary shows that oil had given way to spittle, in accordance with the Lord's action in healing the deaf and dumb man.[91] Spittle is specified also an hundred years later in *Ordo* XI.[92] Finally, the *Hadrianum* is obscure as to the material used in touching the organs of sense, though it speaks of an unction with oil on the shoulders and breast.[93]

The Blessing of the Water

The blessing of the water is always an important element in the initiation rite, and is reserved to the bishop when he is present.[94] The Old Gelasian gives the full form of the prayers for accomplishing this blessing.[95] The ceremony is described in more detail in *Ordo* XI.[96] The pope leaves the church in procession, with lights and incense, and comes to the baptistery, which is a separate building. The litany is sung in this procession, as is also prescribed by the Old Gelasian.[97] The singing ceases when all have arrived at the font; and the bishop then

---

[88] *Ap. Trad.* ch. 20, ed. Dix, p. 32; ed. Botte, p. 42: 'And when he has finished exorcizing, let him breathe on (their faces) and seal their foreheads and ears and noses, and (then) let him raise them up.'

[89] Cf. *De mysteriis*, quoted above, n. 87, and *De sacramentis* I.i.2: 'quae mysteria celebrata sunt apertionis, quando tibi aures tetigit sacerdos et nares' (CSEL LXXIII, 15).

[90] *Ep. ad Sen.* 4,5: 'tanguntur sanctificationis oleo aures eorum, tanguntur et nares'.

[91] *Gel.* I, ed. Mohlberg, 419-20. In § 420 we read the rubric: 'Inde tanges ei nares et aures de sputo, et dicis ei ad aurem: *Effeta*, quod est, Adaperire, in odorem suauitatis. Tu autem effugare, diabole, adpropinquauit enim iudicium Dei.'

[92] *Ordo* XI.85.

[93] *Hadr.* 83: 'post hoc tangit singulis nares et aures, et dicit eis: *Effeta*. Postea tangit de oleo sancto scapulas et pectus, et dicit. . .' (there follow the questions concerning renunciation).

[94] *Ap. Trad.* ch. 21 (SAE): prayer is first made over the water. Cf. Ambrose, *De mysteriis* 20; Tertullian, *De baptismo* 4: the waters have been in a manner imbued with medicinal virtue through the intervention of the angel.

[95] *Gel.* I.xliv, 444-8. And the use of the second person singular in the rubrics shows this section to belong to the earliest stratum, from the mid sixth century, e.g., 'Inde descendis cum laetania ad fontes . . .'

[96] *Ordo* XI.90-5.

[97] *Gel.* I. xliv, 444.

begins the blessing of the water saying, 'The Lord be with you. And with thy spirit. Let us pray. Almighty and everlasting God', etc. After the prayer, he pours oil into the font from a golden vessel. This is the chrism or fragrant oil, and is poured in the form of a cross; and he mingles the chrism into the water with his hand, and sprinkles the mixture over all the baptistery, and the people who stand by. After this, and before any candidates are baptized, the people have liberty to abstract from the font water for sprinkling at home upon their fruits or in their fields and vineyards. *Hadrianum* 85 also has the form for blessing the water.

Renunciation and First Unction

After the water has been blessed, and before the baptism, the candidates at Rome were questioned whether they renounced evil, and were given the first of the three unctions which characterized the Roman rite in the early centuries. This unction was performed by the priest with the oil of exorcism, and was apotropaic in character, designed, that is, to expel demons from the candidate, and to prepare him for reception into the Church by baptism. The two ceremonies, which are not mentioned in Justin's account, make their first appearance at Rome in the *Apostolic Tradition* of Hippolytus.[98] The act of renunciation is mentioned by Tertullian.[99] Tertullian does not mention this first unction, but it is noted by Ambrose at Milan. However, he places the unction first and the renunciation second. But Ambrose's order is not to be relied on.[100] The placing of unction before renunciation may not have any significance.[101] John the Deacon speaks of the renunciation, and the unction with oil of consecration, an unusual term. Elsewhere it is oil of exorcism which is used for this purpose.[102] In the Gelasian Sacramentary, when the scrutinies were increased from

---

[98] *Ap. Trad.* ch. 21 (SAE): 'And when the priest takes hold of each one of those who are to be baptized, let him bid him to renounce saying, I renounce thee, Satan, and all thy service and all thy works. And when he has said this, let him anoint him with the oil of exorcism, saying, Let all evil spirits depart far from thee.'

[99] *De spectaculis* 4; *De corona* 3.

[100] *De sacramentis* II.iv.12: 'etsi non ordinem tenemus . . .'

[101] Unction: *De sacramentis* I.4: 'uenimus ad fontem, ingressus es, unctus es'. Renunciation: *ibid.* I.5: 'quando te interrogauit: "Abrenuntias diabolo et operibus eius?" quid respondisti? "Abrenuntio." "Abrenuntias saeculo et uoluptatibus eius?" quid respondisti? "Abrenuntio".' The renunciation is mentioned also in *De mysteriis*, 5.

[102] *Ep. ad Sen.* 6: 'dehinc pectus eorum oleo consecrationis perunguitur, in quo est sedes et habitaculum cordis, ut intellegant firma se conscientia et puro corde debere promittere quod iam relicto diabolo christi mandata secrantur.'

three to seven, the renunciations were attached to the seventh and final scrutiny, which takes place in the forenoon of Holy Saturday.[103] The unction accompanies the renunciation.[104] *Ordo* XI does not mention renunciations or this preliminary unction in the baptismal rite, doubtless because it is not part of the rite of the Easter Vigil, but, as in the Gelasian, belongs to Saturday morning, and to the seventh scrutiny. *Hadrianum* has the renunciations in terms identical with the Gelasian Sacramentary.[105]

The Baptism

In all the sources the candidates are now baptized in the water. The sources vary slightly in the details which they give, but are agreed upon the fundamentals. The candidates go into the font naked, are asked the threefold question of belief, based upon the Apostles' Creed. Each is asked whether be believes in the Father, and he is then immersed in the water the first time. Then he is asked whether he believes in the Son, and is immersed a second time. And so for the third time, after professing his belief in the Holy Ghost in answer to the third question. The declaratory form, 'I baptize thee in the Name of the Father, and of the Son, and of the Holy Ghost' does not make an appearance until two or three centuries after St Gregory, and so does not concern us here. There is greater agreement on this central ceremony among our pre-Gregorian sources than in most other parts of the rite. Justin speaks of the washing in the threefold Name.[106] Hippolytus gives much more detail, but most of ch. 21, which treats of baptism, is missing from the Latin Verona palimpsest, and we are dependent mainly on the Sahidic (S), and on the Arabic (A) and Ethiopic (E), which derive from it. The Sahidic of this chapter is not complete, and a long lacuna in the middle of it has to be supplied from the Bohairic version (B), which was made as recently as 1804. A little evidence is also available from the Syriac *Testamentum Domini* (T).[107] The deficiency of some of the

---

[103] *Gel.* I.xlii, 421-4.

[104] *Ibid.* 421: 'tangis ei pectus et inter scapulas de oleo exorcizato, et uocato nomine singulis dicis: "Abrenuntias satanae?" ', etc.

[105] *Hadrianum*, 83: 'post hoc tangit singulis nares et aures, et dicit eis, *Effeta*. postea tangit de oleo sancto scapulas et pectus et dicit, "Abrenuntias Satanae?" et respondet: "Abrenuntio." "Et omnibus operibus eius?" respondit "Abrenuntio". "Et omnibus pompis eius?" respondit "Abrenuntio".'

[106] *Apol.*, ch. 61.

[107] See Botte, *La tradition apostolique*, pp. 44-59.

sources in this chapter is regrettable, but the main outlines are clear
enough to show that the rite of *Apostolic Tradition* is in line with all that
we know of the Roman baptismal tradition before Gregory. The deacon
hands the candidate over to the priest or the bishop, who stands by the
water and is to be the minister of baptism. TSAE says that the deacon
takes him into the water; L attests the threefold question of faith which
is put to him,[108] and L says that he is then immersed thrice by the
deacon. The text of L is much clearer at this point than that of the
Coptic, and has therefore been followed in this account. Tertullian attests
the triple interrogation concerning faith, and the triple immersion.[109] The
cermony is the same at Milan as in Rome and Africa.[110] The questions are
also mentioned in *De mysteriis*, ch. 28.[111] John the Deacon at Rome
mentions the threefold immersion.[112] The traditional early Roman rite is
seen clearly in the Old Gelasian.[113] Hippolytus states that the deacons
baptize the candidates, and stand with them in the water, while the bishop
presides on the edge of the font. *Ordo* XI, however, prescribes that the
bishop himself baptize the first two or three candidates, or as many as he
wishes, and that the rest shall be baptized by the deacons.[114]

The Second Unction

Justin says nothing of this unction nor of the third unction which
occurs at the end of the rite. No doubt this is due to his observance of
the *disciplina arcani*. He may have thought that pagan readers would be
misled by references to anointing, and in the case of the final anointing,
with its reference to the Holy Spirit, into supposing that Christianity
was a disreputable mystery religion. Over two hundred years later,

---

[108] See Botte, *ibid.*, pp. 48-50.

[109] *Aduersus Praxeam*, 26; *De spectaculis*, 4; *De corona*, 3.

[110] Ambrose, *De sacramentis* II.vii.20 (CSEL LXXIII, 34).

[111] *Ibid.* p. 100.

[112] *Ep. ad Sen.* 6: 'in quo sacramento baptizatus trina demersione perficitur, et recte.
Nam qui in nomine Trinitatis baptizandus accedit, ipsam utique Trinitatem trina debet
mersione signari, et illius se agnoscere beneficiis debitorem qui tertia pro eo die
resurrexit a mortuis.'

[113] *Gel.* I.xliv, 449: 'inde benedicto fonte baptizas unumquemque in ordine suo sub has
interrogationes: "Credis in Deum Patrem omnipotentem?" Respondit: "Credo".
"Credis et in Iesum Christum Filium eius unicum Dominum nostrum natum et passum?"
Respondit: "Credo". "Credis et in Spiritum sanctum, sanctam aecclesiam, remissionem
peccatorum, carnis resurrectionem?" Respondit: "Credo". Deinde per singulas uices
mergis eum tertio in aqua.'

[114] *Ordo* XI.96: 'Deinde pontifex baptizat unum aut duos uel quantos ei placuerit de ipsis
infantibus, caeterique a diacono cui ipse iusserit baptizantur.'

Ambrose is still very reticent about the unction and the gift of the Spirit. In the rest of the Roman tradition down to the present day, the purpose and the position of the second anointing have remained constant. Justin simply says that the candidates are led from the bath to those whom we call brethren.[115] This must refer to their being brought back from the private ceremonies in the baptistery to the church for their confirmation in the presence of the whole assembly of the faithful, and their sharing in the general communion which concluded the rites of initiation. Hippolytus tells us that the candidates came out of the water after the baptism,[116] and were anointed by the priest with the oil of thanksgiving. Like the third unction, this anointing is with chrism, fragrant balsam or ointment, not the plain olive oil used in the preliminary anointing before the washing. It was not, like the first, administered all over the body, nor on the forehead, like the third, but on the crown of the head (*in uertice*[117] or *in cerebro*).[118] The first and second unctions are administered by the priest, but in all sources the third is reserved to the bishop, and this is the rite of confirmation, conferring the indwelling gift of the Holy Ghost. Hippolytus gives us the form used by the priest for this rite: 'Ungueo te oleo sancto in nomine Iesu Christi'.[119] The candidates then dress, and return to the church. In John the Deacon's account, they dress after emerging from the bath and before having their heads anointed, and this would have been a practical possibility, but it does not seem possible to know what the practice was at any particular time, or whether it remained constant. Tertullian speaks of this anointing,[120] and so apparently does Cyprian,[121] but it is not possible to be quite sure whether this reference is to the post-baptismal unction by the priest, or to the episcopal confirmation unction. Ambrose mentions the second unction.[122] From *De mysteriis* it is clear that the unction was administered on the head, *supra caput*, and here Ambrose quotes the form: 'Deus, Pater omnipotens, qui te regenerauit ex aqua et Spiritu, concessitque tibi peccata tua, ipse te unguet in uitam aeternam.' The second unction was not, like the third, intended to

---

[115] *Apol.*, ch. 65.
[116] *Ap. Trad.*, ch. 21 (LBAE).
[117] *Ordo* XI.97.
[118] *Gel.* I.xliv, 449-50.
[119] *Ap. Trad.* (LBAE).
[120] *De baptismo*, 7.
[121] *Ep.* LXX.2 (CSEL III, 768).
[122] *De sacramentis* II.vii.24 – III.1 (CSEL LXXIII, 36-7); *De mysteriis* 29-30 (*ibid.* p. 101).

bestow the Holy Spirit, but it is connected with the candidate becoming a member of the royal priesthood of the Church, which is the holy people of God.[123] In the Old Testament kings and priests were anointed upon the head.[124] Aaron was anointed on his head as a priest so abundantly that the oil invaded his person, and ran down to Aaron's beard, even to the skirts of his clothing (Ps. CXXXIII.2). After this unction, according to Ambrose, as according to Hippolytus, the candidate assumed white robes.[125] John the Deacon explicitly connects this anointing with the royal priesthood.[126] After this he mentions the white garment, but here, as we noted earlier, the garment is mentioned before the oil. The Old Gelasian provides for this unction[127] and appoints a collect to be said at this point. *Hadrianum* has the following rubric, 'et linit eum presbyter de chrismate in cerebro',[128] and provides a collect, which is almost identical with that of *Gelasianum*.[129] In *Ordo XI*, the candidate leaves the water, and is then anointed by a priest with chrism *in uertice*, and returns to church, where the pope gives each candidate a baptismal robe and outer garment, presumably to keep him warm during the night in an unheated church, and a linen head-covering to preserve the oil, and ten shekels.[130] It does not seem to be known what is the purpose of giving money, but the suggestion has been made that it was to encourage the presentation of children for baptism. Ambrose states[131] that the feet of the candidates are washed by the bishop. This ceremony is mentioned by Augustine,[132] but does not occur elsewhere in our sources. Ambrose acknowledges that this ceremony is not practised at Rome, but makes a sort of apology for it by recalling that St Peter, the first bishop of Rome, had his feet washed by the Lord himself. Ambrose therefore practised this ceremony at Milan, and no doubt it was an established baptismal custom there, which he

---

[123] Cf. I. Pet. II.9. The terms *sacerdotium* and *regnum* occur in Ambrose, *De sacramentis* IV.3 (CSEL LXXIII, 47): 'unguitur in sacerdotium, unguitur in regnum.' They also occur together in John the Deacon, *Ep. ad Sen.*, 6.

[124] For example, Saul and David, I Sam. X.1; I Sam. XVI.2.

[125] *De sacramentis* IV.v. 6; *De mysteriis*, 34: 'accepisti post haec uestimenta candida' (CSEL LXXIII, 102).

[126] *Ep. ad Sen.* 6: 'ut intellegat baptizatus regnum in se ac sacerdotale conuenisse mysterium.'

[127] *Gel.* I.xliv, 449: 'signatur a presbytero in cerebro de chrismate'.

[128] *Hadrianum*, 85.

[129] *Gel.* I.xliv, 449.

[130] *Ordo* XI.97-9: 'stola, casula, et chrismale, et decem siclos'.

[131] *De sacramentis* III. 4-7; *De mysteriis*, 31-4.

[132] Augustine, *Ep.* LV.xviii.33.

inherited when he became bishop on a sudden, and which he did not care to suppress in order to come into line with Roman practice. It is not difficult to understand that Ambrose should have been prepared to retain a non-Roman custom which he considered edifying, but it is astonishing that he would have attributed to the foot-washing a quasi-sacramental significance, declaring that while the bath washes away actual sin, the foot-washing purges away original sin. The logical conclusion of this theory would be that persons who had the misfortune to be baptized at Rome, like his own sister Marcellina, were still encumbered with original sin. The fact that he does so illustrates the limitations of this former civil servant as a theologian.

Confirmation

When all have returned to the church in their white robes, and joined the congregation of the faithful, who in the meantime have apparently been occupied with lessons and chants, there is conferred upon the neophytes the third unction with chrism on the forehead for the bestowal of the Holy Ghost, which later came to be called confirmation, though we shall not find the name in our documents. Nothing is said of it by Justin, but careful details are given by Hippolytus, including the matter and form. The candidates are placed in order before the bishop, who stands facing them with hands outstretched towards them for the gift of the Holy Ghost. The form is:

Domine Deus, qui dignos fecisti eos remissionem mereri peccatorum, per lauacrum regenerationis Spiritus sancti, immitte in eos tuam gratiam, ut tibi seruiant secundum voluntatem tuam, quoniam tibi est gloria, Patri et Filio cum Spiritu sancto in sancta ecclesia, et nunc et in saecula saeculorum. Amen.

The fact that this prayer is in the plural, by contrast with the succeeding formula for the unction of each candidate, which is in the singular, proves that *inponere manus* does not necessarily mean a tactual imposition of the hand upon each candidate, but covers a blessing conveyed to them all at once by extending the hands towards them and over them. The chrismation, of course, has to be administered to each candidate separately. The bishop then pours some oil of thanksgiving on to his hand, and transfers it to the head of the candidate, saying, 'Ungueo te sancto oleo in Domino Patre omnipotente et Christo Iesu et Spiritu sancto.' He then signs him on the forehead and kisses him, saying, 'The Lord be with you'. This account follows the text of L. The version in BAE differs slightly, and S is deficient at this point. Tertullian mentions no unction, but says that the hand is laid on the candidates in blessing and in invocation of the Spirit,[133] and Cyprian speaks of imposition of hands and prayer, but not of unction.[134] This *manus impositio* in Tertullian may, as we have seen, imply a collective blessing over all the candidates at once. Ambrose is nearly as reticent as Justin about unction, but doubtless it was in his rite at Milan. He has passing references to the kiss[135] and consignation.[136] John the Deacon has a reference to consignation, and to an episcopal blessing, but no detail.[137] The Gelasian has the prayer by the bishop for the conferring of the Holy Spirit.[138] After this the Gelasian has the consignation and the *Pax*.[139] The collect in *Hadrianum* 86, *Oratio ad infantes consignandos*, which is substantially the same as that in Gelasianum, shows the persistence of the confirmation form in Roman liturgy.[140] In *Ordo* XI the bishop pronounces over the candidates the prayer for the sevenfold gifts of the Spirit, and then consigns each of them and gives each the *Pax*, to which the candidate replies *Amen*.[141]

The Mass

Evidence for the form of baptismal mass may be grouped under several headings.

(i) *The Prayer of the Faithful*. When all the candidates have been confirmed, the bishop begins the mass of the day, whether it be of Easter Day or Whitsun Day. Our two earliest sources, and they alone,

---

[133] *De baptismo*, 8.

[134] *Ep.* LXXIII.9.

[135] *De sacramentis* V.5.

[136] *Ibid.* VI.6.

[137] *Ep. ad Sen.* 14, ed. Wilmart, *Analecta Reginensia*, p. 178.

[138] *Gel.* I.xliv, 450: 'Deus omnipotens, Pater Domini nostri Iesu Christi, qui regenerasti famulos tuos ex aqua et Spiritu sancto, quique dedisti eis remissionem omnium peccatorum, tu, Domine, inmitte in eos Spiritum sanctum tuum paraclitum et da eis spiritum sapientiae, et intellectus, spiritum consilii et fortitudinis, spiritum scientiae et pietatis, adimple eos spiritu timoris Dei: In nomine Domini nostri Iesu Christi, cum quo uiuis et regnas Deus semper cum Spiritu sancto per omnia saecula saeculorum. Amen.'

[139] *Ibid.* 451-2: 'Postea signat eos in fronte de crismate dicens: Signum Christi in uitam aeternam. Respondit: Amen. Pax tecum. Respondit: Et cum spiritu tuo.'

[140] Ed. Lietzmann, *Das Sacramentarium Gregorianum*, p. 54.

[141] *Ordo* XI.100-1: 'Induti uero ordinantur per ordinem, sicut scripti sunt, in circuitu, et dat orationem pontifex super eos, confirmans eos cum inuocatione septiformis gratiae Spiritus sancti. Oratione expleta, facit crucem cum pollice et crisma in singulorum frontibus, ita dicendo: In nomine Patris et Filii et Spiritus sancti. Pax tibi. et respondent, Amen.'

state that the first item of this mass, before the Offertory, is the prayer of the faithful. The neophytes have, during their catechumenate, been excluded from the church before this prayer began, and now they take part in it for the first time.[142] Justin's is the first reference to this general intercession of the faithful.[143]

(ii) *The Offertory*. Our only source explicitly to mention the Offertory in the baptismal mass is Hippolytus, who notes that it is now brought to the bishop by the deacons.[144]

(iii) *The Blessing of the Elements*. The bishop at this point blesses bread, wine, milk and honey.[145] It is not clear whether the *Apostolic Tradition* makes any distinction between the bread and wine mingled with water for the eucharist, and the blessing of the milk and honey, which are to be given to the neophytes at the time of their first communion, in token that they have now become part of the Church, and inherited the land of promise, which the Old Testament describes as flowing with milk and honey.

(iv) *The Canon*. The Canon had on this occasion proper clauses for *Communicantes* and *Hanc igitur oblationem*, the text of which is given in the Old Gelasian[146] and *Hadrianum* in almost identical terms, and these forms have continued till the present time in the Roman Missal.

(v) *The Fraction*. Only Hippolytus mentions this[147] in describing the baptismal mass.

(vi) *The Communion*. Hippolytus says that the bishop administers the bread, while the chalice is administered by priests or deacons.[148]

(vii) *Administration of milk and honey*. It is clear that these are given to the neophytes only, and at the time of their reception of the communion.[149] Tertullian also mentions the tasting of milk and honey

---

[142] See Willis, *Essays in Early Roman Liturgy*, pp. 3-10.

[143] Justin, *Apol*, ch. 65; cf. Hippolytus, *Ap. Trad.* ch. 21 (LBAE): 'et iam simul cum omni populo orent'.

[144] *Ap. Trad.*, ch. 21 (LBAE).

[145] *Ibid*.

[146] *Gel*. I, 459-60; *Hadr*. 87.

[147] *Ap. Trad.* ch. 21 (LSAE): 'cum ergo episcopus fregit panem, det partem ex eo singulis . . .'

[148] *Ibid*.

[149] *Ibid*. It is clear from L that milk and honey are mixed in one chalice, but SAE, at a later point in the text, suggest two separate chalices for milk and honey.

after baptism.[150] Ambrose is reticent about the matter, as he is on several points of the baptismal rites, but in *De sacramentis* he has an apt quotation from the Song of Songs (*Cant.* V.1) which makes it certain that the rite of Milan bestowed milk and honey on the neophytes.[151] This quotation shows that the bestowal of milk and honey took place at the same time as the communion, and John the Deacon seems to imply that an additional chalice containing a mixture of milk and honey was given to the neophytes, and not that milk and honey were administered separately from two chalices.[152] The neophytes came with their sponsors to mass for seven days, till the Saturday of Easter Week, which later acquired the name of *Sabbatum in albis depositis* since they wore their white baptismal robes each day until then. It was usual in many places for the bishop to give instructions daily to the neophytes at this mass, and the *Mystagogical Catecheses* of Cyril at Jerusalem, the *De sacramentis* and *De mysteriis* of Ambrose at Milan, and sermons of Augustine in Africa, are examples of such catechesis.[153]

---

[150] *De corona*, 3.

[151] *De sacramentis* V.15 (CSEL LXXIII, 64): 'manducaui panem meum cum melle meo; bibi uinum meum cum lacte meo'.

[152] *Ep. ad Sen*. 12, ed. Wilmart, p. 177: '. . . in . . . calicem lac mittatur et mel . . .'

[153] See *Ordo* XI.103.

V

Ordination

Before the end of the first century St Clement of Rome speaks of the bishops as 'those who offer the gifts',[1] and these gifts to which he refers are to be identified with the gifts of bread and wine which the Church offers in the eucharist. In a city church at that time the bishop was the normal celebrant of the eucharist. There appears to exist in Clement's mind a close parallel between this sacrifice of the Church on earth, offered by the bishop, and the offering which Christ the eternal priest offers at the heavenly altar, and that offering consists in himself, whom he gave as an offering for the sins of the world, and now presents at the heavenly altar. Nearly a century later we find Irenaeus in southern Gaul asserting that there is an altar in heaven, to which our earthly prayers and offerings are directed.[2]

So the notion of the Church's sacrifice, which it offers by the agency of its sacred ministers, is present in Roman theology from a very early date; but the earliest full description of the election and ordination of ministers is to be found in the *Apostolic Tradition* of Hippolytus. The original Greek of this treatise may be dated about 215, but, as we have seen, this text has disappeared and the earliest evidence of it which is available is the Latin version in the Verona palimpsest, which can be dated palaeographically to about 420, and will perhaps represent a Greek original of about the end of the fourth century. It is, however, likely, though not susceptible of conclusive demonstration, that the ordination prayers and the details about the ordination ceremonies which the treatise supplies do, in fact, represent Roman practice of the early third century, perhaps of the end of the second. It will appear later in this chapter that some distinctive Roman features of the rite, which are to be found in the

---

[1] Clement I.36 (Corinthians); cf. Hippolytus, *Apostolic Tradition*, ch. 3: '. . . et offerre dona sanctae ecclesiae tuae . . .'
[2] Irenaeus, *Adv. Haer.* IV.18 '. . . est ergo altare in caelis. Illuc enim preces nostrae et oblationes nostrae diriguntur'.

Apostolic Tradition, make their appearance in later Roman documents. Our next detailed information comes from *Ordines Romani* XXXIV and XLA.[3] *Ordo* XXXIV describes the procedure for the election and consecration of a suburbicarian bishop by the pope at Rome, and also ordination of priests and deacons at Rome by the pope, and the *ordo* dates from *c*. 750 at the latest. *Ordo* XLA, which probably dates from the sixth century, is for the consecration of a bishop of Rome by three suburbicarian bishops, but it does not provide for ordinations to the orders of priest and deacon. It was later included in *Liber Diurnus*,[4] a collection of papal legal and liturgical forms of the Roman chancery, going back to the sixth century, and therefore to the period shortly before St Gregory. We have included in our enquiry information about ordination derived from the *Statuta ecclesiae antiqua*.[5] This sixth-century document is not from Rome but comes from southern Gaul, probably from the church of Arles, but inclusion here in a treatment of Roman rites may be justified by the closeness of some of its wording to the earliest Roman authority, the *Apostolic Tradition*, and to later Roman practice. Accordingly the details of these four rites are set out in tabular form (Table III, below, pp. 152-4), and will be discussed in greater detail in this present chapter. The table follows the order of *Ordo* XXXIV as being the fullest description of the early Roman rite. *Ordo* XXXIV treats the three major orders of the ministry, deacons, priests, bishops. *Ordo* XL is limited to the consecration of a pope, and the *Apostolic Tradition* deals with the matter in the reverse order.

ORDINATION OF DEACONS

In *Ordo* XXXIV.4 the mass at the ordination of deacons begins, as usual, with the Introit, but the *Kyrie* is not then said, but is postponed and said as part of the litany which is later recited on behalf of the candidates. The collect follows,[6] and then the Epistle, which is I Tim.

---

[3] The text of these *ordines*, with introductions, will be found respectively in Andrieu III, pp. 536-99 (introduction) and 603-13 (text), and IV, pp. 289-94 (introduction), and 297 (text).

[4] Ed. T. Sickel, *Liber Diurnus Romanorum Pontificum* (Vienna, 1889), pp. 46-7.

[5] Andrieu III, pp. 615-19.

[6] *Ordo* XXXIV.5.

III.8-13, and the gradual. The bishop then begins the ordination by bidding the people to prayer, and all say the litany.[7] At the end of this the bishop pronounces the consecration prayer asking for the outpouring of the Holy Spirit upon the candidates for the diaconate.[8] It is significant that in the early sources, Roman and non-Roman, the word used in this prayer is 'send upon (them) . . . the Holy Spirit': 'Emitte in eos, domine, quaesumus spiritum sanctum . . .'[9] What is envisaged is a creative act of God the Father in pouring forth the Holy Spirit upon the candidates as they come out of the general body of the faithful into the lowest order of the sacred ministry. But when, within the sacred ministry, they are raised from the order of deacons to that of priests, the word 'send' is replaced by the word 'renew': '. . . Innova in visceribus eorum spiritum sanctitatis'.[10] In the ordination of bishops, however, neither of these verbs is used, and in the *Consecratio* prayer there is no explicit mention of the sending or renewal of the Holy Spirit: it is a prayer for the bestowal of the gifts and graces appropriate to the work of a bishop.[11] This distinction appears very early in the Roman rite because although the Latin version of the *Apostolic Tradition* does not express it clearly, yet in the Arabic *Canons of Hippolytus* the words used in the prayer over deacons may be translated 'pour out thy Holy Spirit upon .N.'[12] During the consecration prayer for a deacon the bishop lays his hands upon the candidate's head, and he does this alone, not being joined, as in the ordination of bishops and priests, by other bishops or priests. This, Hippolytus explains, is because the deacon is ordained to service (*ministerium*) and not to a priestly office (*sacerdotium*), and because he is to perform such functions as the bishop may assign to him. The practice of the bishop alone ordaining the deacon has continued ever since, and it is mentioned, in words very close to those used by Hippolytus, in the Gallican *Statuta ecclesiae antiqua*.[13]

[7] *Ibid.* 8.

[8] *Ibid.* 9. Cf. Verona Sacrmentary, 951: '. . . emitte in eos, domine, quaesumus spiritum sanctum . . .'

[9] Cf. Verona 951; *Gel.* 152; *Hadr.* 4, 3/6; and see G. G. Willis, 'The Petition for the Spirit in Roman Ordination Prayers', *Downside Review* XCII (1974), 265-8.

[10] Verona, 954; *Gel.* 145; *Hadr.* 3, 3/6.

[11] Verona, 942; *Gel.* 769; *Hadr.* 2, 3.

[12] *Canons of Hippolytus*, ch. 5, ed. R. Coquin, *Patrologia Orientalis* XXXI (Paris, 1966).

[13] *Apostolic Tradition*, ch. 8, ed. Botte, p. 22: 'In diacono ordinando solus episcopus imponat manus, propterea quia non in sacerdotio ordinatur, sed in ministerio episcopi, ut faciat ea quae ab ipso iubentur'; *Statuta ecclesiae antiqua*, ed. Andrieu III, p. 617:

After the imposition of the bishop's hands the new deacon rises, kisses the bishop and the priests present, and stands at the right of the bishop.[14]

ORDINATION OF PRIESTS

In *Ordo* XXXIV, when a deacon is to be ordained priest, the archdeacon takes him outside the sanctuary rails and removes his dalmatic and replaces it by a chasuble. He then brings him back into the sanctuary and presents him to the bishop.[15] The bishop lays his hands on the candidate as he recites the consecration prayer; and the other priests present join the bishop in laying on their hands.[16] The ceremony of the imposition of the bishop's hands accompanied by the imposition of the priests' hands is constant in all witnesses of the early Roman rite, and has continued ever since. The *Statuta ecclesiae antiqua* provides for it in terms very similar to those of the *Apostolic Tradition*.[17] *Apostolic Tradition* (ch. 7) states that in ordaining priests the bishop expresses himself, 'in accordance with what has already been stated in the ordination of a bishop'.[18] Hippolytus then quotes the prayer said over

'Diaconus cum ordinatur, solus episcopus, qui eum benedicit, manus suas super caput eius ponat, quia non ad sacerdotium, sed ad ministerium consecratur.'

[14] *Ordo* XXXIV.10. The *ordo* says, '. . . ad dexteram episcoporum'. The plural may be a mere slip: V reads *episcopi*.

[15] *Ibid.* 11: 'Si vero voluerit eum consecrare presbyterum, tenens eum archidiaconus ducit foras rugas altaris, exuit eum dalmatica et sic eum induit planeta et ducit iterum ad episcopum.' Andrieu discusses whether the text of this section envisages a man being made priest at the same service as he is made deacon or on a different occasion (III, p. 562).

[16] *Ibid.* 12; cf. *Apostolic Tradition*, ch. 7: 'Cum autem praesbyter ordinatur, imponat manum super caput eius episcopus, contingentibus etiam praesbyteris, et dicat secundum ea quae praedicta sunt, sicut praediximus super episcopum, orans et dicens: Deus et pater domini nostri Iesu Christi, respice super servum tuum istum et inpartire spiritum gratiae et consilii praesbyteris ut adiubet et gubernet plebem tuam in corde mundo, sicuti respexisti super populum electionis tuae et praecepisti Moysi ut elegeret praesbyteros quos replesti de spiritu tuo quod tu donasti famulo tuo. Et nunc, domine, praesta indeficienter conservari in nobis spiritum gratiae tuae et dignos effice ut credentes tibi ministremus in simplicitate cordis, laudantes te per puerum tuum Christum Iesum, per quem tibi gloria et virtus, patri et filio cum spiritu sancto in sancta ecclesia et nunc et in saecula saeculorum. Amen.'

[17] *Statuta ecclesiae antiqua*, ch. 3: 'Presbyter cum ordinatur, episcopo benedicente et manus super caput eius tenente, etiam omnes presbyteri qui praesentes sunt, manus suas iuxta manus episcopi super caput illius teneant.'

[18] That is, in *Apostolic Tradition*, ch. 3.

the priest which was cited above (n. 16). But this is not the same prayer as he cites for the ordination of a bishop in ch. 3, and the words *sicut praecepimus super episcopum* must therefore be interpreted as having the general meaning that the ordaining bishop says over a new priest, as over a new bishop, a prayer for the gift of the Holy Spirit for the office and work of his order, and that this prayer is accompanied by the imposition of the hands of the ordaining bishop. The bishop, having thus ordained him, gives him the kiss of peace, and the new priest takes his place in the ranks of the other priests present.[19] The mass then resumes with the *Alleluia* or Tract, according to the season.[20]

ORDINATION OF BISHOPS

Ordinations of priests and deacons were usually performed at Rome during vigil night masses on the Saturdays in the Ember Weeks, or on Easter night at the vigil mass, or on the Sunday *in Mediana*. These occasions are specified by Pope Gelasius (492-6).[21] Consecrations of bishops were not confined to these days, but it was a very early rule that they should always be performed on Sunday. This was the rule in the West from the time of the *Apostolic Tradition* till about the tenth century, when ordinations of bishops began to be permitted on holy days which were not Sundays. The universality and persistence of this rule suggests that it was a primitive rule, and it seems reasonable to guess that in the *Apostolic Tradition* it is part of the original text and not a fourth-century addition.[22] In our present sources this document states that the rite is performed on Sunday.[23] This is also the case with *Ordo* XXXIV.[24]

---

[19] *Ordo* XXXIV.12: 'Et tunc alia illi dante orationem, consecrat illum presbiterum, dans osculum episcopo vel ceteris sacerdotibus, et stat in ordine presbiterii'.

[20] *Ibid.* 13: 'Et dicitur Alleluia vel tractus et evangelium et quod sequitur, et completa missa ordine suo.'

[21] Gelasius, *Ep.* XV.3: 'Ordinationes vero presbyterorum seu diaconorum non nisi quarti septimi vel decimi mensium ieiuniis, sed et in ingressu quadragesimali atque medianae vespere sabbati noverit celebrandas'. See also Willis, *Essays in Early Roman Liturgy*, p. 79.

[22] On Ember Days, see Willis, *ibid.*, pp. 49-98.

[23] *Apostolic Tradition*, ch. 2: 'conveniet populus una cum praesbyterio et his qui praesentes fuerint episcopi, die dominica'.

[24] *Ordo* XXXIV.32: 'Alia vero die, quod est dominica, procedit domnus apostolicus in ecclesia . . .'

Ordo XXXIV describes the consecration of a suburbicarian bishop by the pope, and is a purely Roman order. It includes the presentation and election of the new bishop, his examination, and his consecration. The clergy and people of the vacant diocese elect a man to be their bishop.[25] This procedure seems to be identical with that envisaged in the *Apostolic Tradition*, of which the Latin version only survives.[26] The candidate is brought to Rome and presented to the pope by representatives of the clergy and laity of the vacant church.[27] When they have presented the candidate to the pope, together with a formal written request for his consecration, the pope remits the candidate to the archdeacon for examination as to his innocence from the four capital sexual crimes which are an impediment to holy orders. These are sodomy, defilement of sacred virgins, conjunction with animals, and marriage with women who have already been married to another.[28] These were the grave sins for which in former times public penance had been imposed. Before the time of St Gregory such public penance had fallen into desuetude, but when it was in use nobody who had performed penance for these sins could be admitted to Holy Orders. This is why for centuries afterward an oath that they had not been committed was required of *all* candidates for Holy Orders. After the archdeacon has questioned him on the subject of these *quattuor capitula*, the candidate swears on the book of the gospels that he has committed none of these crimes.[29] The subdeacon then takes him to the tomb of the blessed apostle St Peter, where he takes the same oath upon the Apostle's bones.[30] The pope then questions the representatives of the local church about the candidate, how old he is, how long he has served as a priest or deacon, whether he is married, and whether he has made a disposition of his property.[31] The candidate then comes in, and

---

[25] *Ibid.* 14: 'Dum a civitate et loco episcopus fuerit defunctus, a populo civitatis elegitur alius et fiat a sacerdotibus, clero et populo decretus.'

[26] *Apostolic Tradition*, ch. 2: 'Episcopus ordinetur electus ab omni populo, quique cum nominatus fuerit et placuerit omnibus, conveniet populum una cum praesbyterio et his qui praesentes fuerint episcopi, die dominica. Consentientibus omnibus, inponant super eum manus, et praesbyterium adstet quiescens. Omnes autem silentium habeant, orantes in corde propter descensionem spiritus. Ex quibus unus de praesentibus episcopis, ab omnibus rogatus, inponens manum ei qui ordinatur episcopus, oret ita dicens . . .'

[27] *Ordo* XXXIV.15 'Veniunt ad domnum apostolicum, adducentes secum et suggestionem, hoc est rogatorias litteras, ut eis episcopum consecret, quam secum deportati sunt.'

[28] *Ibid.* 16. See Andrieu III, pp. 549-50.

[29] *Ordo* XXXIV.17.

[30] *Ibid.* 18.

[31] *Ibid.* 22 and 23.

prostrates himself.[32] The pope examines the candidate as to his condition and status, with questions similar to those already put by the pope to the representatives of the church which presents him.[33] This is the end of the proceedings on Saturday, and the candidate is sent away and told to present himself on Sunday.[34] On Sunday morning the pope comes to church, with the participating bishops, the priests and others of the clergy and the people.[35] *Kyrie eleison* is not said, being required later for the litany, but the mass begins with the collect.[36] The Epistle is I Tim III.1 ff.[37] During the singing of the gradual the archdeacon departs with the acolytes and subdeacons, and vests the candidate in a dalmatic, chasuble and boots, and brings him into church.[38] The pope then calls the people to prayer for the candidate.[39] The litany is said.[40] At the end of the litany the candidate is ordained by imposition of hands with prayer.[41] In *Apostolic Tradition* this prayer is both silent and vocal.[42]

In the early sixth century the *Statuta ecclesiae antiqua* state that the gospelbook is held open over the kneeling candidate by two bishops, and while one bishop pronounces the prayer – this must be the

---

[32] *Ibid.* 24-5.
[33] *Ibid.* 27-8.
[34] *Ibid.* 31.
[35] *Ibid.* 32.
[36] *Ibid.* 35.
[37] *Ibid.* 36.
[38] *Ibid.* 37.
[39] *Ibid.* 38.
[40] *Ibid.* 39.
[41] *Ibid.* 40.
[42] *Apostolic Tradition*, ch. 2 (quoted above, n. 26). the prayer continues as follows in ch. 3: 'Deus et Pater domini nostri Iesu Christi, Pater misericordiarum et Deus totius consolationis, qui in excelsis habitas, et humilia respicis, qui cognoscis omnia antequam nascantur, tu qui dedisti terminos in ecclesia per uerbum gratiae tuae, praedestinas ex principio genus iustorum Abraham, principes et sacerdotes constituens et sanctum tuum sine ministerio non derelinquens, ex initio saeculi bene tibi placuit in his quos elegisti dari: nunc effunde eam uirtutem quae a te est, principalis spiritus, quem dedisti dilecto filio tuo Iesu Christo, quod donauit sanctis apostolis, qui constituerunt ecclesiam per singula loca in sanctificationem tuam, in gloriam et laudem indeficientem nomini tuo. Da, cordis cognitor Pater, super hunc seruum tuum, quem elegisti ad episcopatum, pascere gregem sanctam tuam, et primatu sacerdotii tibi exhibere sine repraehensione, seruientem noctu et die, incessanter repropitiare uultum tuum et offerre dona sancta ecclesiae tuae, spiritum primatus sacerdotii habere potestatem dimittere peccata secundum mandatum tuum, dare sortes secundum praeceptum tuum soluere etiam omnem colligationem secundum potestatem quam dedisti apostolis, placere autem tibi in mansuetudine et mundo corde, offerentem tibi odorem suauitatis per puerum tuum Iesum Christum, per quem tibi gloria et potentia et honor, Patri et Filio cum Spiritu sancto et nunc et in saecula saeculorum. Amen.'

archbishop or the prinicpal consecrator – the other bishops present touch the head of the candidate. In the consecration of the pope, *Ordo* XLA prescribes that the gospels be held over the candidate by two deacons, and not two bishops, as in the *Statuta*.[43] Three bishops consecrate the pope. The first prayer is said by the bishop of Alba, the second by the bishop of Ortus, and the third by the bishop of Ostia, the principal consecrator.[44] The *pallium* is then placed upon the pope by the archdeacon.[45]

After the consecration, *Ordo* XXXIV.41 states that the chief consecrator gives the bishop the kiss of peace, which he, conducted by the archdeacon, then bestows upon the bishops and priests present. This represents a practice as old as the *Apostolic Tradition*.[46] In *Ordo* XLA the new pontiff ascends his throne, and gives the kiss to all the priests, and begins the mass with *Gloria in excelsis Deo*. This implies that the consecration comes earlier in the rite than it does in *Ordo* XXXIV, where it follows the gradual.

In the consecration of a bishop in *Ordo* XXXIV.42, the consecrator causes the newly consecrated bishop to sit in a position of precedence over the other bishops present. In ch. 43 the mass then resumes with the *Alleluia* and the gospel. In *Apostolic Tradition* the new bishop, and not the consecrator, is the celebrant of the mass, and to him the deacons bring the oblations, upon which he lays his hands and says the Anaphora.[47] When the Canon is finished the pope, before the communion, gives the new bishop his letters of orders[48] and a consecrated host, and he takes this home and communicates from it for the ensuing forty days. Finally the new bishop communicates the people present at his ordination mass.[49]

---

[43] *Ordo* XLA.5; cf. *Statuta ecclesiae antiqua*, ch. 3: 'Episcopus cum ordinatur, duo episcopi exponant et teneant euangeliorum codicem super caput eius et, uno super eum fundente benedictionem, reliqui omnes episcopi qui adsunt manibus suis caput eius tangant.'

[44] *Ordo* XLA.3, 4 and 6.

[45] *Ibid.* 7.

[46] *Apostolic Tradition*, ch. 4: 'Quicumque factus fuerit episcopus, omnes os offerant pacis . . .'

[47] *Ibid.*: 'Illi vero offerant diacones oblationes, quique inponens manus in eas cum omni praesbyterio dicat gratias agens. . . .'

[48] See Andrieu III, p. 587.

[49] *Ordo* XXXIV.44-5: 'dum uero uenerit ad communicandum, domnus apostolicus porrigit ei formatam atque sacratam oblationem, et eam suscipiens ipse episcopus ex ea communicat super altare et caeterum ex ea sibi reseruat ad communicandum usque ad dies quadraginta . . . et postmodum ex praecepto domni apostolici communicat omnem populum.'

CONCLUSION: THE MAJOR ORDERS

The general theme of the Roman ordination prayers remains constant through our period. The episcopate is the order of the sovereign priesthood, and the bishop is compared with the Jewish High Priest of the Aaronic dispensation, upon whom the Spirit is poured; with Moses as a ruler of the people; and with the Apostles as a teacher occupying the *cathedra*, or throne, which is the teacher's chair, and the symbol of his disciplinary authority over the Church. The priests are fellow workers with the bishop. They share his priesthood in its three aspects, sacerdotal, regal and magisterial; and are often described as 'priests of the second order'. They are the assistants of the bishop, as Eleazar and Ithamar were of Aaron, the seventy elders of Moses, and the disciples of the Apostles. The diaconate, as its name implies, is the order of service, not of government. The deacon's antitype in the Old Dispensation is the Levite.

MINOR ORDERS

Writing to Fabius, bishop of Antioch, in 251 Pope Cornelius states that at that time the church of Rome possessed the following ministers: forty-six priests; seven deacons and seven subdeacons; forty-two acolytes; fifty-two exorcists, readers and doorkeepers.[50] A century and more later the same orders existed at Rome, for prayer is bidden on behalf of them in the solemn prayers of Good Friday: 'Oremus et pro omnibus episcopis, presbyteris, diaconibus, sub-diaconibus, acolytis, exorcistis, lectoribus, ostiariis . . .' Further evidence, also probably from the third century, may be adduced from the bidding of the third of the solemn prayers of Good Friday.[51] Unfortunately there is no evidence earlier than the sixth century as to how candidates for certain of these orders of ministers were admitted to their sacred office. The early Roman evidence which exists does however state clearly, even emphatically, that candidates were not admitted to minor orders by prayer with the imposition of hands, as they were to the major orders of

---

[50] Eusebius of Caesarea, *Historia ecclesiastica* VI.xliii.11.
[51] For a critical text, see Willis, *Essays in Early Roman Liturgy*, p. 15.

bishop, priest and deacon. The general practice was for the bishop to admit them to office by giving them some instrument appropriate to it, with or without a charge or blessing (see Table IV, below, p. 155). In the earliest source concerned with minor orders, the *Apostolic Tradition*, the only orders dealt with are reader and subdeacon. The reader is admitted by the bishop giving him a book, presumably containing the lesson which he will have to read.[52] The Coptic version states that this book is the 'Apostle', that is to say an epistolary, but the Arabic *Canons of Hippolytus* state that the gospel is given. The subdeacon appears to be given no instrument but is nominated to be in attendance on the deacon.[53] The next evidence from Rome about ordination to minor orders is that of John the Deacon whose letter to Senarius at Ravenna is to be dated about 500.[54] He states that the acolyte is given a bag (in which he will carry the blessed sacrament when for instance he takes the *fermentum* from the pope's mass to the priests in the *tituli* in the city). The subdeacon receives a chalice and precisely the same instruments are mentioned by *Ordo* XXXIV, also a purely Roman document but about 250 years later than the Letter to Senarius.[55] This adds to John's information the facts that the acolyte is ordained at the communion of the people and is given a blessing and that the subdeacon, like a deacon, is required to swear that he has not committed any of the *quattuor capitula* which are an impediment to holy orders.

Thus far the sources dealt with are purely Roman but there are two sources which are partly Gallican but which have a Roman base – namely *Statuta ecclesiae antiqua* and the Old Gelasian Sacramentary.[56] In both of these the reader is given a book and a charge by the bishop: the acolyte is given instruction as to his duty by the bishop, is handed a candlestick and candle by the archdeacon, and is given a water cruet for adding water to the chalice: and the subdeacon is given an empty paten and chalice by the bishop and an ewer, basin and towel by the archdeacon. In none of these orders is there any imposition of hand or prayer for the Holy Spirit, and they are therefore clearly distinguished from the major orders of bishop, priest and deacon. The *Statuta* and the

---

[52] *Apostolic Tradition*, ch. 11.
[53] *Ibid*. 13.
[54] *Ep. ad Sen*. 10, ed. Wilmart, *Analecta Reginensia*, p. 176.
[55] *Ordo* XXXIV.1-3.
[56] See Gelasian I.xcv, 741-6, and *Statuta ecclesiae antiqua*, chs. 5-10 (Andrieu II, pp. 618-19).

Old Gelasian also make provision for admitting candidates to the orders of exorcist, doorkeeper and psalmist. The exorcist is given a book of exorcisms and a formula giving him authority; the doorkeeper (*Ostiarius*) is given a door-key and a charge by the archdeacon; and the psalmist is given a charge by the priest.

From *Ordo* XXXIV it appears that the conferment of minor orders, unlike that of major, was not confined to Sunday, nor to the Sundays (or the Saturday vigil) following the four Ember Weeks.

Table I. St Cyprian's text of the Institution narrative (see above, pp. 45-50)

HIPPOLYTUS	CYPRIAN - MATTHEW	CYPRIAN - CORINTHIANS	ROMAN
accipiens panem		accepit panem	accepit panem + in sanctas ac uenerabiles manus suas eleuatis oculis in caelum ad te deum patrem suum omnipotentem
gratias tibi agens		et gratias egit	tibi gratias agens
		et fregit	benedixit fregit dedit discipulis suis dicens
hoc est corpus meum quod pro uobis confringetur		hoc est corpus meum quod pro uobis est	accipite et manducate ex hoc omnes: hoc est enim corpus meum
similiter et calicem dicens	calicem etenim sub die passionis accipiens benedixit et dedit discipulis suis dicens	simili modo et calicem postquam cenatum est accepit dicens	simili modo posteaquam caenatum est accipiens et hunc praeclarum calicem in sanctas ac uenerabiles manus suas item tibi gratias agens benedixit dedit discipulis suis dicens
om.	bibite ex hoc omnes		accipite et bibite ex eo omnes
hic est sanguis meus qui pro uobis effunditur	hic est enim sanguis testamenti qui pro multis effundetur in remissionem peccatorum	hic calix nouum testamentum est in meo sanguine	hic est enim calix sanguinis mei noui et aeterni testamenti mysterium fidei qui pro uobis et pro multis effundetur in remissionem peccatorum
quando hoc facitis meam commemorationem facitis		quotienscumque enim ederitis panem istum et calicem biberitis mortem domini adnuntiatis quoadusque ueniat	haec quotiescumque feceritis in mei memoriam facietis

Table II. Written evidence for the baptismal ceremony

A: Preliminaries (see above, pp. 119-26)

	Justin I	Hippolytus	Tertullian	Cyprian	Ambrose	Augustine	John the Deacon	Gelasianum	Ordo XI	Hadrianum
1. Scrutinies		AT 20 S(AE)				Exorcism: Ep. 194, 46		I.26, 193-9 1st Scrutiny, Lent III; I.27, 225-8 2nd Scrutiny, Lent IV; I.28, 254-7 3rd Scrutiny, Lent V; I.29, 283-4 Notice of Scrutinia; I.30, 285-7 Prayers ad cat. fac.	7 Scrutinies [§§28ff; 38; 40; 77; 79; 80; 81ff]	81, 82
2. Instruction		AT 20 S(AE)				Tradition of Creed & Lord's Prayer, Serm. 58 — No tradition of Gospels		I.34, 299-309 Expositio Evangeliorum; I.35, 310-?8 Praefatio Symboli; I.36, 319-28 Pater Noster; I.42, 422 Credo	§44 Evangelia; §61 Symbolum; §69 Pater Noster	
3 Imposition of hands and blessing		AT 20 S(AE)								
4. The salt						Council of Carthage III, Canon 5		I.31, 288-9; I.32, 290	§5 ff	80
5. Blessing of the oils		AT 21 S(AE)								

B: Baptismal Ceremonies Proper (see above, pp. 126-36)

	Justin I	Hippolytus	Tertullian	Cyprian	Ambrose	Augustine	John the Deacon	Gelasianum	Ordo XI	Hadrianum
1. Effeta		AT 20 S(AE)			De Sacr. 1, 2-3 De Myst. 3-4		4-5	I.42, 419-20 (Sat. a. m.)	85	83
2. Blessing of the water		AT 21 S(AE)	De Bapt. 4		cf. De Myst. 20			I.44, 444-8	92-95	85
3. Renunciation and first unction		AT 21 S(AE)	Renunciation: - in the water: De Spect. 4 - before the water: De Cor. 3		De Sacr. 1, 4-5 De Myst. 5		6	I.42, 421-4 (Sat. a. m.)		83
4. The baptism	Apol. 65	*AT 21 SB(AE)TL	De Spect. 4 Adv. Prax. 26 De Cor. 3	Ep. 70, 2	De Sacr. 2, 20 De Myst. 28		6	I.44, 449	96	85
5. Second unction		AT 21 LB(AE)	De Bapt. 7	Ep. 70, 2	De Sacr. 2, 24-3, 1 De Myst. 29-30		6	I.44, 449-50	97	85
6. Confirmation or third unction		AT 21 LB(AE)	De Bapt. 8	Ep. 73, 9	De Sacr. 5, 5		14	I.44, 450-2	100	86
7. The mass	Apol. 65-6	AT 21 LSB(AE)	De Cor. 3		De Sacr. 5, 15-17		12	I.44, 452, 459-60	103	87

* vide Botte, pp. 48-50

Table III. Written evidence for ordination ceremonies (see above, pp. 138-45)

ORDO XXXIV	Apostolic Tradition	ORDO XL A	Statula ecclesiae antiqua
Ordination of deacon			
1. 4 At introit - Kyrie postponed 5 Collect Ep. I Tim 3.8-14 Gradual	1. 8L eligatur secundum ea quae praedicta sunt	(Incorporated in 7th century into Liber Diurnus Formula LVII)	
2. 8 Bidding and Litany (form of bidding given)			
3. 9 Consecration prayer	3. 8L Imposition by bishop alone sicuti praecipimus		3. Solus episcopus …
4. 10 Kisses bishop and priests. Stands at right of bishops (sic)			
Ordination of priest			
5. 11 Presentation by archdeacon			
6. 12 Consecration prayer	6. 7L Imposition of hands by bishop and other priests Prayer secundus ea quae praedicta sunt sicut praediximus super episcopum (same content, different form)		6. Bishop … etiam omnes presbyteri
7. 12 Kisses episcopo uel ceteris sacerdotibus et stat in ordine presbyterii			

ORDO XXXIV	Apostolic Tradition	ORDO XL A	Statuta ecclesiae antiqua
8. 13 Mass resumes with Alleluia uel tractus			
Ordination of bishop			
9. 14 Election by local church	9. 2L elecrus ab omni populo		
10. 15 Presentation to Pope with request for ordination			
11. 16 Pope sends him to archdeacon for examination de IV capitulis Oath on gospels & on St. Peter's body			
12. 20 Pope questions local church's representative about candidate			
13. 24 Entry and prostration of candidate Pope 'protegat nos dominus'			
14. 27 Pope questions candidate			
15. 30 Ordered to fast till next day 31 Kissed by Pope			

153

ORDQ XXXIV	Apostolic Tradition	ORDQ XL A	Statuta ecclesiae antiqua
16. 32 Third day - Sunday Ordination Mass Introit. No Kyrie. Collect	16. 2L Die Dominica	16. 1 Entry. To confessio (during introit)	
17. 36 Ep. 1 Tim 3.1			
18. 37 Candidate dressed and presented during gradual			
19. 38 Pope's bidding			
20. 39 Litany and prostrations		20. 2 Litany	
21. 40 Consecration	21. 2L Silent prayer. Prayer by one of the bishops with imposition of hands.	21. 3 Prayer 1 Bp. Albanensis 4 2 Bp. Portuensis 5 Open gospels on his head 6 Consecrated by Bp. of Ostia 7 Archdeacon gives him pallium	21. 2 bishops hold gospels open 1 says prayer All the rest impose hands.
22. 41 Kissed by Pope Kisses bishops and priests.	22. 4L Kiss omnibus	22. 8 Dat pacem omnibus sacerdotibus Gloria (N.B. all this comes earlier in the rite than the consecrations in Ordo XXXIV)	
23. 42 Sits super alios episcopos Alleluia Mass continues.	23. 4L Concelebrates Mass cum omni praesbyterio		
24. 44 Pope gives him formatam atque sacratam oblationem from which he communicates and which he keeps forty days.			
25. 45 Communicates people			

Table IV. The ordination of the minor orders (see above, pp. 145-7)

	Apostolic Tradition	Ordo XXXIV	Gelasian	John the Deacon	Statuta ecclesiae antiqua
Reader	(A.T.11) Bishop gives him a book. No imposition of hands		(l.XCV 744) Bishop gives him a book and a charge.		(8) Bishop gives him a book and a charge. Cf. Gelasian.
Acolyte		(XXXIV, 1-2) Ordained at the Communion. Given a linen bag and a blessing (Intercedente).	(l.XCV 742) Bishop instructs him as to duty. Archdeacon gives him a candlestick and a candle, and a water cruet for adding water to the chalice.	(Ep. ad Sen. X) Given a bag.	(6) Bishop instructs him. Archdeacon gives him a candlestick and candle and water cruet for adding water to the chalice. Cf. Gelasian.
Subdeacon	(A.T.13) Non imponetur manus super subdiaconum ... sed nominabitur ut sequatur diaconum.	(XXXIV, 3) Given an empty chalice by Archdeacon or Bishop after swearing on the Gospels that he has not committed the four capitula.	(l.XCV 741) Imposition of hands. Bishop gives him an empty patten and chalice. Archdeacon gives him an ewer, basin and towel.	(Ep. ad Sen. X) Given a chalice.	(5) No imposition of hands. Bishop gives empty patten and chalice, and archdeacon gives ewer, basin and towel. Cf. Gelasian.
Exorcist			(l.XCV 743) Book of exorcisms included in formula giving authority.		(7) Cf. Gelasian.
Ostiarius (Doorkeeper)			(l.XCV 745) Archdeacon gives him a doordey and a charge.		(9) Cf. Gelasian.
Psalmist			(l.XCV 746) Priest gives him a charge.		(10) Cf. Gelasian.

INDEX OF LESSONS

GENERAL INDEX

Abdon and Sennes, SS: cult of (30 July), 106, 109
Abyssinia: liturgy of, 14
acolytes, 69, 70, 72, 73-4, 75, 76, 77, 120, 123, 124, 125, 143, 145; ordination of, 146
Acontus, St: cult of (5 Sept.), 106
Addai and Mari, SS, of Edessa: liturgy of, 65
Advent, 93, 94, 104, 105, 113, 115
Africa, St: cult of (14 Sept.), 106
Africa: liturgy of, 6, 11, 14, 16, 18, 20, 22, 25, 34, 35, 36, 39, 55, 58, 61, 64, 80, 84, 87, 90, 113, 114, 117, 125, 130; *and see* Augustine, Cyprian, Tertullian; councils: of Hippo, of Carthage
Agapitus [and Felicissimus], SS: cult of (6 Aug.), 106
Agnes, St: cult of (21 Jan.), 105, 113; octave (28 Jan.), 107, 113
Agnus Dei, 58, 72, 76
Alcuin: lectionary of, 95, 97, 98, 100, 102, 103, 105, 108, 109, 110, 111; liturgical revisions of, 40, 60
Alexandria: liturgy of, 10, 35, 36; *and see* Sarapion
Alexander: *see* Martialis
All Saints: cult of (1 Nov.), 103, 110
alleluia, 63, 64, 74, 92, 101, 141, 144
Amalarius, 54
ambo, 74
Ambrose, St (of Milan), 2, 15, 20, 36, 51, 52, 74, 134; *De mysteriis*, 23, 123, 126, 127, 130, 131, 132, 136; *De sacramentis*, 7, 8, 14, 15, 16, 21, 22, 23-32, 34, 38, 44, 45,
48, 51, 62, 118, 123, 127, 128, 132, 136; *Explanationes in psalmos*, 23
anamnesis, 12-13, 30, 51
anaphora, 8, 10, 35, 39, 53, 144; of Addai and Mari (eastern Syria), 22
Anastasia, St: cult of (25 Dec.), 81-2; *and see* stational churches (in Rome)
Anastasius I, Pope (399-401), 81, 99
Andreas, St: cult of (30 Nov.), 57, 94, 111, 113; vigil, 111; *and see* stational churches (in Rome)
anointing, 132; *and see* baptism: unctions
antiphons, 74; *and see* communion chant; Gradual, Introit, Offertory
antiphonary, 87, 93, 104; revisions of, 95
apocrisarius, 55
Apostles: cult of [SS Petrus and Paulus] (29 June), 94, 104, 105, 106, 108, 109, 110, 113; *and see* stational churches (in Rome): Holy Apostles
Apostolic Constitutions, 11, 55, 64
Apostolic Fathers, 3
Apostolic Tradition: *see* Hippolytus
aquarianism, 16
Arab invasions, 16
archbishop, 144
archdeacon, 56, 58, 60, 73, 75, 76, 77, 109, 140, 142, 144, 146, 147
Arianism, 14-15, 34, 65
Ariston, St: cult of (13 Dec.), 106
Arles, 138
Arnobius Junior, 81, 87
Ascension, 43, 53, 62, 79, 91, 92, 97, 101, 102, 112, 115

oblation, 11

Offertory (antiphon), 6, 7, 58, 63, 64, 75, 76, 77, 90; during baptismal mass, 135

oil, use of: after baptismal immersion, 131; at baptism, 53, 126, 128, 132; during confirmation, 133-4; for baptismal *effeta*, 127; for exorcism, 128

Old Gelasian: *see* sacramentary: Old Gelasian

oratio ad collectam: *see* stational liturgy (at Rome), *collecta*

oratio super populum, 61, 66-7, 77; in Lent, 89-90

orationes fidelium (commemorations of the living and the dead), 6, 18, 39-40, 89, 122

orationes sollemnes: *see* Good Friday

ordinations, 2, 51, 64, 67, 79, 86, 92-3, 99, 102, 103, 105, 137-47; of an acolyte, 146; of a bishop, 10, 138, 139, 140, 141-4; of a deacon, 10, 138-40; of a doorkeeper, 147; of an exorcist, 147; of a pope, 138; of a priest, 10, 138; 140-1; of a psalmist, 147; of a reader, 146; of a subdeacon, 146; of Aaron, Eleazar, and Ithamar, 51; *and see* consecration

Ordines Romani: Ordo Romanus Primus, 6, 36, 55-6, 58-9, 60, 66, 67, 70, 72, 75, 76; *Ordo* II, 69; *Ordo* III, 36; *Ordo* VII, 60; *Ordo* XI, 90, 118, 120, 121, 123, 124, 125, 127, 129, 130, 132, 134, 136; *Ordo* XIV (of Mabillon), 66; *Ordo* XXXIV, 138, 140, 141, 142, 144, 146, 147; *Ordo* XL, 138; *Ordo* XLA, 73, 138, 144

Origen, 35

paganism, 8, 27, 28, 80, 81, 116, 130

pallium, 144

Palm Sunday, 88, 100

Pammachius: *titulus* of (in Rome), 70

Pancratius [and Nereus, Achilleus], SS: cult of (12 May), 113

papal correspondence: language characteristic of, 28

parrochia, 68

Parthenus [and Calocerus], SS: cult of (19 May), 105

Pascha Annotina, 91, 101, 102

paten, 77, 76, 146

patriarchium (papal residence in Rome), 72

Paul the Deacon: *Life* of Gregory the Great, 93

Paul, St: cult of (in Rome), 57, 83; influence of letters on liturgy, 17, 28, 48; *and see* Apostles: cult of, stational churches (in Rome)

Pax Domini, 5, 6, 57, 58, 59, 60, 69, 72, 76

Pelagius II, Pope, 83

penance: public, 67, 142; *and see* penitence

penitents: reconciliation for, 90, 100; *and see* Lent, penance

Pentecost, 6, 44, 43, 53, 79, 89, 90, 91, 92, 92-3, 97, 101, 102-3, 115, 133; administration of baptismal rites, 119, 134; mid-Pentecost, 91; octave of, 92, 93, 102, 103; Sundays after, 67, 94, 104-5, 110, 113, 115; Wednesday in, 71

pericope: *see* lessons

Perpetua [and Felicitas], SS: cult of (7 Mar.), 105, 108

Peter, St: cult of (in Rome), 57, 83; tomb of (in Rome), 142; *and see* Apostles: cult of, stational churches (in Rome)

Petrus [and Paulus], SS: *see* Apostles: cult of

Petrus, St: *in cathedra*, cult of (22 Feb.), 105, 108

Philippus [and Iacobus], SS: cult of (1 May), 108; *and see* stational churches (in Rome)

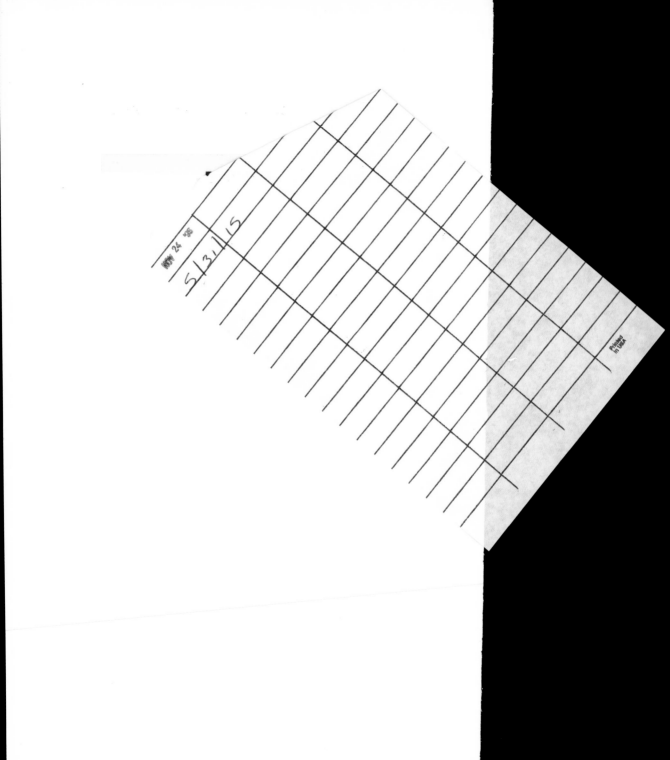